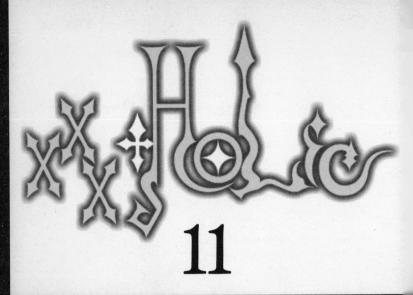

11

CLAMP

TRANSLATED AND ADAPTED BY

William Flanagan

LETTERED BY

Dana Hayward

BALLANTINE BOOKS • NEW YORK

A Del Rey Manga/Kodansha Trade Paperback Original

xxxHOLiC, volume 11 copyright © 2007 by CLAMP
English translation copyright © 2008 by CLAMP

Published in the United States by Del Rey Books, an imprint of The Random House Publishing Group, a division of Random House, Inc., New York.

Del Rey is a registered trademark and the Del Rey colophon is a trademark of Random House, Inc.

Publication rights arranged through Kodansha Ltd.

First published in Japan in 2007 by Kodansha Ltd., Tokyo.

ISBN 978-0-345-50163-9

Printed in the United States of America

www.delreymanga.com

9 8 7 6 5 4 3 2 1

Translator and Adaptor—William Flanagan
Lettering—Dana Hayward

xxxHOLiC crosses over with *Tsubasa*. Although it isn't necessary to read *Tsubasa* to understand the events in *xxxHOLiC*, you'll get to see the same events from different perspectives if you read both series!

Contents

Honorifics Explained

Throughout the Del Rey Manga books, you will find Japanese honorifics left intact in the translations. For those not familiar with how the Japanese use honorifics and, more important, how they differ from American honorifics, we present this brief overview.

Politeness has always been a critical facet of Japanese culture. Ever since the feudal era, when Japan was a highly stratified society, use of honorifics—which can be defined as polite speech that indicates relationship or status—has played an essential role in the Japanese language. When addressing someone in Japanese, an honorific usually takes the form of a suffix attached to one's name (example: "Asuna-san"), is used as a title at the end of one's name, or appears in place of the name itself (example: "Negi-sensei," or simply "Sensei!").

Honorifics can be expressions of respect or endearment. In the context of manga and anime, honorifics give insight into the nature of the relationship between characters. Many English translations leave out these important honorifics and therefore distort the feel of the original Japanese. Because Japanese honorifics contain nuances that English honorifics lack, it is our policy at Del Rey not to translate them. Here, instead, is a guide to some of the honorifics you may encounter in Del Rey Manga.

-san: This is the most common honorific and is equivalent to Mr., Miss, Ms., or Mrs. It is the all-purpose honorific and can be used in any situation where politeness is required.

-sama: This is one level higher than "-san" and is used to confer great respect.

-dono: This comes from the word "tono," which means "lord." It is an even higher level than "-sama" and confers utmost respect.

-kun: This suffix is used at the end of boys' names to express familiarity or endearment. It is also sometimes used by men among friends, or when addressing someone younger or of a lower station.

-chan: This is used to express endearment, mostly toward girls. It is also used for little boys, pets, and even among lovers. It gives a sense of childish cuteness.

Bozu: This is an informal way to refer to a boy, similar to the English terms "kid" and "squirt."

Sempai/Senpai: This title suggests that the addressee is one's senior in a group or organization. It is most often used in a school setting, where underclassmen refer to their upperclassmen as "sempai." It can also be used in the workplace, such as when a newer employee addresses an employee who has seniority in the company.

Kohai: This is the opposite of "sempai" and is used toward underclassmen in school or newcomers in the workplace. It connotes that the addressee is of a lower station.

Sensei: Literally meaning "one who has come before," this title is used for teachers, doctors, or masters of any profession or art.

-[blank]: This is usually forgotten in these lists, but it is perhaps the most significant difference between Japanese and English. The lack of honorific means that the speaker has permission to address the person in a very intimate way. Usually, only family, spouses, or very close friends have this kind of permission. Known as yobisute, it can be gratifying when someone who has earned the intimacy starts to call one by one's name without an honorific. But when that intimacy hasn't been earned, it can be very insulting.

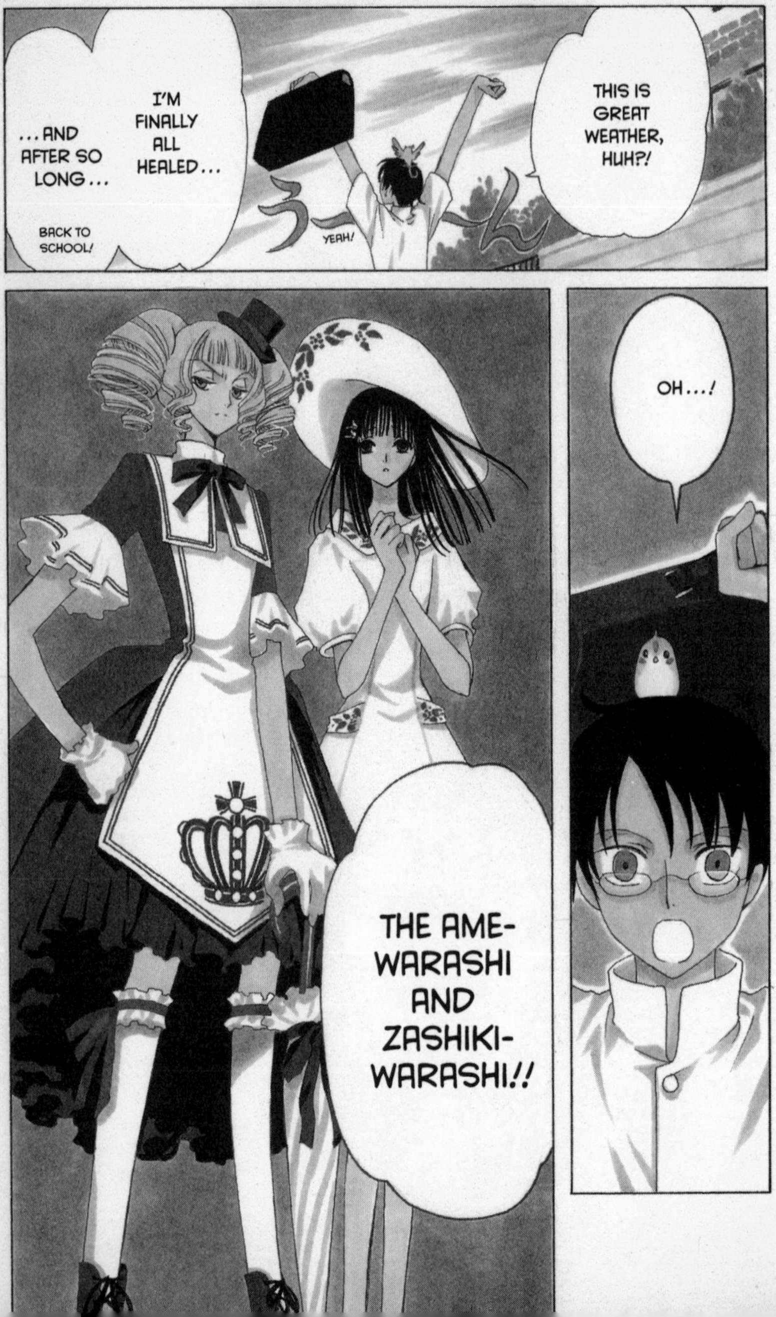
THIS IS GREAT WEATHER, HUH?!
うーん
YEAH!
I'M FINALLY ALL HEALED...
...AND AFTER SO LONG...
BACK TO SCHOOL!
OH...!
THE AME-WARASHI AND ZASHIKI-WARASHI!!

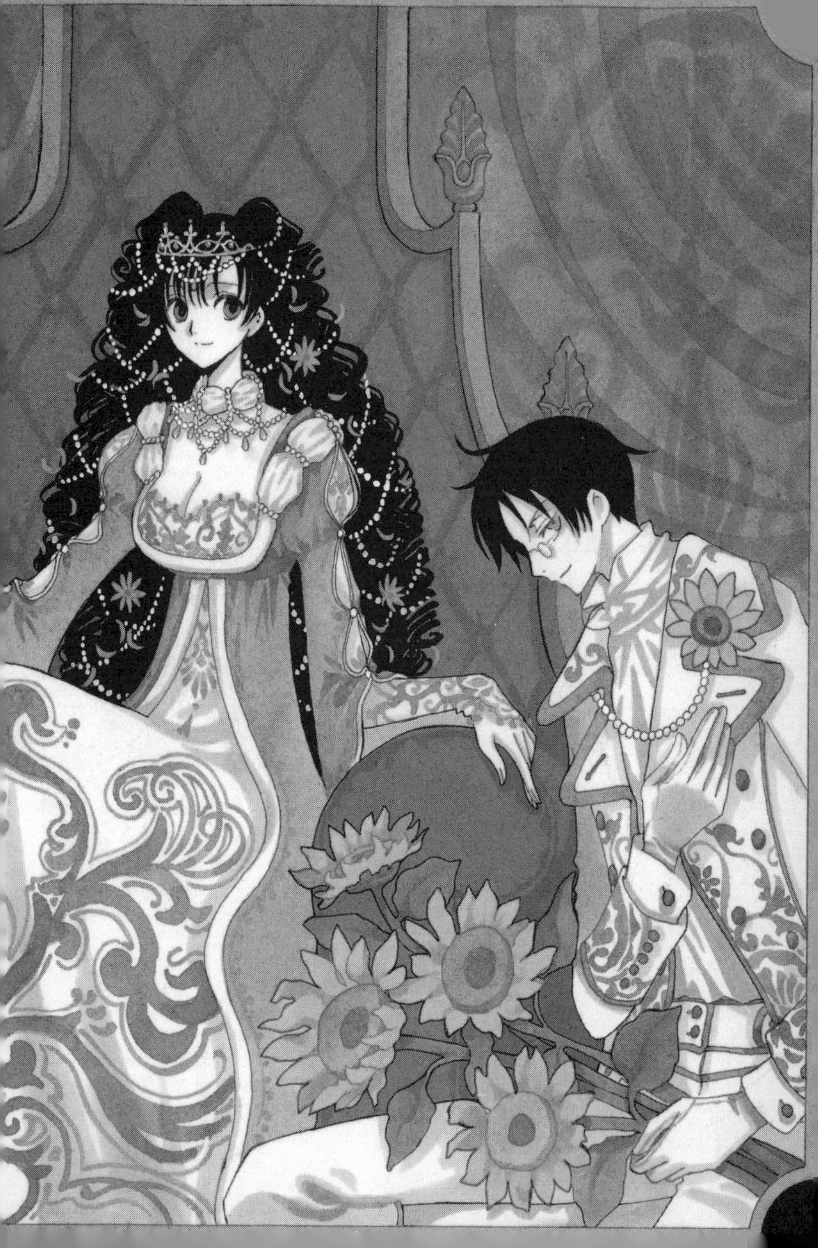

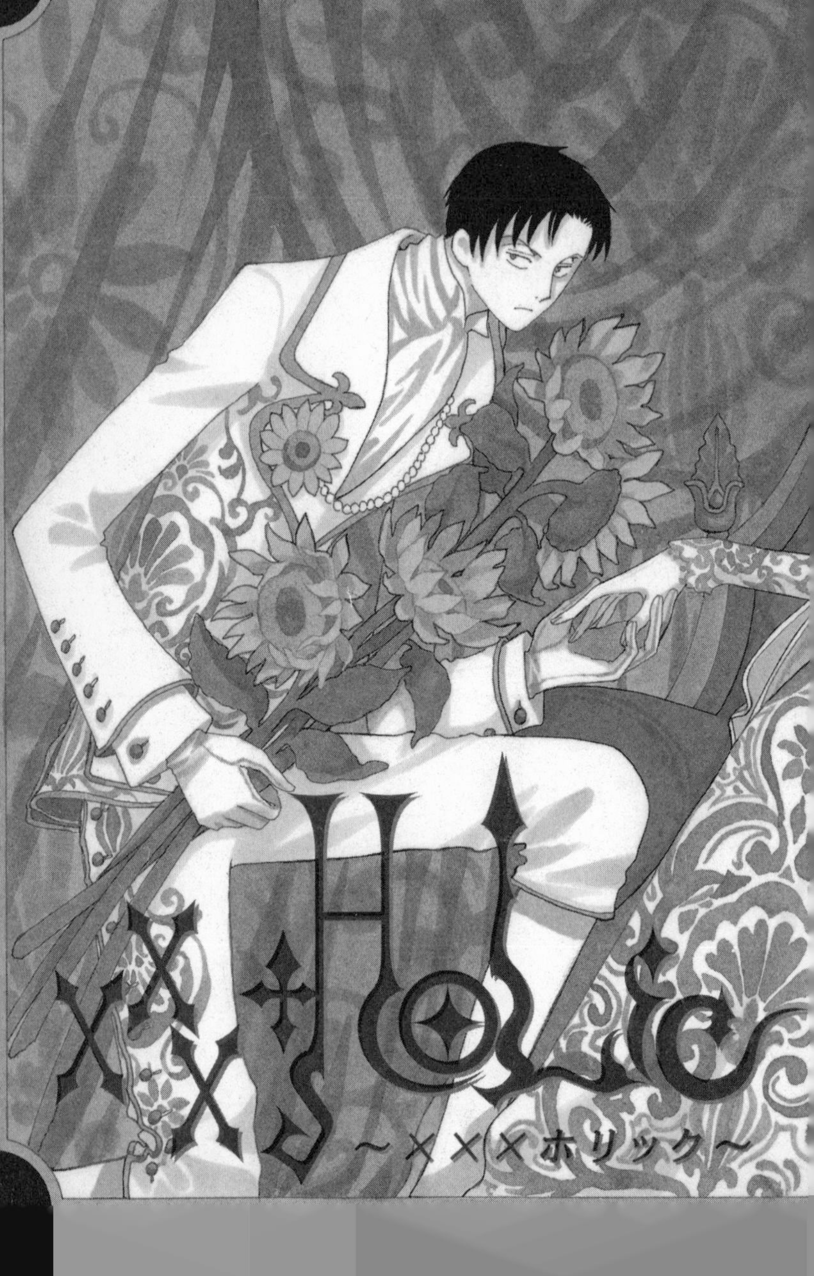
xxxHOLiC
〜×××ホリック〜

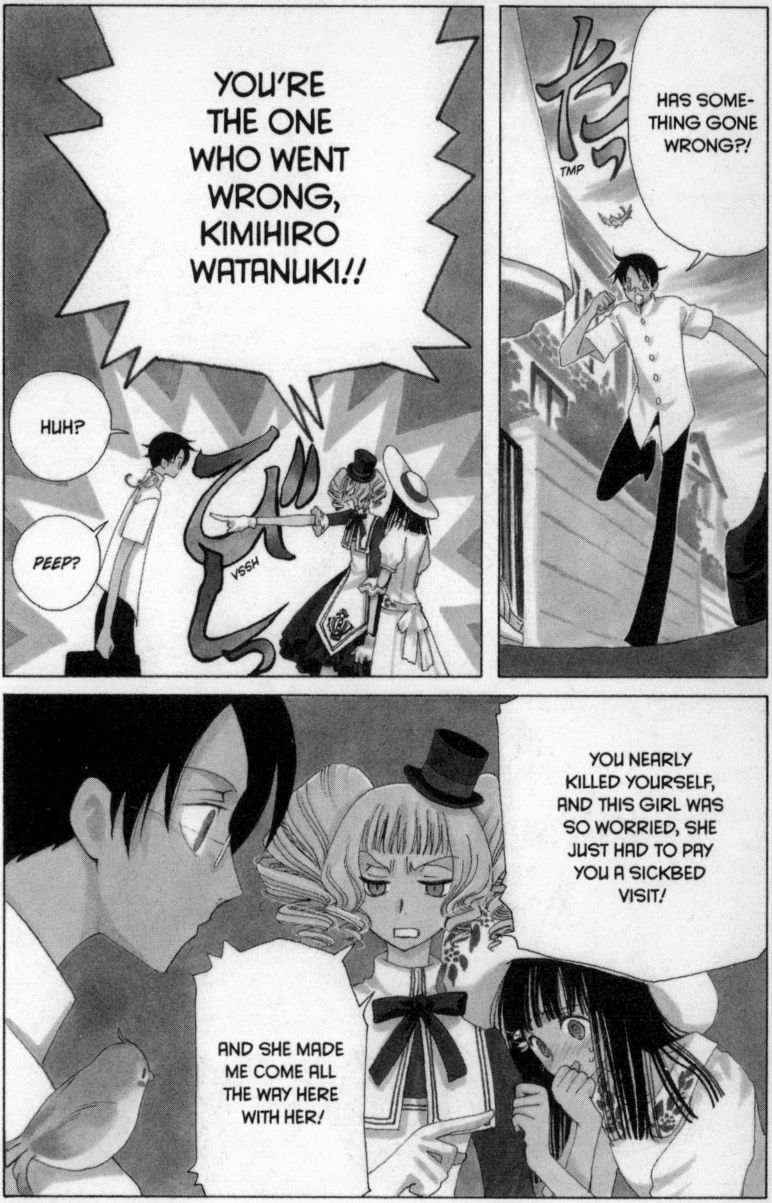
HAS SOME-THING GONE WRONG?!
TMP
YOU'RE THE ONE WHO WENT WRONG, KIMIHIRO WATANUKI!!
HUH?
PEEP?
VSSH
YOU NEARLY KILLED YOURSELF, AND THIS GIRL WAS SO WORRIED, SHE JUST HAD TO PAY YOU A SICKBED VISIT!
AND SHE MADE ME COME ALL THE WAY HERE WITH HER!

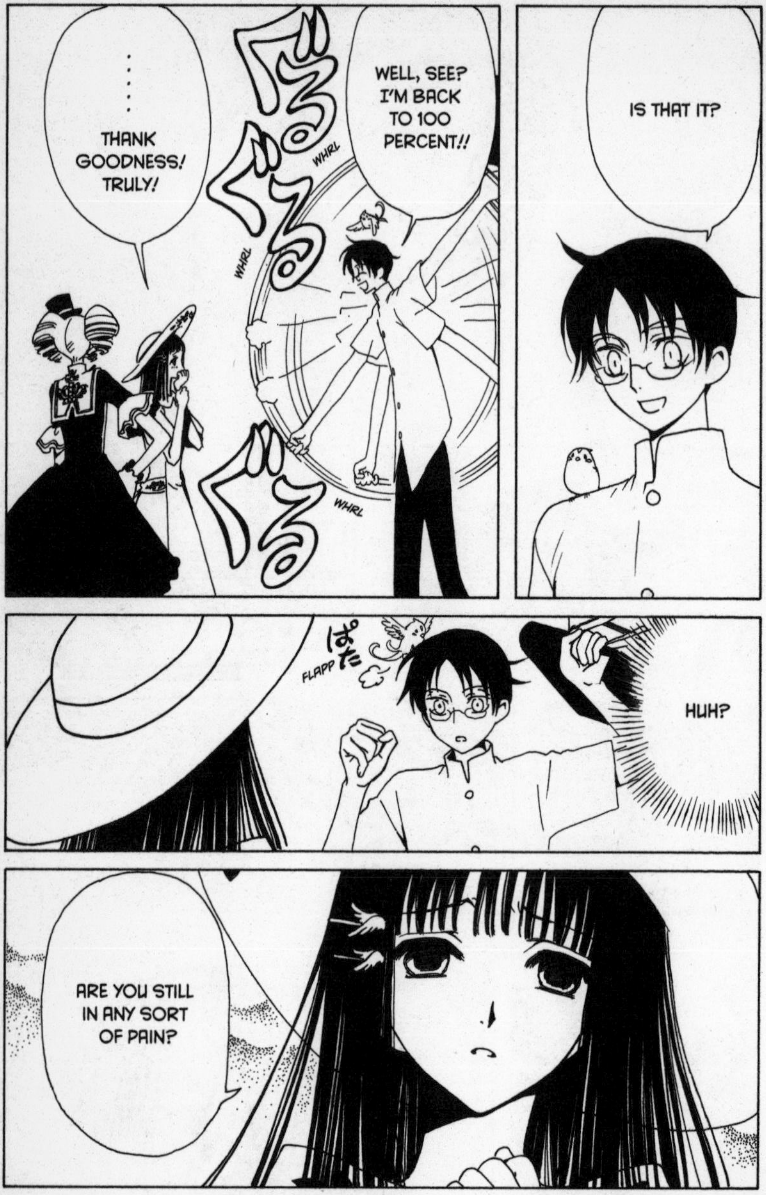
IS THAT IT?
WELL, SEE? I'M BACK TO 100 PERCENT!!
ぐるぐる
WHRL
WHRL
WHRL
..... THANK GOODNESS! TRULY!
HUH?
ぱた
FLAPP
ARE YOU STILL IN ANY SORT OF PAIN?

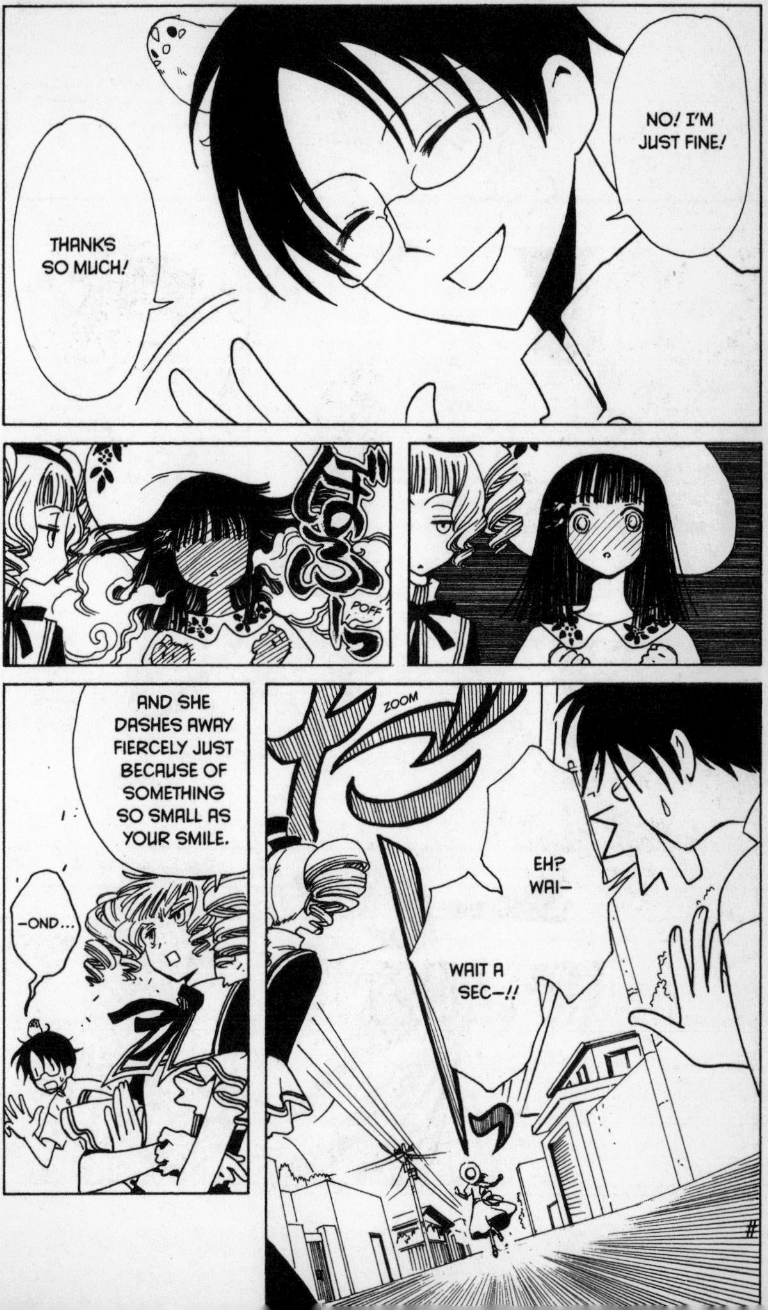
NO! I'M JUST FINE!
THANKS SO MUCH!
POFF
ZOOM
EH? WAI-
WAIT A SEC-!!
AND SHE DASHES AWAY FIERCELY JUST BECAUSE OF SOMETHING SO SMALL AS YOUR SMILE.
-OND...

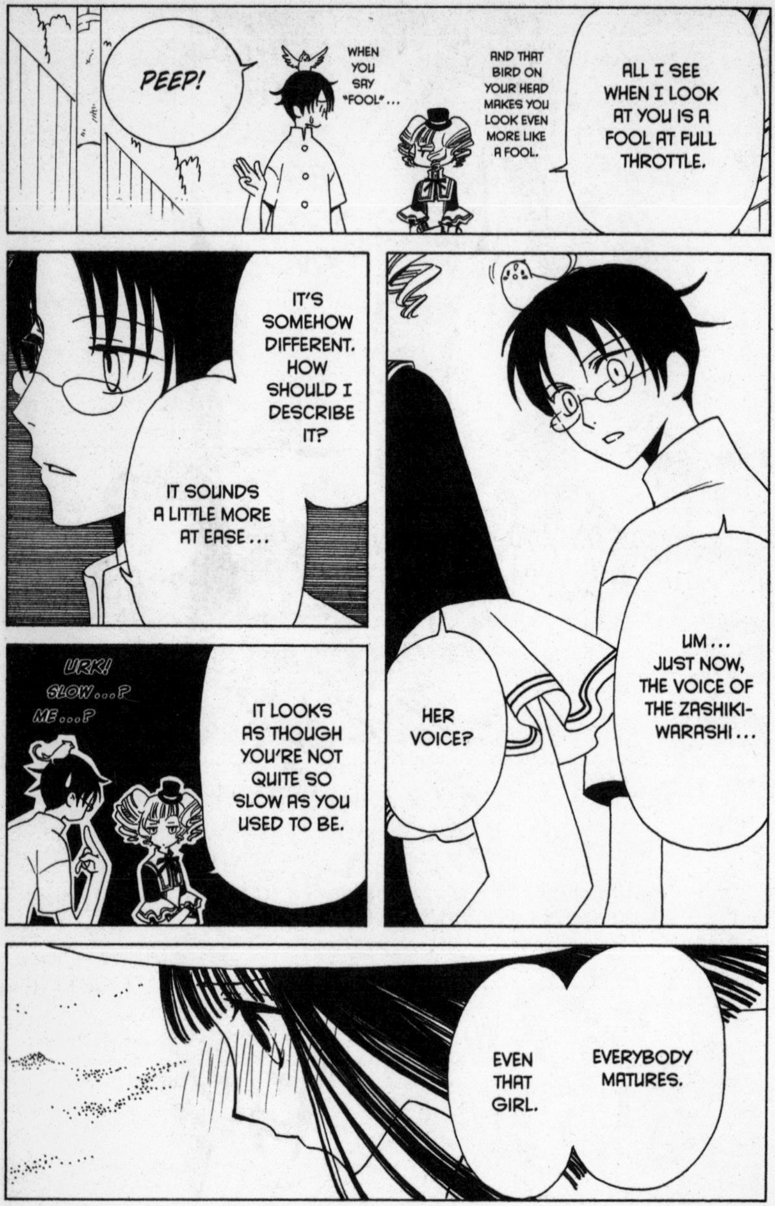
ALL I SEE WHEN I LOOK AT YOU IS A FOOL AT FULL THROTTLE.
AND THAT BIRD ON YOUR HEAD MAKES YOU LOOK EVEN MORE LIKE A FOOL.
WHEN YOU SAY "FOOL"...
PEEP!
UM... JUST NOW, THE VOICE OF THE ZASHIKI-WARASHI...
HER VOICE?
IT'S SOMEHOW DIFFERENT. HOW SHOULD I DESCRIBE IT?
IT SOUNDS A LITTLE MORE AT EASE...
IT LOOKS AS THOUGH YOU'RE NOT QUITE SO SLOW AS YOU USED TO BE.
URK! SLOW...? ME...?
EVERYBODY MATURES.
EVEN THAT GIRL.

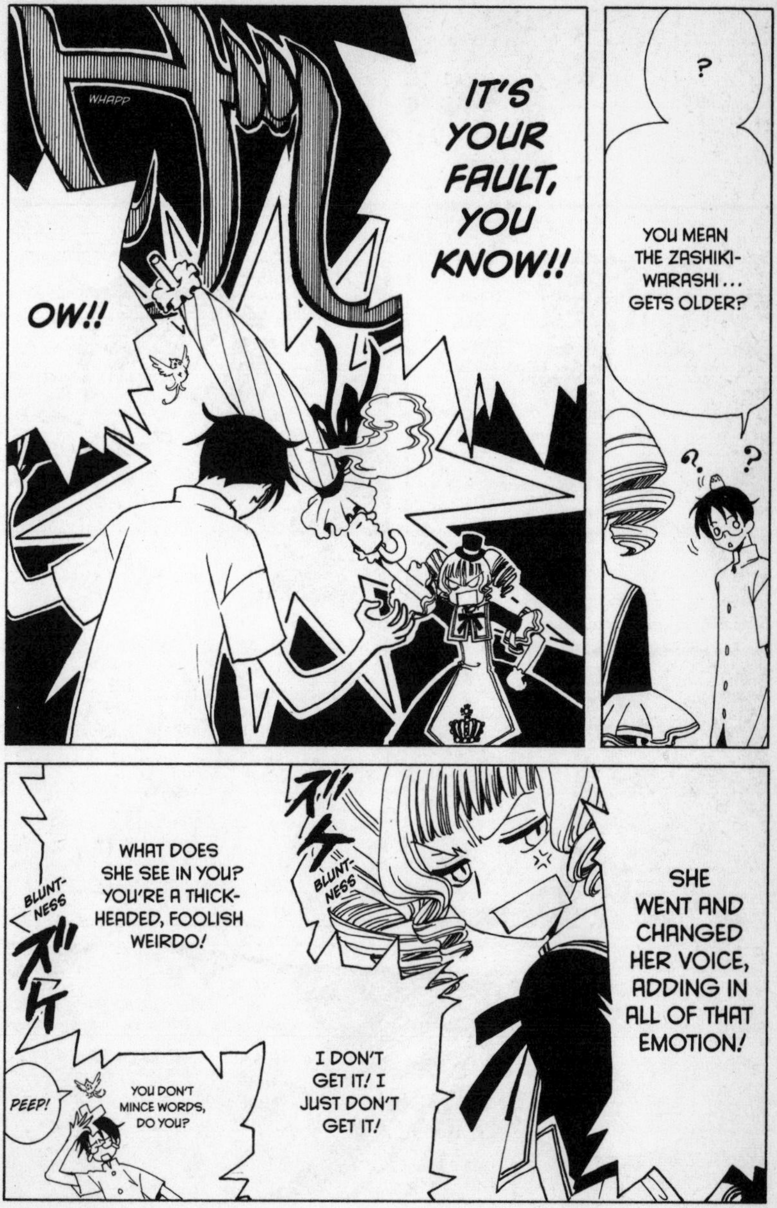
?
YOU MEAN THE ZASHIKI-WARASHI... GETS OLDER?
?
?
IT'S YOUR FAULT, YOU KNOW!!
WHAPP
OW!!
SHE WENT AND CHANGED HER VOICE, ADDING IN ALL OF THAT EMOTION!
BLUNT-NESS
WHAT DOES SHE SEE IN YOU? YOU'RE A THICK-HEADED, FOOLISH WEIRDO!
BLUNT-NESS
I DON'T GET IT! I JUST DON'T GET IT!
YOU DON'T MINCE WORDS, DO YOU?
PEEP!

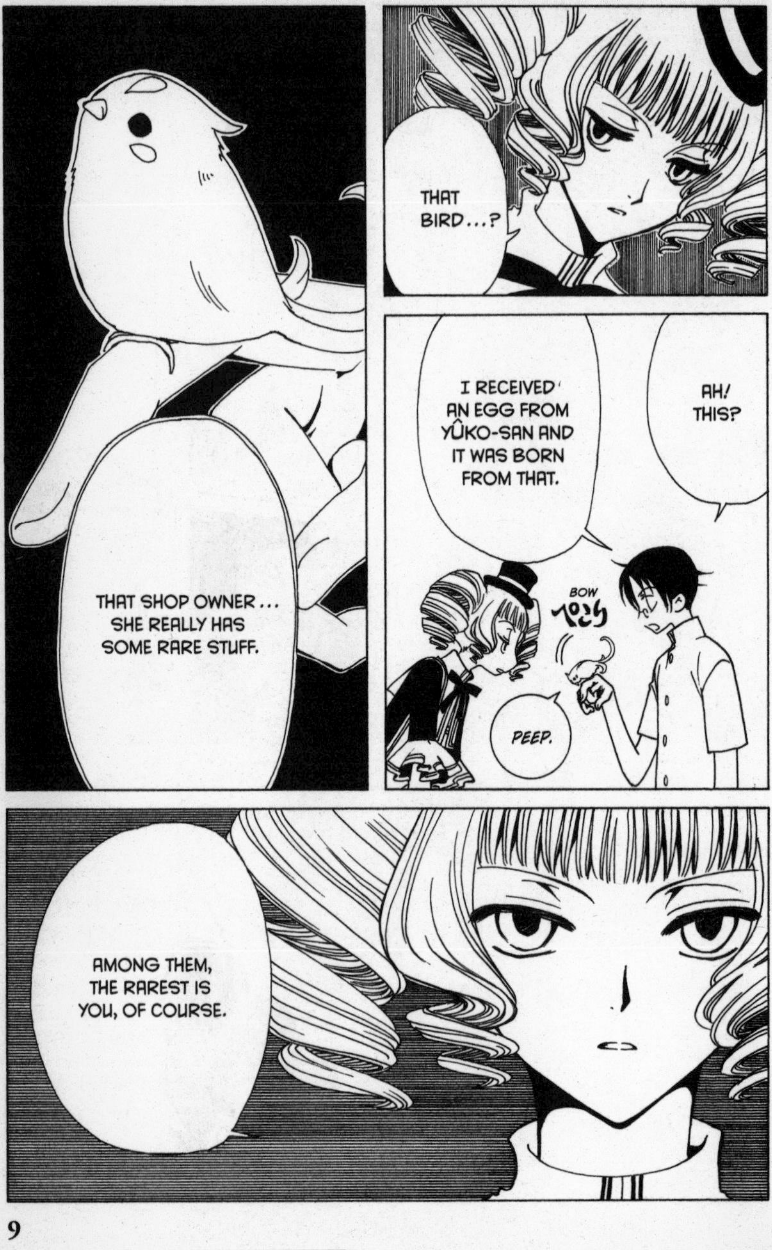
THAT BIRD...?
AH! THIS?
I RECEIVED AN EGG FROM YÛKO-SAN AND IT WAS BORN FROM THAT.
BOW
PEEP.
THAT SHOP OWNER... SHE REALLY HAS SOME RARE STUFF.
AMONG THEM, THE RAREST IS YOU, OF COURSE.

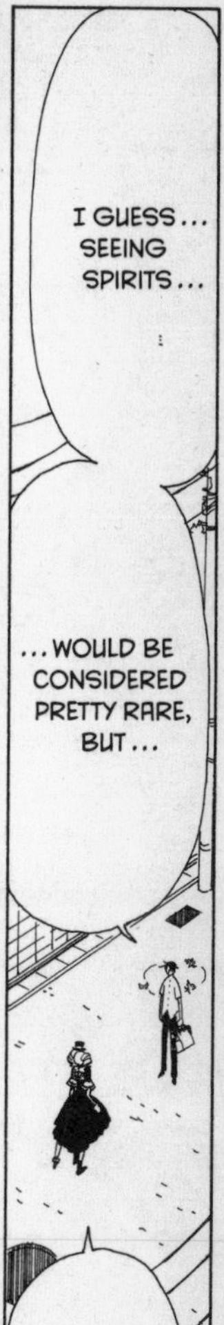
I GUESS... SEEING SPIRITS...
...WOULD BE CONSIDERED PRETTY RARE, BUT...
THERE ARE PLENTY WHO CAN DO THAT.
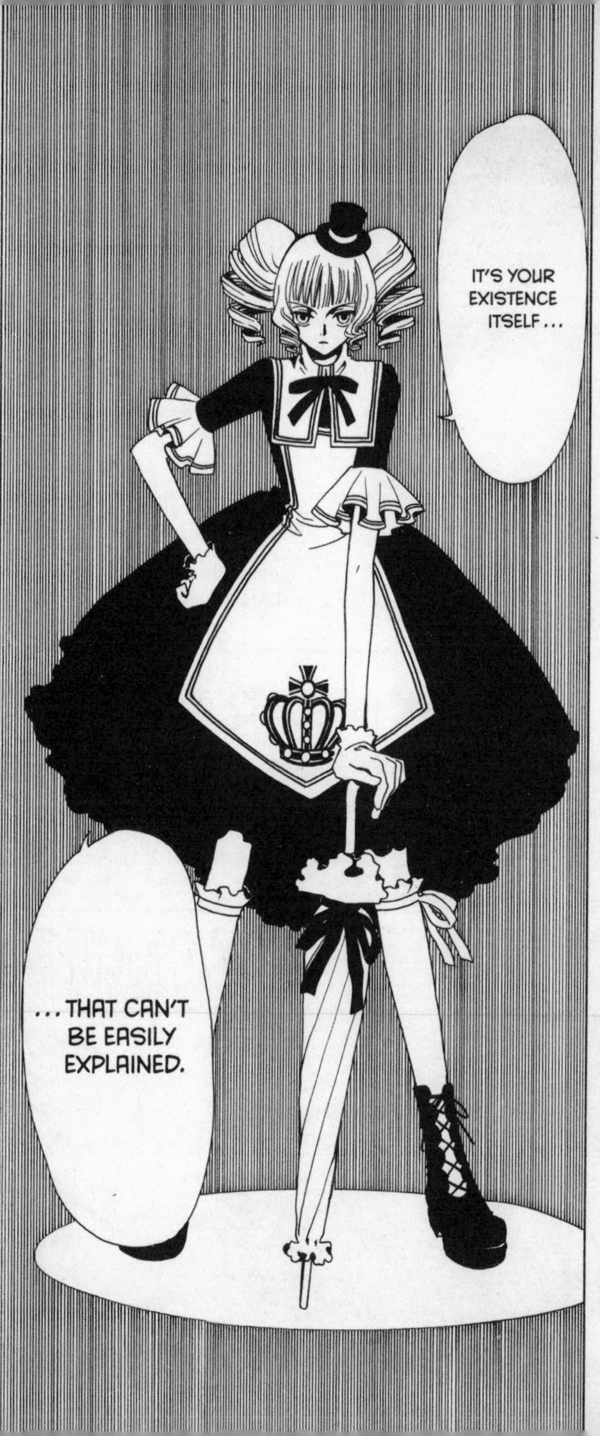
IT'S YOUR EXISTENCE ITSELF...
...THAT CAN'T BE EASILY EXPLAINED.

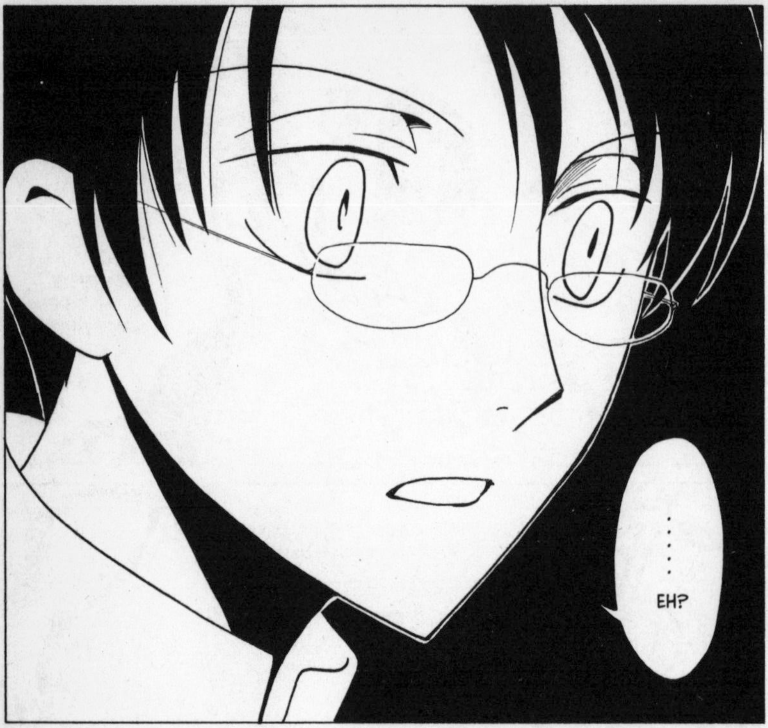
......
EH?

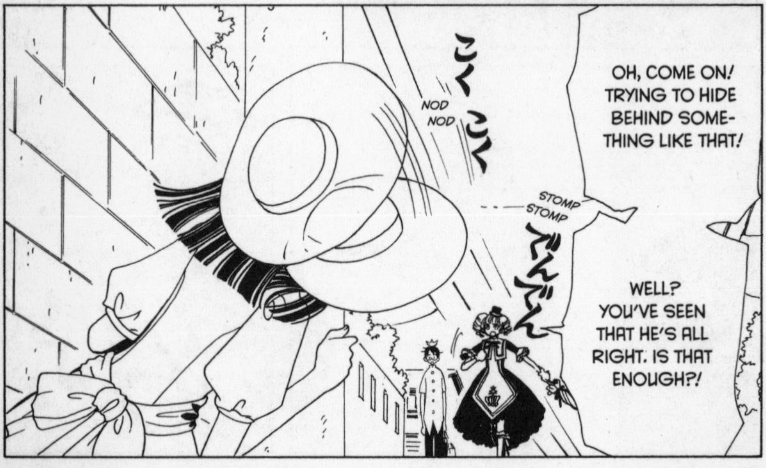
OH, COME ON! TRYING TO HIDE BEHIND SOME-THING LIKE THAT!
こくこく
NOD NOD
STOMP STOMP
でんでん
WELL? YOU'VE SEEN THAT HE'S ALL RIGHT. IS THAT ENOUGH?!

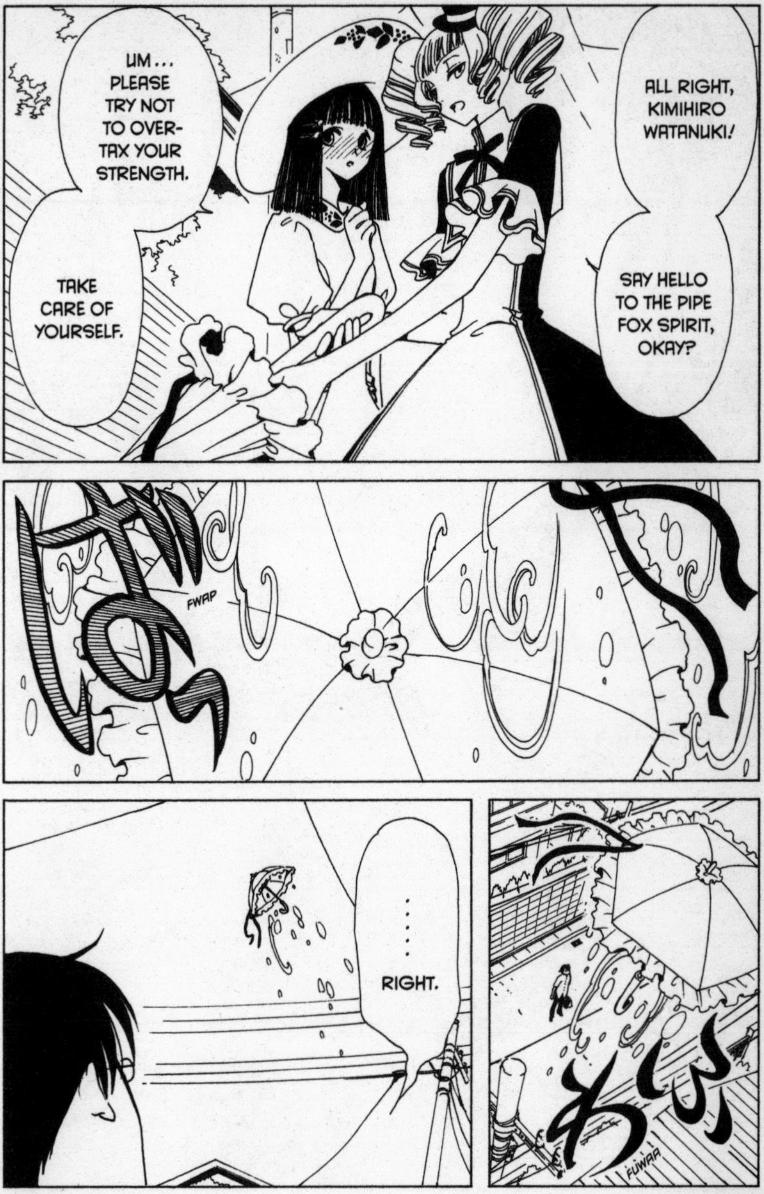
ALL RIGHT, KIMIHIRO WATANUKI!
SAY HELLO TO THE PIPE FOX SPIRIT, OKAY?
UM... PLEASE TRY NOT TO OVER-TAX YOUR STRENGTH.
TAKE CARE OF YOURSELF.
FWAP
FUWAA
..... RIGHT.

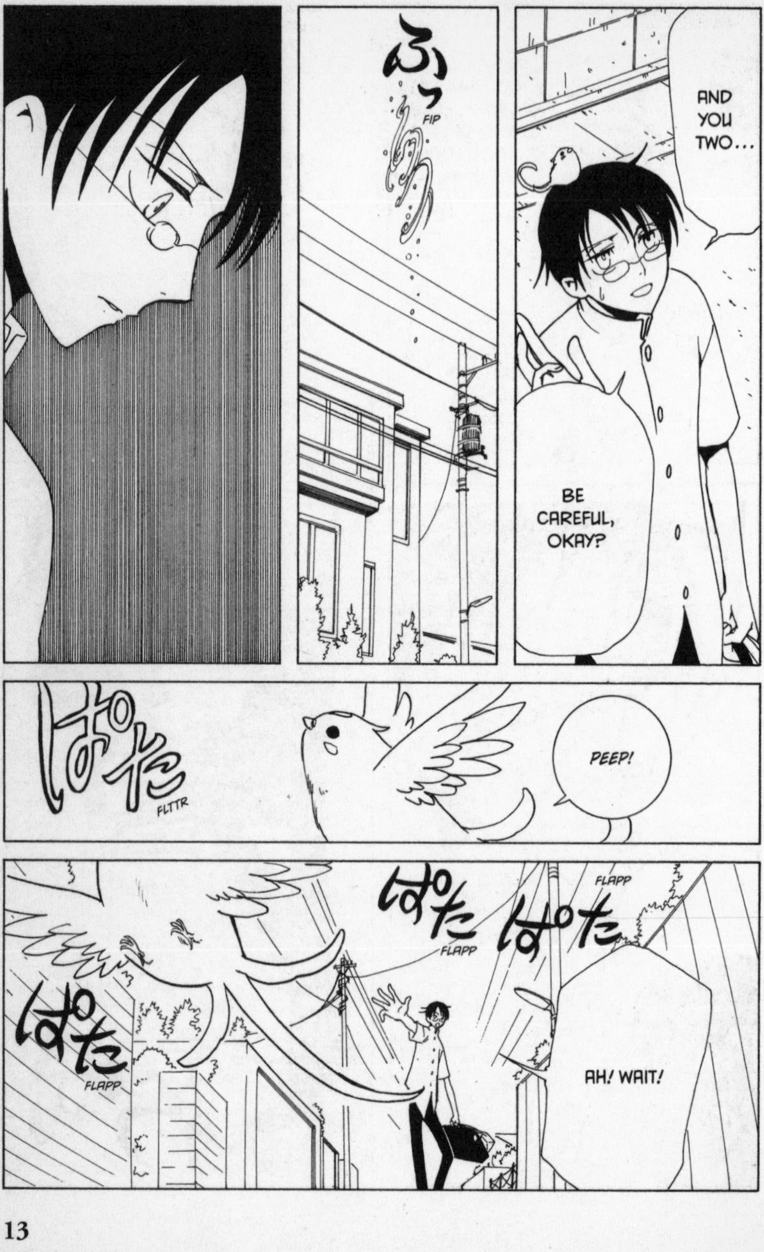
AND YOU TWO...
BE CAREFUL, OKAY?
ふっ
FIP
PEEP!
ぱた
FLTTR
AH! WAIT!
ぱた
FLAPP
ぱた
FLAPP
ぱた
FLAPP

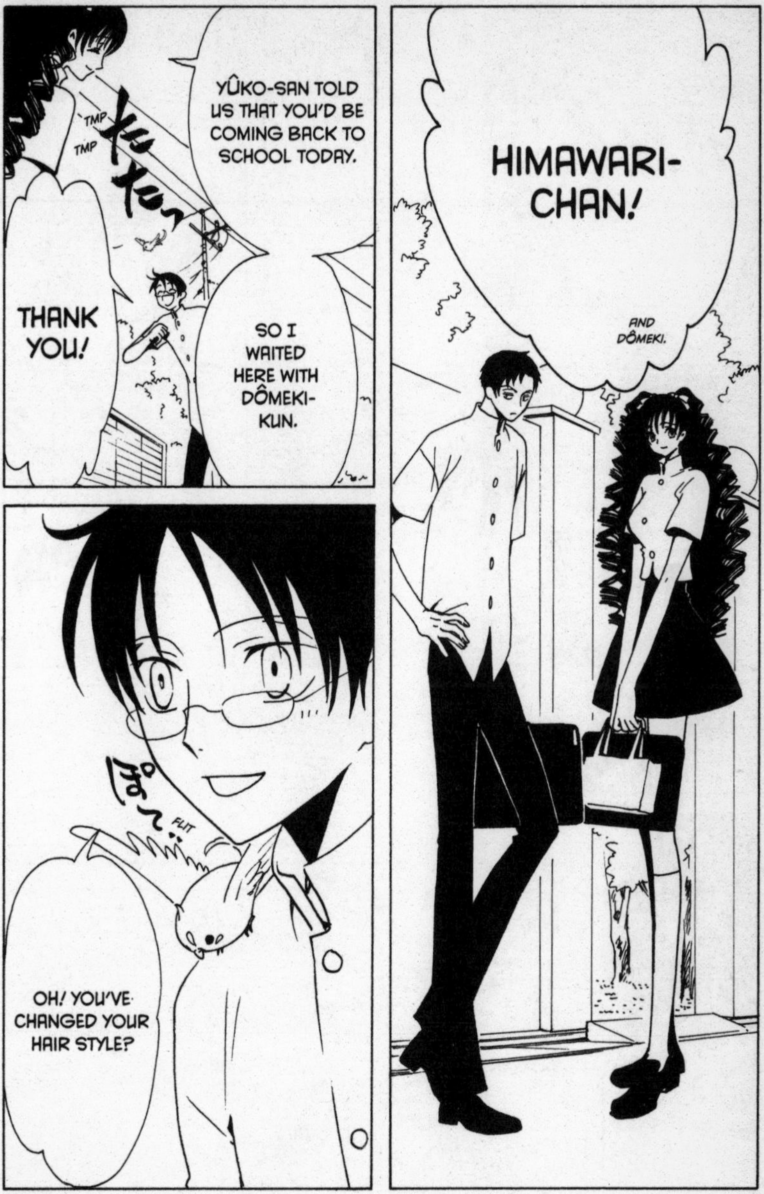
HIMAWARI-CHAN!
AND DÔMEKI.
YÛKO-SAN TOLD US THAT YOU'D BE COMING BACK TO SCHOOL TODAY.
TMP
TMP
SO I WAITED HERE WITH DÔMEKI-KUN.
THANK YOU!
FLIT
OH! YOU'VE CHANGED YOUR HAIR STYLE?

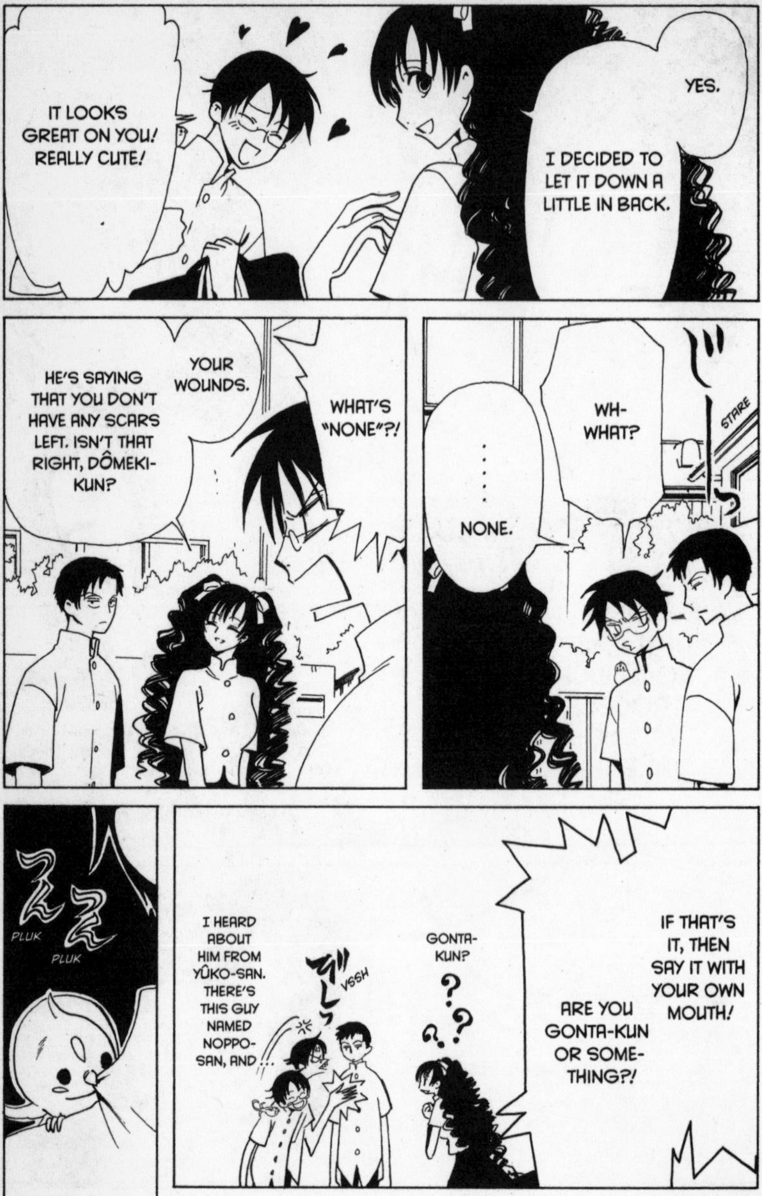
YES.
I DECIDED TO LET IT DOWN A LITTLE IN BACK.
IT LOOKS GREAT ON YOU! REALLY CUTE!
STARE
WH- WHAT?
...... NONE.
WHAT'S "NONE"?!
YOUR WOUNDS.
HE'S SAYING THAT YOU DON'T HAVE ANY SCARS LEFT. ISN'T THAT RIGHT, DÔMEKI-KUN?
IF THAT'S IT, THEN SAY IT WITH YOUR OWN MOUTH!
ARE YOU GONTA-KUN OR SOME-THING?!
GONTA-KUN?
VSSH
I HEARD ABOUT HIM FROM YÛKO-SAN. THERE'S THIS GUY NAMED NOPPO-SAN, AND...
PLUK
PLUK

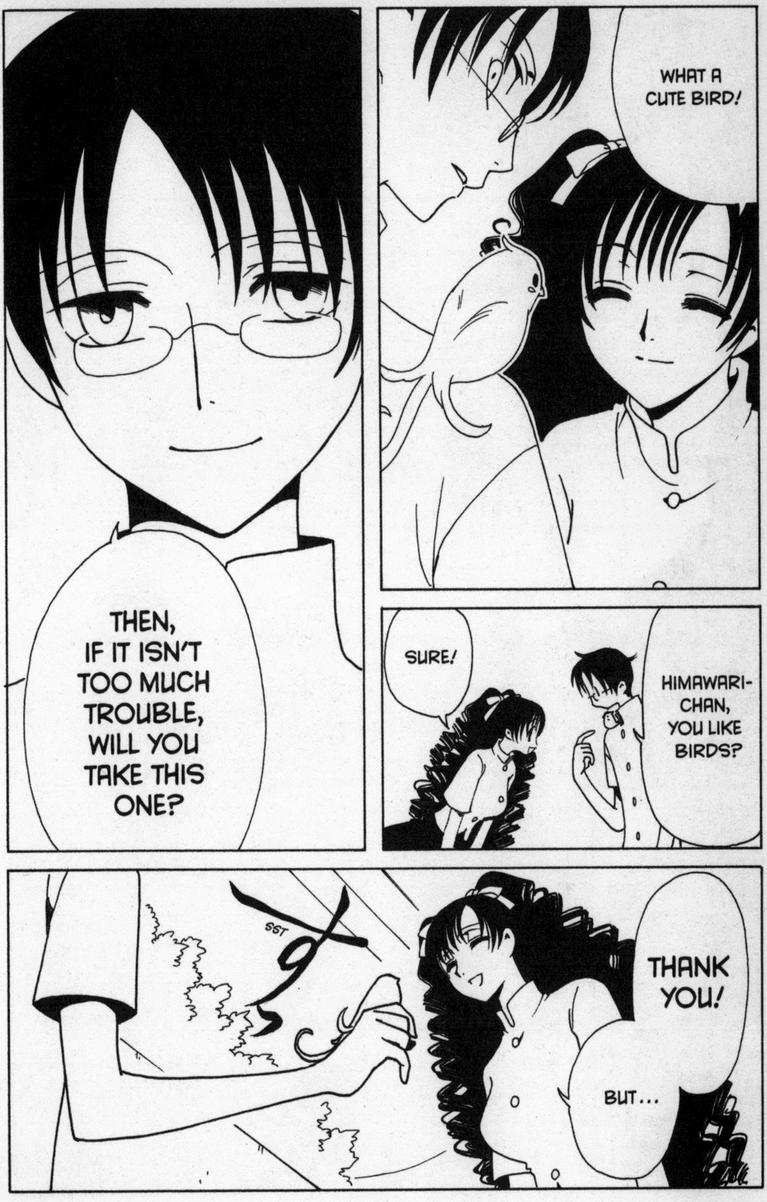
WHAT A CUTE BIRD!
HIMAWARI-CHAN, YOU LIKE BIRDS?
SURE!
THEN, IF IT ISN'T TOO MUCH TROUBLE, WILL YOU TAKE THIS ONE?
THANK YOU!
BUT...
SST

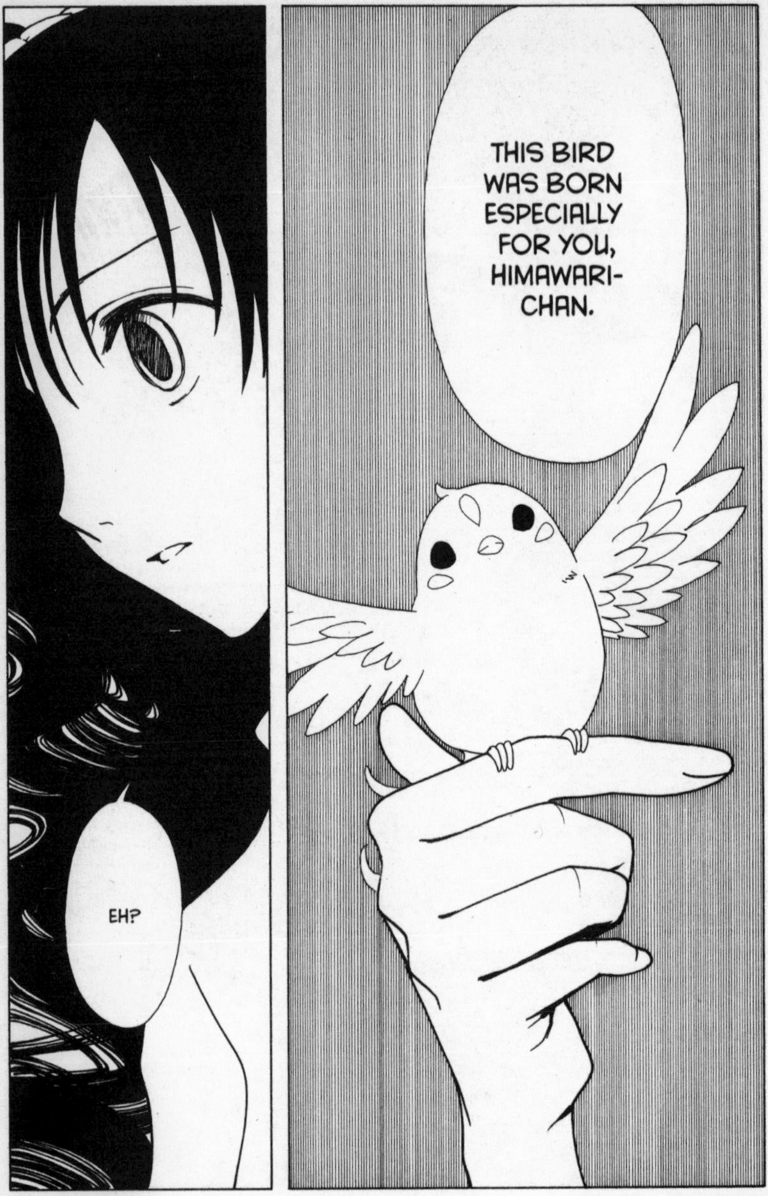
THIS BIRD WAS BORN ESPECIALLY FOR YOU, HIMAWARI-CHAN.
EH?

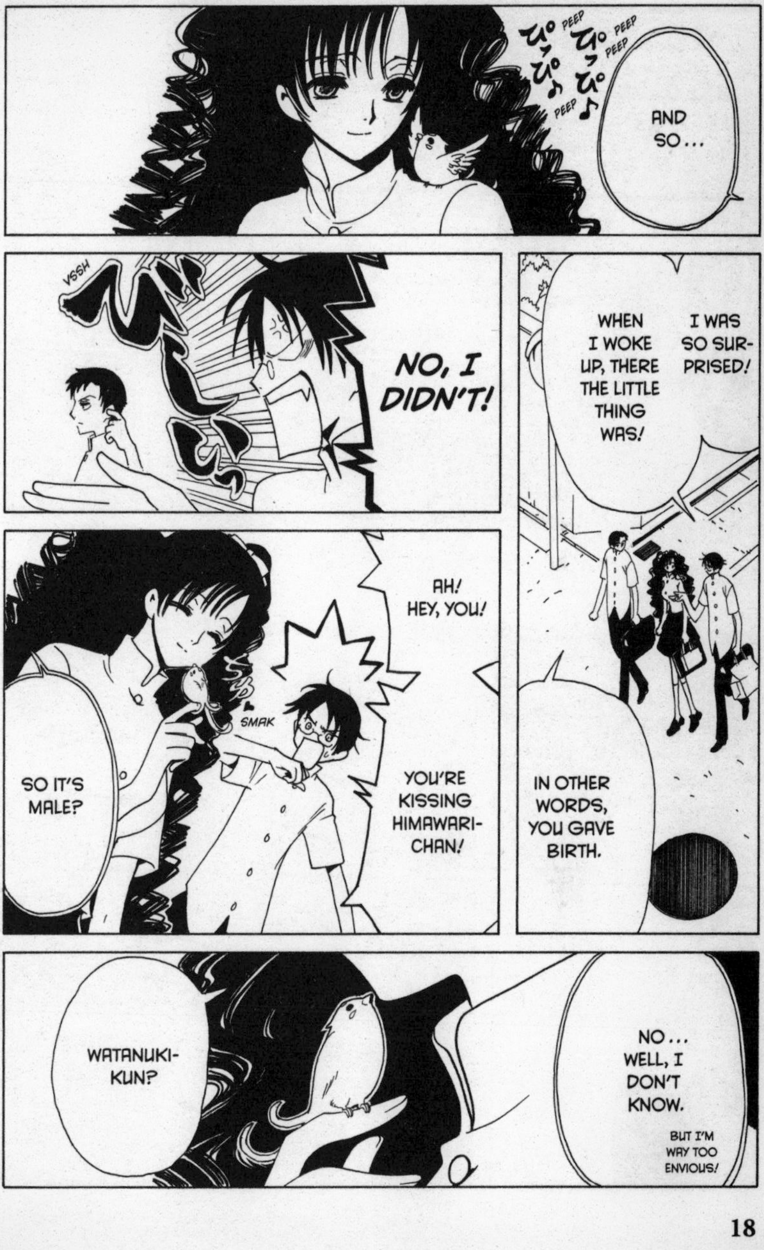

ぴっぴ♪ PEEP PEEP
ぴっぴ♪ PEEP PEEP
AND SO...
I WAS SO SURPRISED!
WHEN I WOKE UP, THERE THE LITTLE THING WAS!
IN OTHER WORDS, YOU GAVE BIRTH.
NO, I DIDN'T!
VSSH
AH! HEY, YOU!
YOU'RE KISSING HIMAWARI-CHAN!
SMAK
SO IT'S MALE?
NO... WELL, I DON'T KNOW.
BUT I'M WAY TOO ENVIOUS!
WATANUKI-KUN?

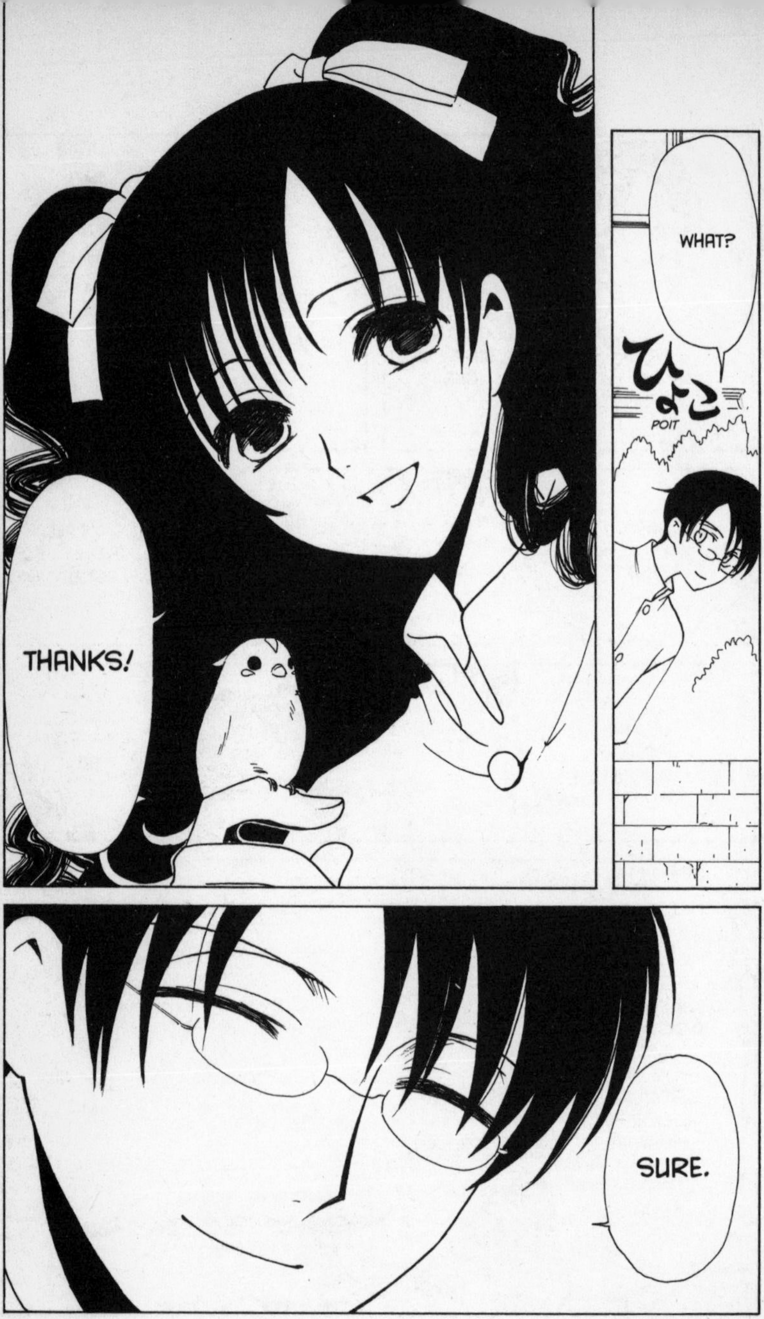
WHAT?
ひょこ
POIT
THANKS!
SURE.

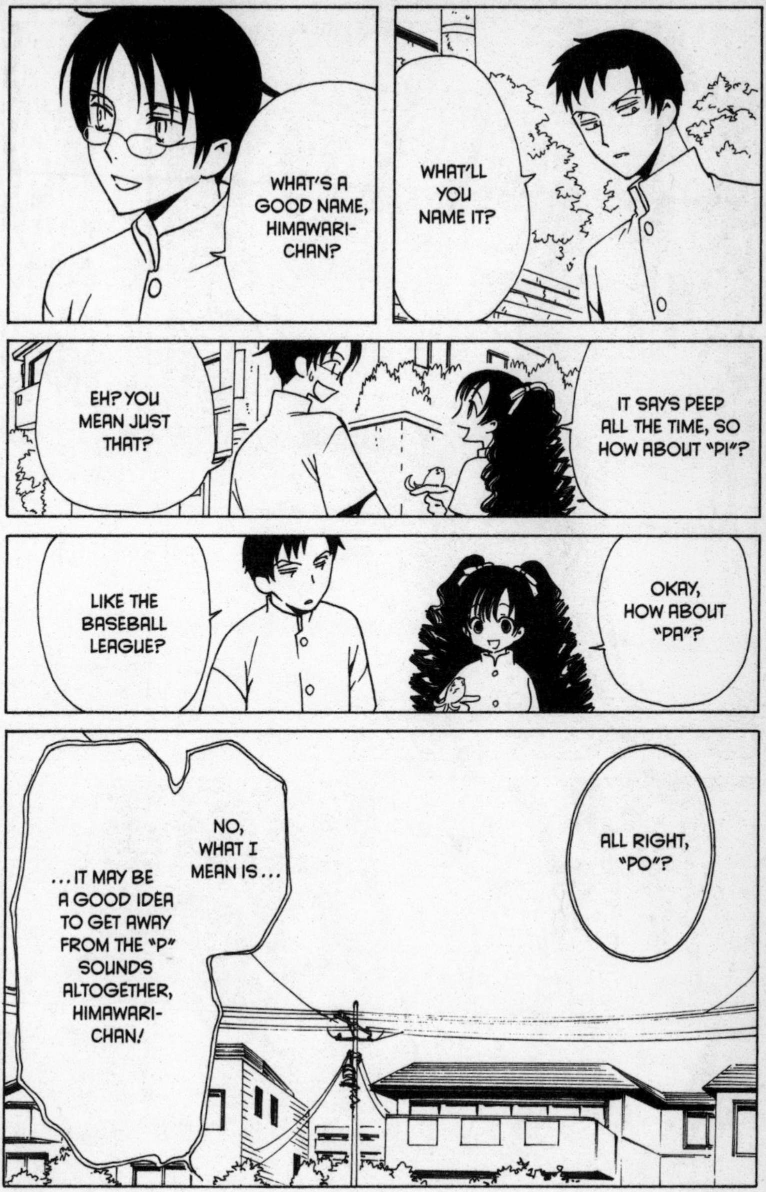
WHAT'LL YOU NAME IT?
WHAT'S A GOOD NAME, HIMAWARI-CHAN?
IT SAYS PEEP ALL THE TIME, SO HOW ABOUT "PI"?
EH? YOU MEAN JUST THAT?
OKAY, HOW ABOUT "PA"?
LIKE THE BASEBALL LEAGUE?
ALL RIGHT, "PO"?
NO, WHAT I MEAN IS...
...IT MAY BE A GOOD IDEA TO GET AWAY FROM THE "P" SOUNDS ALTOGETHER, HIMAWARI-CHAN!

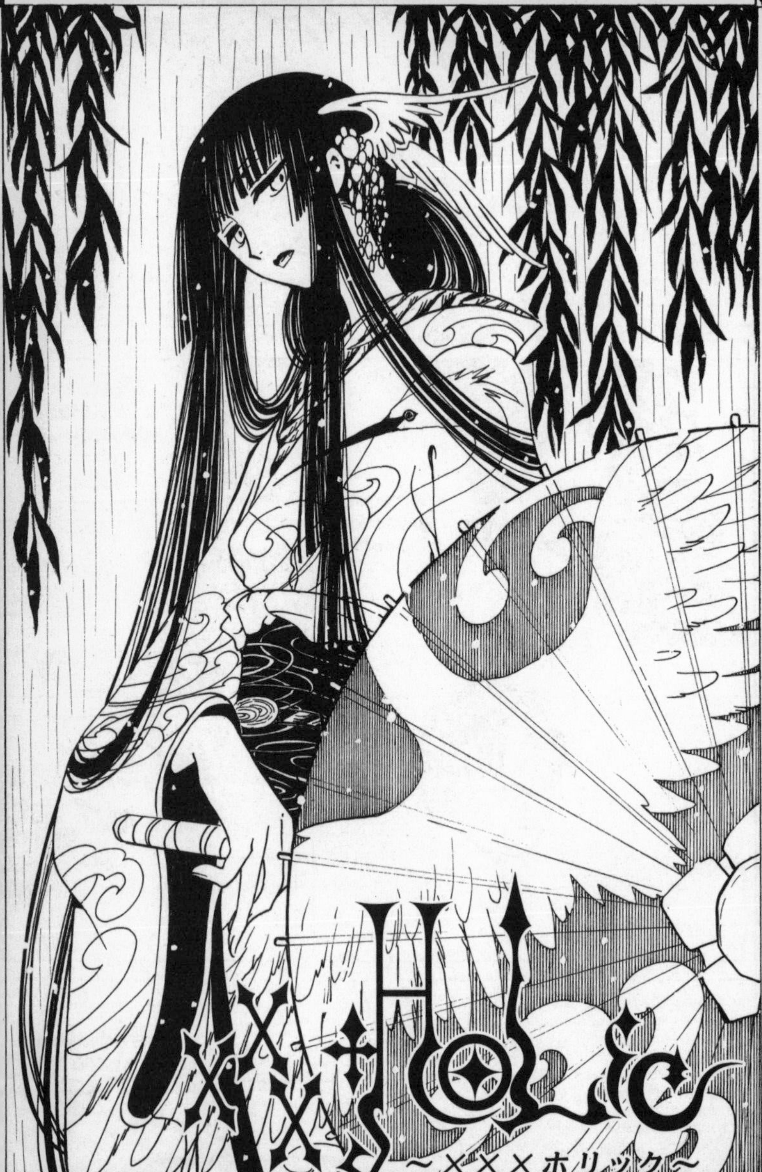
xxxHOLiC
~×××ホリック~

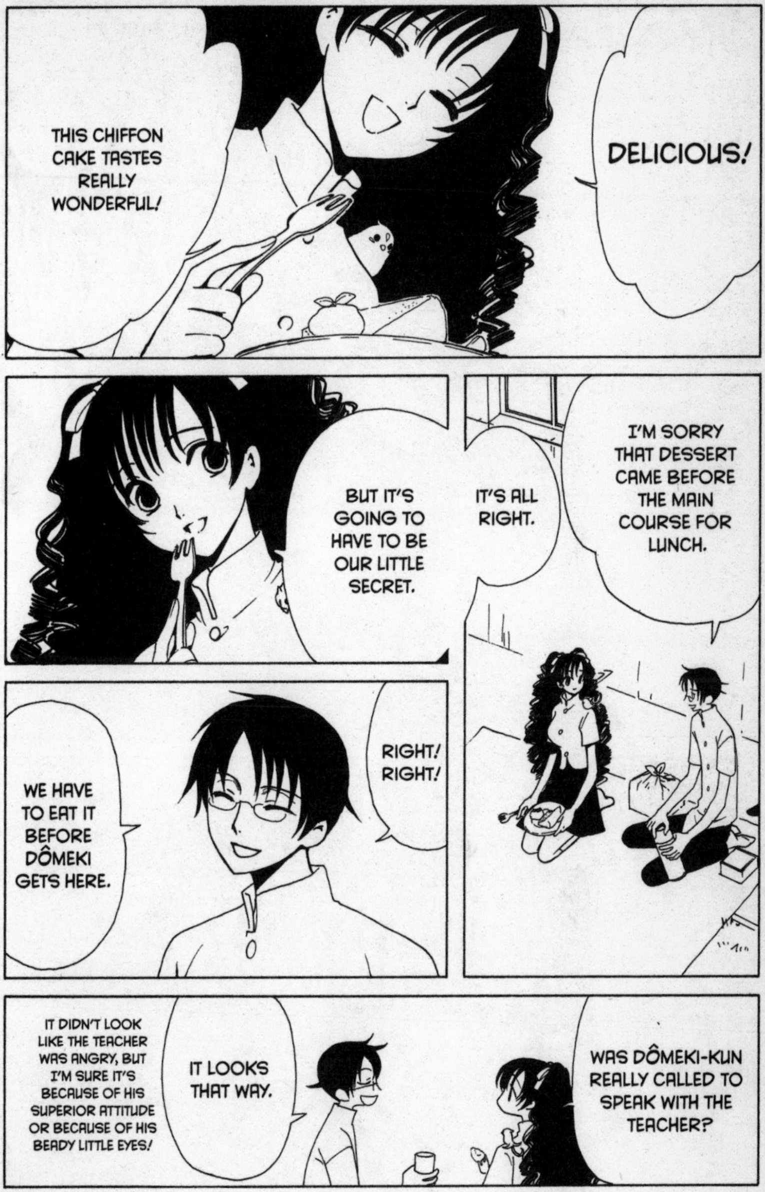
DELICIOUS!
THIS CHIFFON CAKE TASTES REALLY WONDERFUL!
I'M SORRY THAT DESSERT CAME BEFORE THE MAIN COURSE FOR LUNCH.
IT'S ALL RIGHT.
BUT IT'S GOING TO HAVE TO BE OUR LITTLE SECRET.
RIGHT! RIGHT!
WE HAVE TO EAT IT BEFORE DÔMEKI GETS HERE.
WAS DÔMEKI-KUN REALLY CALLED TO SPEAK WITH THE TEACHER?
IT LOOKS THAT WAY.
IT DIDN'T LOOK LIKE THE TEACHER WAS ANGRY, BUT I'M SURE IT'S BECAUSE OF HIS SUPERIOR ATTITUDE OR BECAUSE OF HIS BEADY LITTLE EYES!

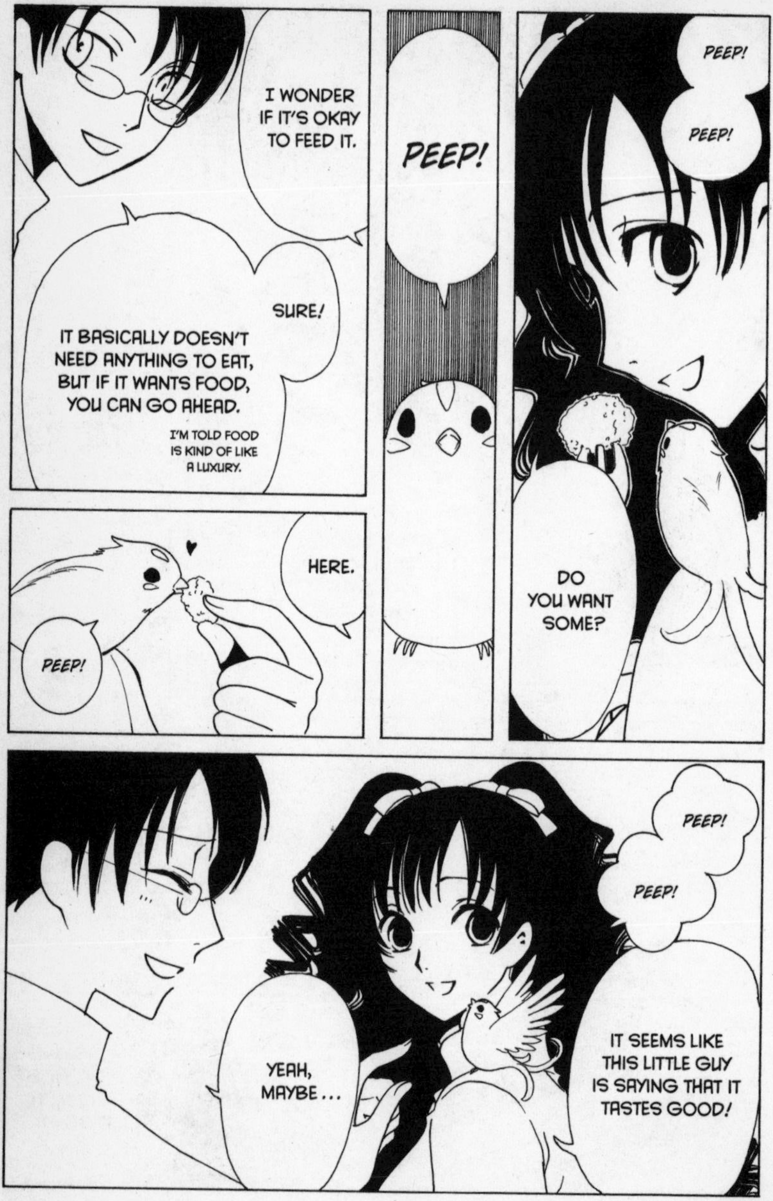
PEEP!
PEEP!
DO YOU WANT SOME?
PEEP!
I WONDER IF IT'S OKAY TO FEED IT.
SURE!
IT BASICALLY DOESN'T NEED ANYTHING TO EAT, BUT IF IT WANTS FOOD, YOU CAN GO AHEAD.
I'M TOLD FOOD IS KIND OF LIKE A LUXURY.
HERE.
PEEP!
PEEP!
PEEP!
IT SEEMS LIKE THIS LITTLE GUY IS SAYING THAT IT TASTES GOOD!
YEAH, MAYBE...

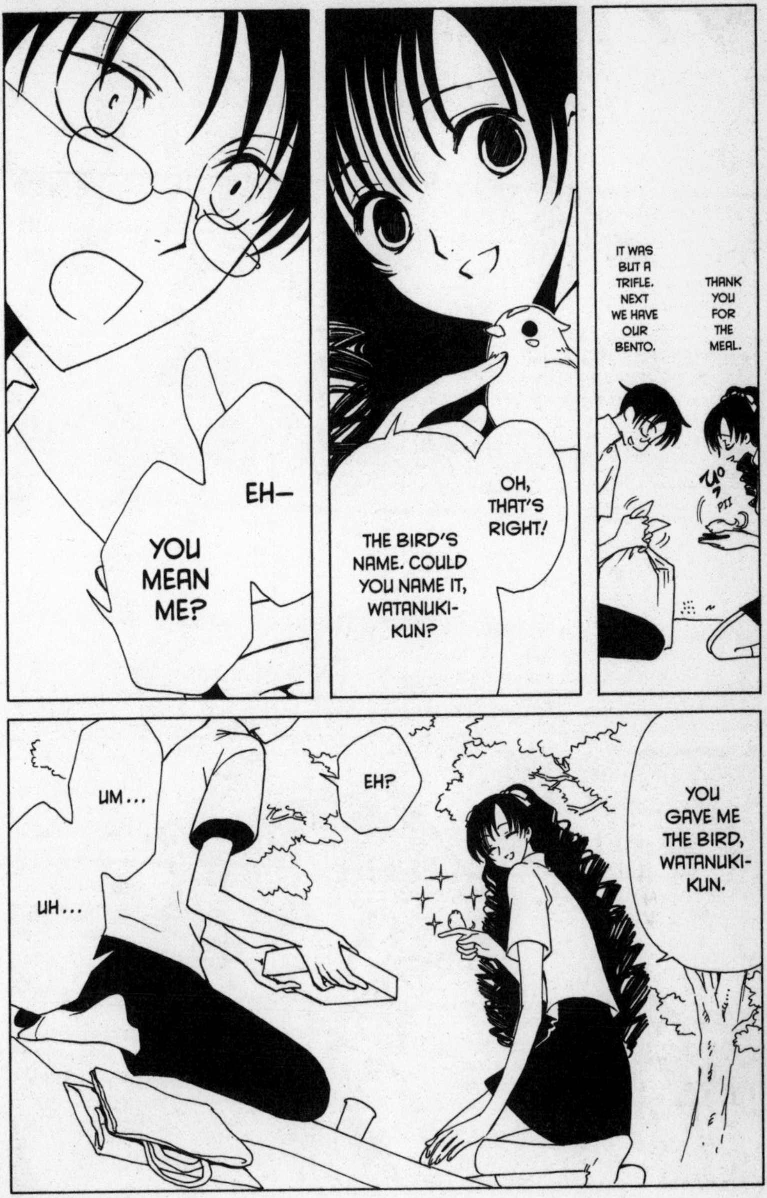
THANK YOU FOR THE MEAL.
IT WAS BUT A TRIFLE. NEXT WE HAVE OUR BENTO.
PII
OH, THAT'S RIGHT!
THE BIRD'S NAME. COULD YOU NAME IT, WATANUKI-KUN?
EH—
YOU MEAN ME?
YOU GAVE ME THE BIRD, WATANUKI-KUN.
EH?
UM...
UH...

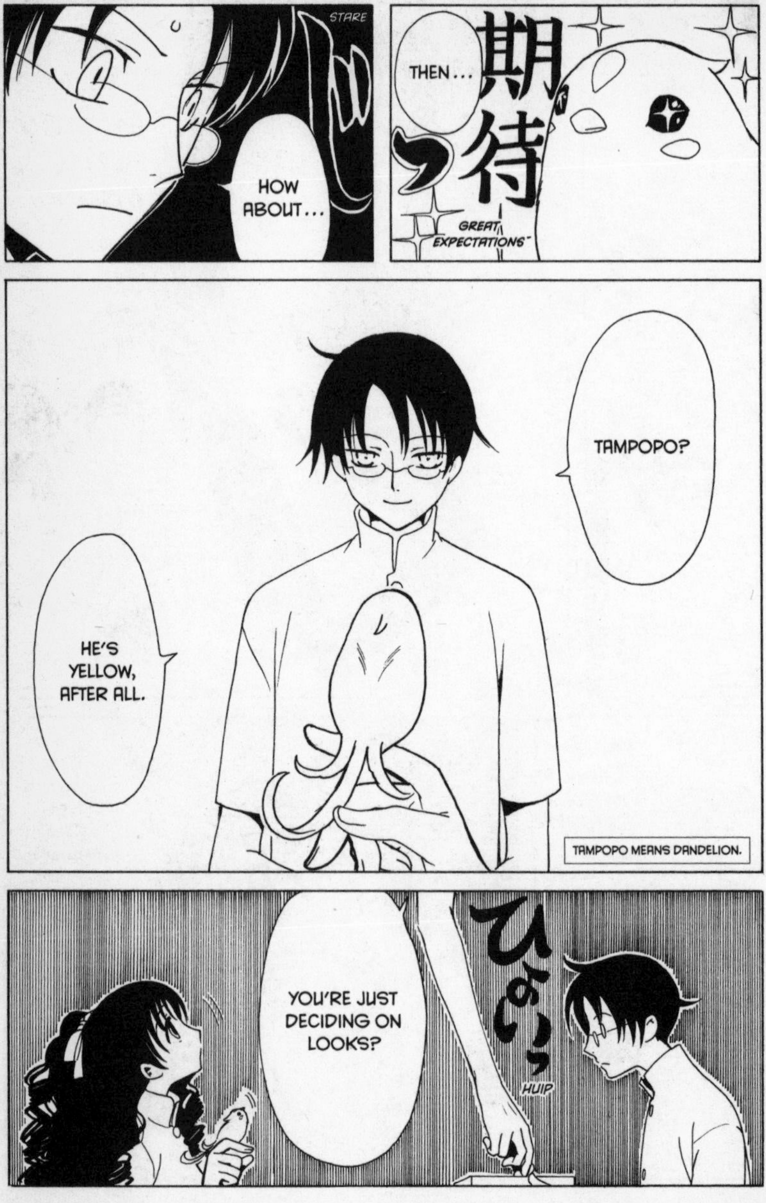
THEN...
期待
GREAT EXPECTATIONS
STARE
HOW ABOUT...
TAMPOPO?
HE'S YELLOW, AFTER ALL.
TAMPOPO MEANS DANDELION.
ひょいっ
HUIP
YOU'RE JUST DECIDING ON LOOKS?

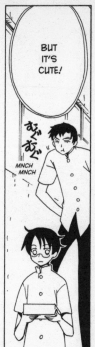

WHY YOU LITTLE ... DÔMEKI!!
むぐむぐ
MNCH MNCH
BUT IT'S CUTE!
むぐむぐ
MNCH MNCH
YOU HAVE A FLOWER NAME, JUST LIKE MINE.
PEEP!
HIMAWARI MEANS SUNFLOWER.
I THINK IT LIKES THE NAME.
PEEP!

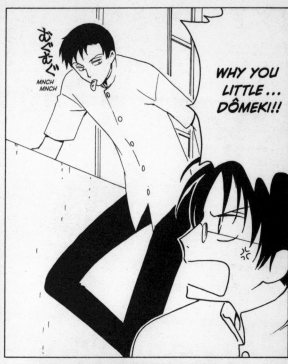

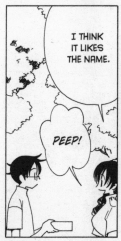

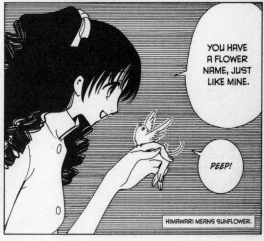

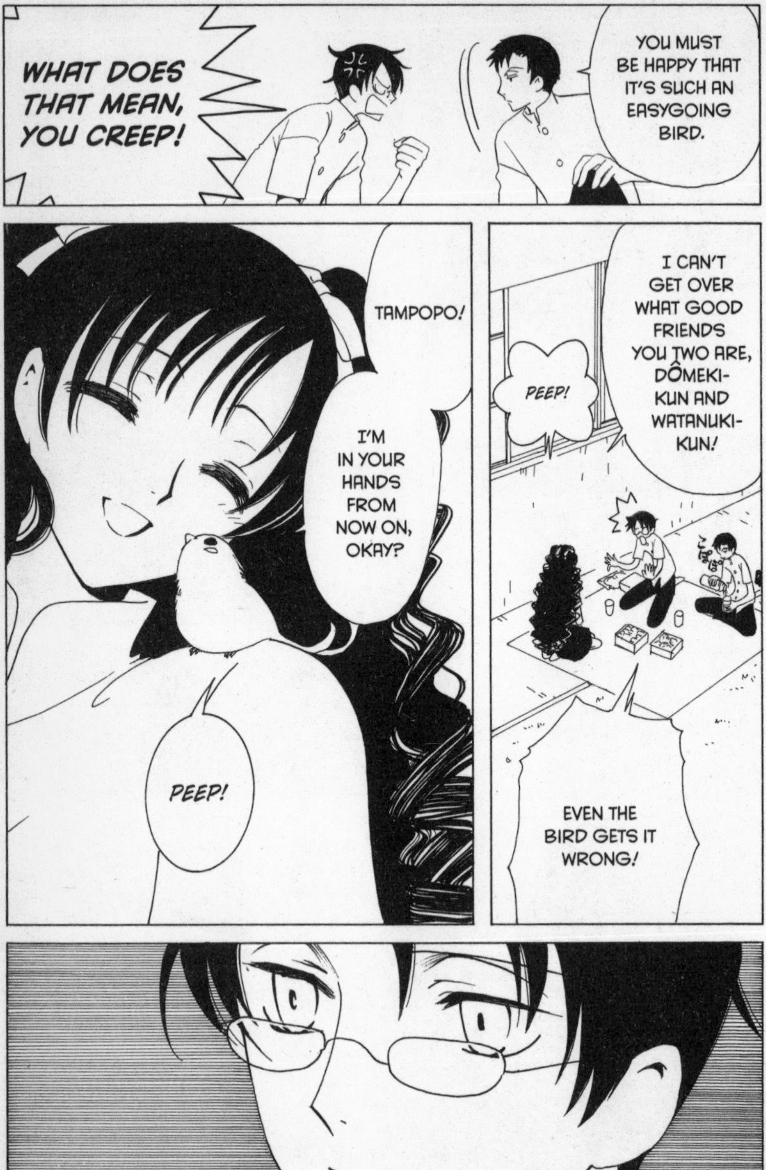
YOU MUST BE HAPPY THAT IT'S SUCH AN EASYGOING BIRD.
WHAT DOES THAT MEAN, YOU CREEP!
I CAN'T GET OVER WHAT GOOD FRIENDS YOU TWO ARE, DÔMEKI-KUN AND WATANUKI-KUN!
PEEP!
EVEN THE BIRD GETS IT WRONG!
TAMPOPO!
I'M IN YOUR HANDS FROM NOW ON, OKAY?
PEEP!

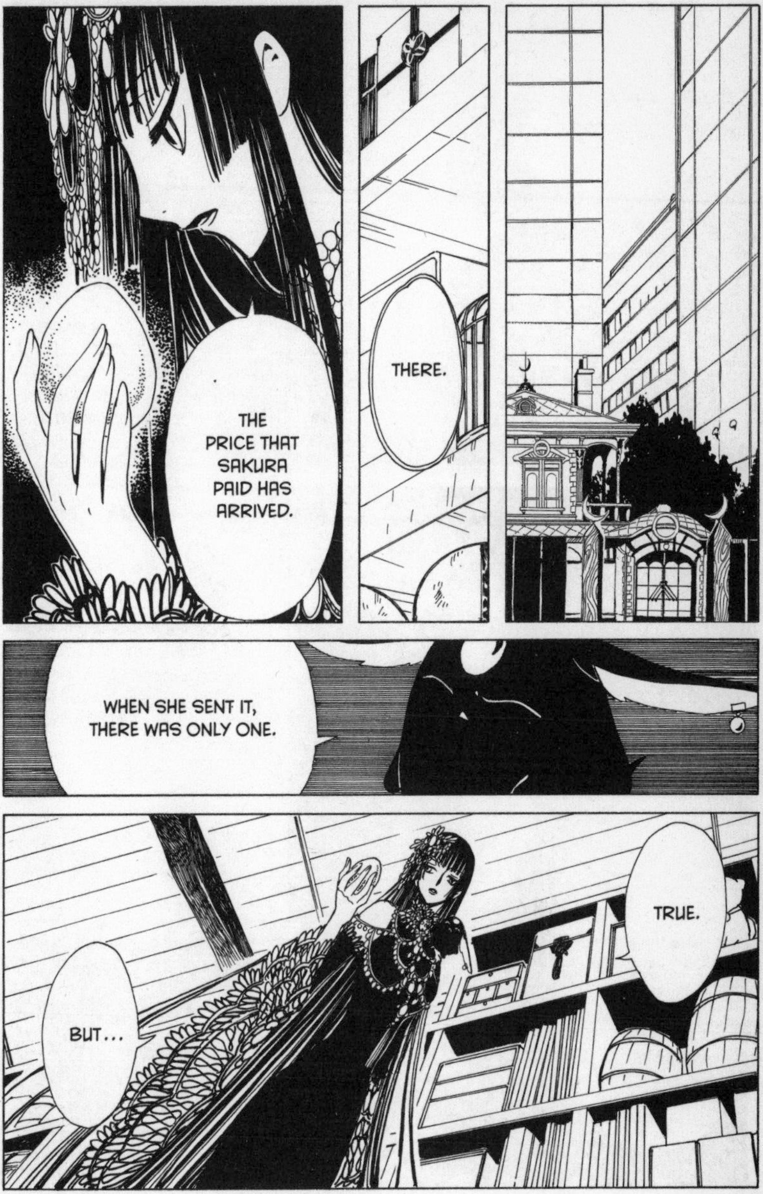
THERE.
THE PRICE THAT SAKURA PAID HAS ARRIVED.
WHEN SHE SENT IT, THERE WAS ONLY ONE.
TRUE.
BUT...

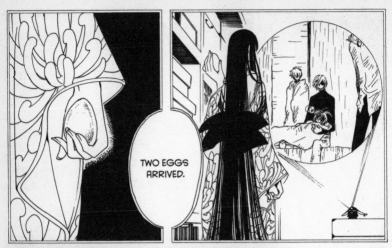

TWO EGGS ARRIVED.
THE WORLD THAT SAKURA-CHAN AND THE OTHERS ARE ON HAS NO PEOPLE WHO USE MAGIC OR EVEN MAGIC ITEMS.
BUT THE EGG THAT WE HANDED OVER TO WATANUKI HAD MAGIC INSIDE IT.
TOO BAD THIS ONE DOESN'T HAVE THE SAME POWER.

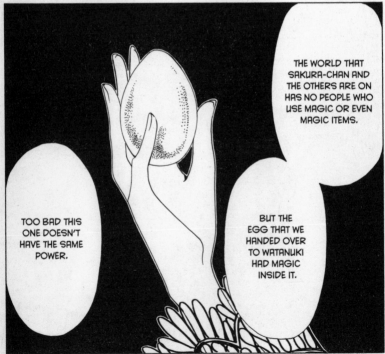

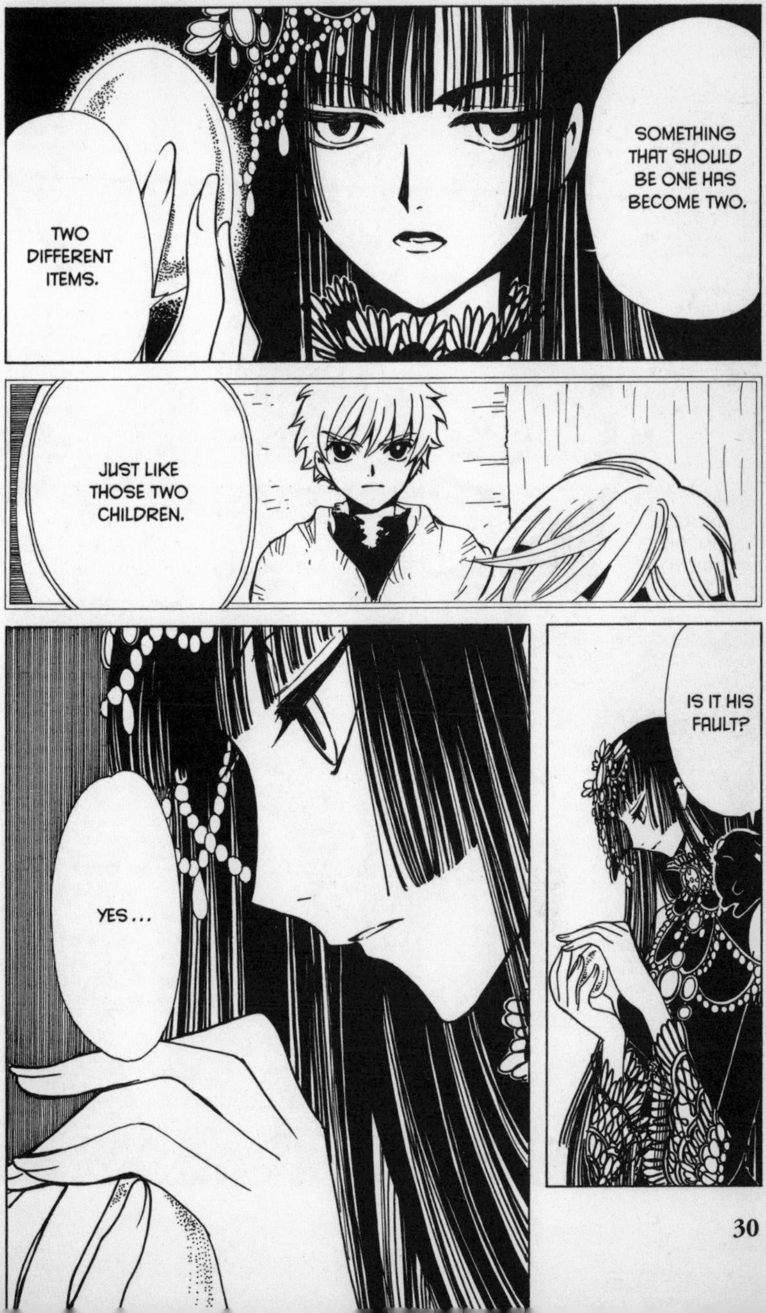
SOMETHING THAT SHOULD BE ONE HAS BECOME TWO.
TWO DIFFERENT ITEMS.
JUST LIKE THOSE TWO CHILDREN.
IS IT HIS FAULT?
YES...

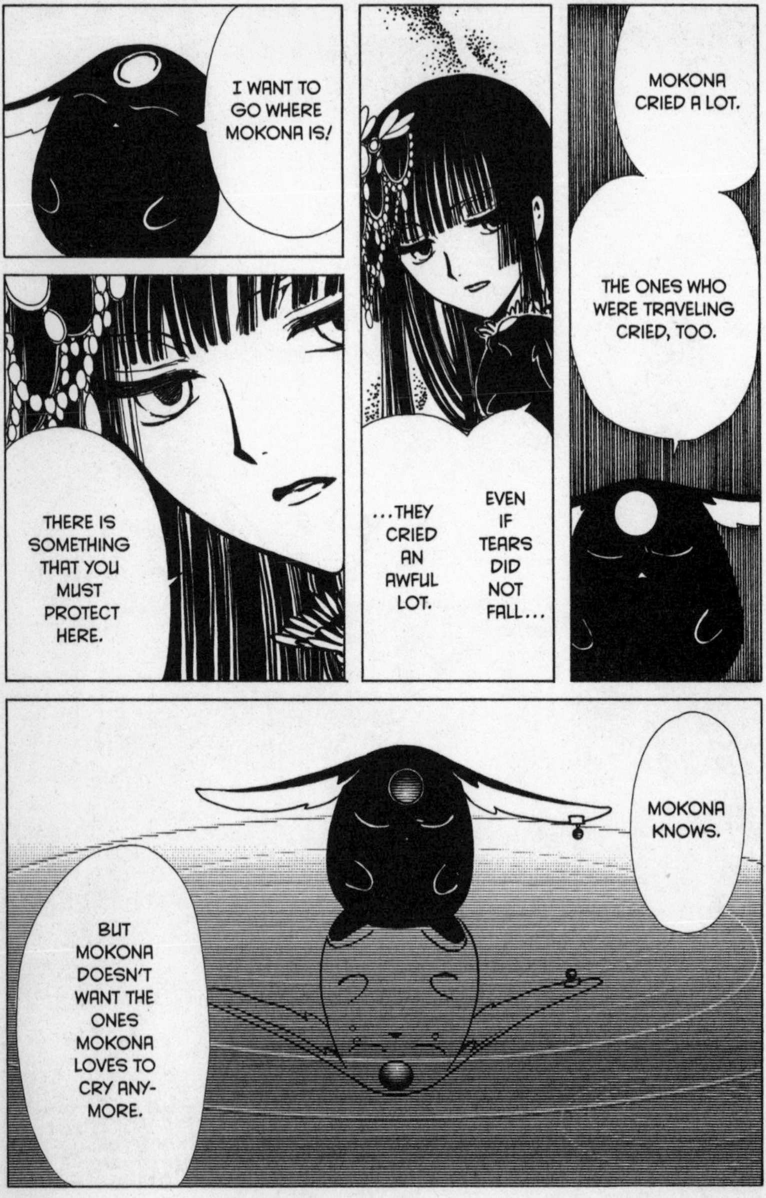

MOKONA CRIED A LOT.
THE ONES WHO WERE TRAVELING CRIED, TOO.
EVEN IF TEARS DID NOT FALL...
...THEY CRIED AN AWFUL LOT.
I WANT TO GO WHERE MOKONA IS!
THERE IS SOMETHING THAT YOU MUST PROTECT HERE.
MOKONA KNOWS.
BUT MOKONA DOESN'T WANT THE ONES MOKONA LOVES TO CRY ANY-MORE.

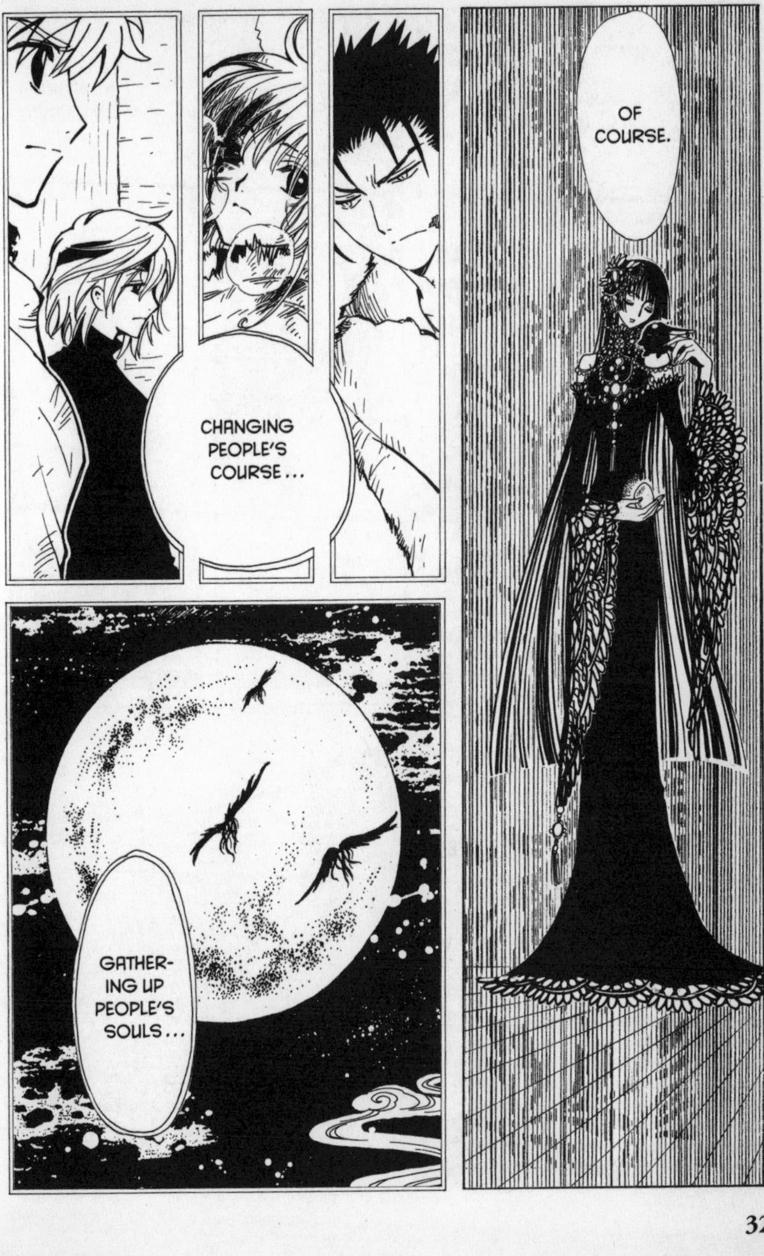
OF COURSE.
CHANGING PEOPLE'S COURSE...
GATHERING UP PEOPLE'S SOULS...

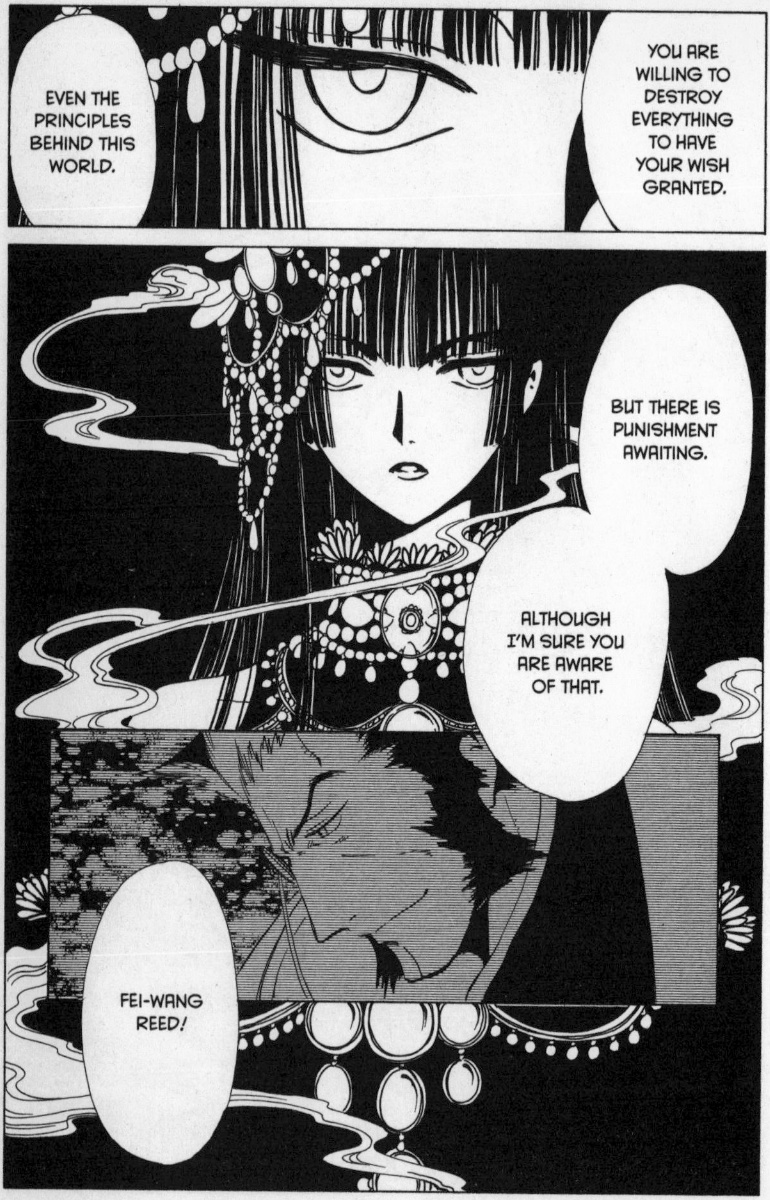
YOU ARE WILLING TO DESTROY EVERYTHING TO HAVE YOUR WISH GRANTED.
EVEN THE PRINCIPLES BEHIND THIS WORLD.
BUT THERE IS PUNISHMENT AWAITING.
ALTHOUGH I'M SURE YOU ARE AWARE OF THAT.
FEI-WANG REED!

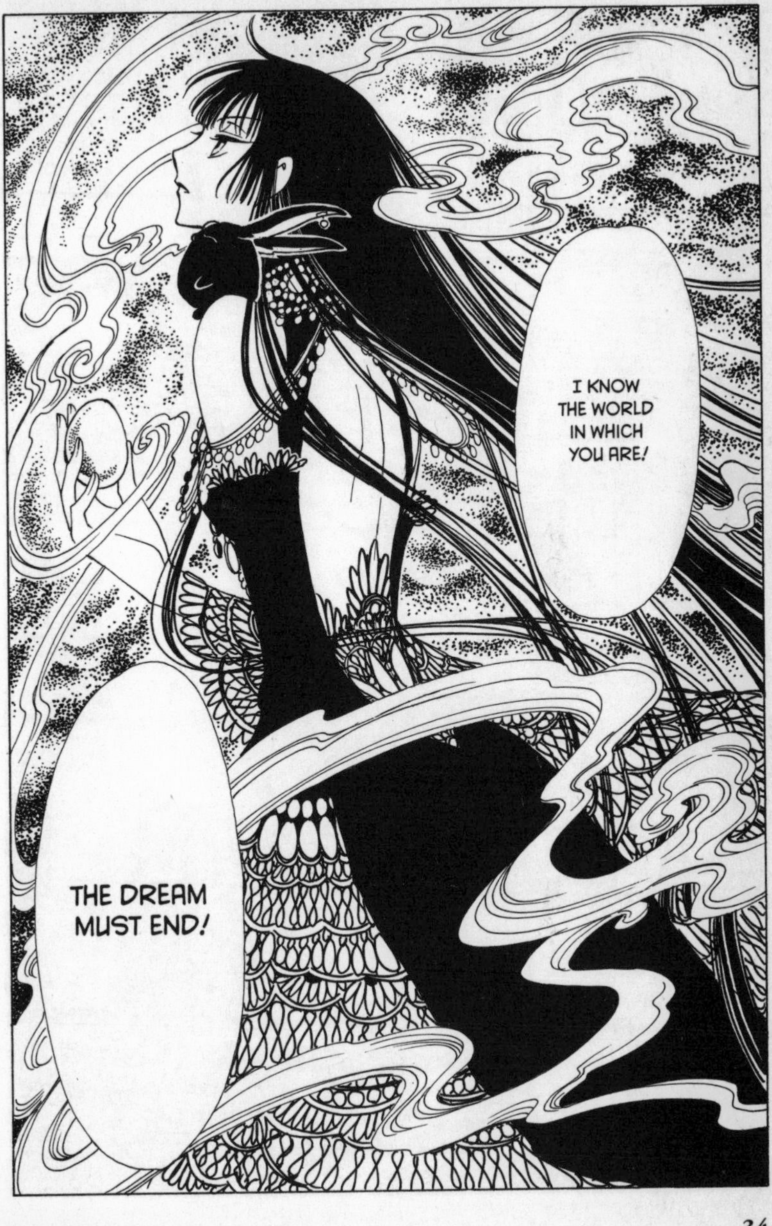
I KNOW THE WORLD IN WHICH YOU ARE!
THE DREAM MUST END!

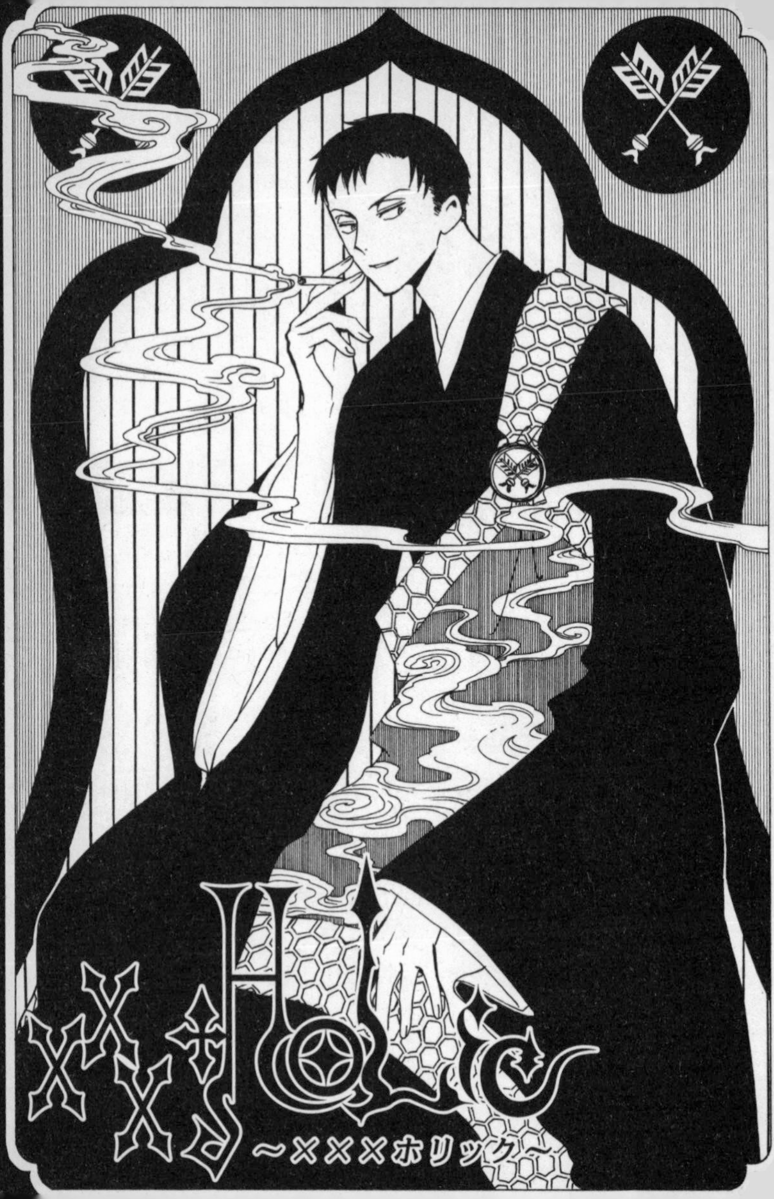
xxxHOLiC
~×××ホリック~

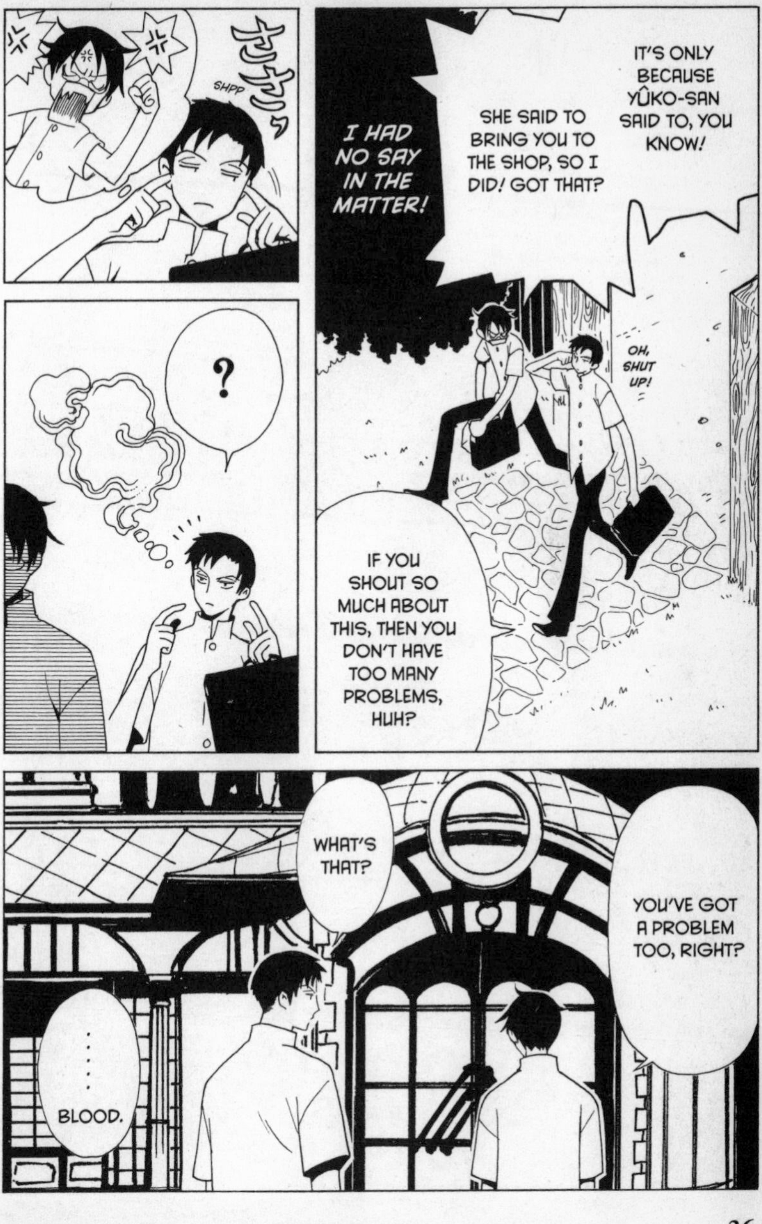
IT'S ONLY BECAUSE YÛKO-SAN SAID TO, YOU KNOW!
SHE SAID TO BRING YOU TO THE SHOP, SO I DID! GOT THAT?
I HAD NO SAY IN THE MATTER!
OH, SHUT UP!
IF YOU SHOUT SO MUCH ABOUT THIS, THEN YOU DON'T HAVE TOO MANY PROBLEMS, HUH?
SHPP
?
YOU'VE GOT A PROBLEM TOO, RIGHT?
WHAT'S THAT?
...... BLOOD.

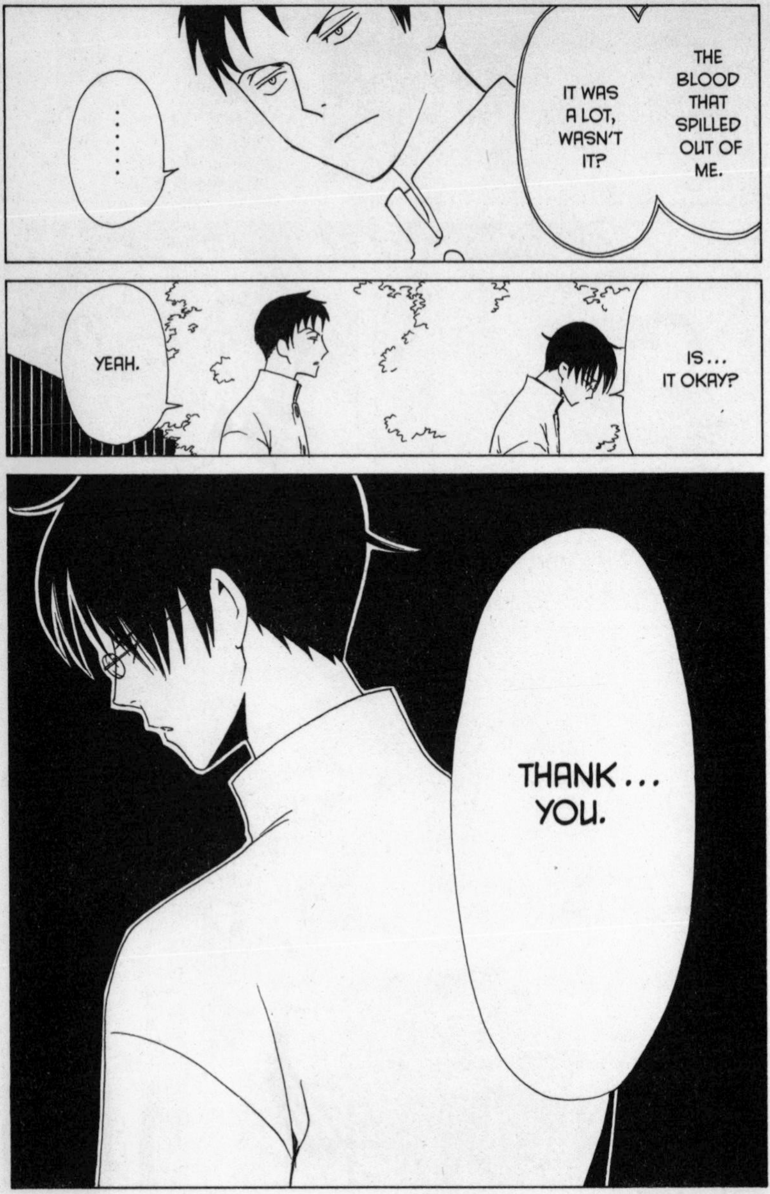
THE BLOOD THAT SPILLED OUT OF ME.
IT WAS A LOT, WASN'T IT?
......
IS... IT OKAY?
YEAH.
THANK... YOU.

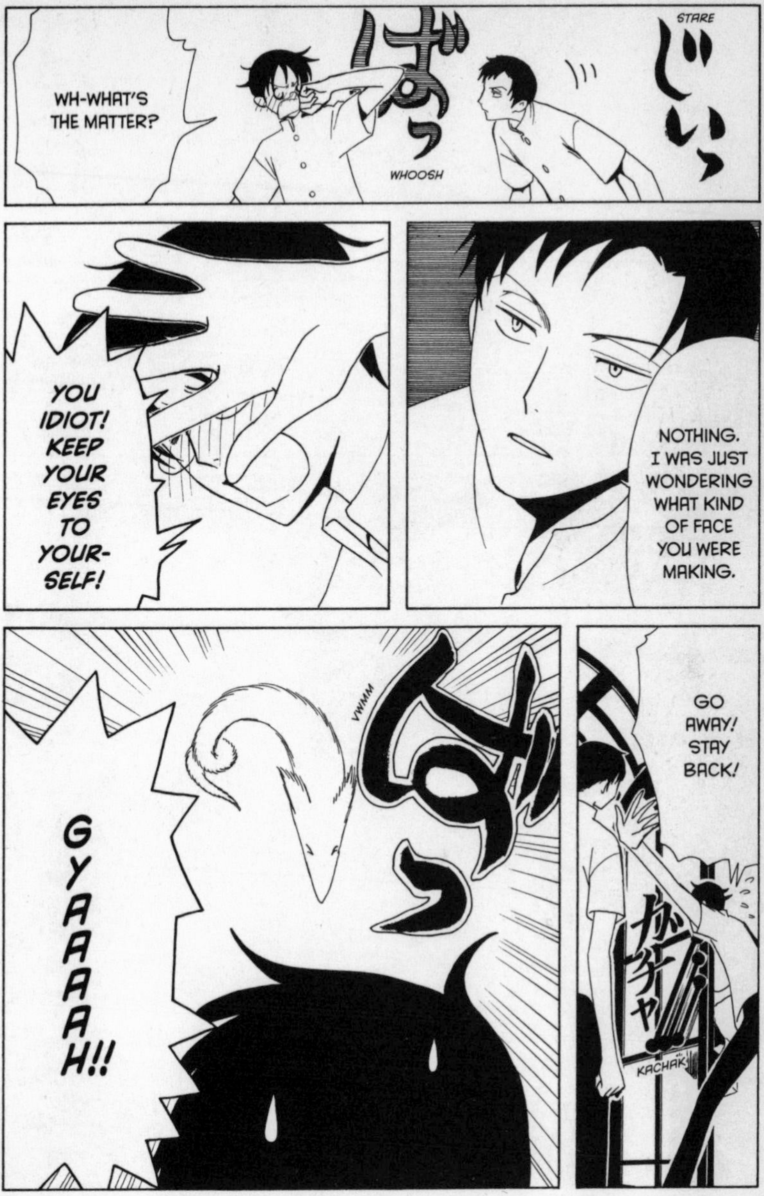
STARE
じいっ
WHOOSH
ばっ
WH-WHAT'S THE MATTER?
NOTHING. I WAS JUST WONDERING WHAT KIND OF FACE YOU WERE MAKING.
YOU IDIOT! KEEP YOUR EYES TO YOUR-SELF!
GO AWAY! STAY BACK!
KACHAK
VWMM
GYAAAAAH!!

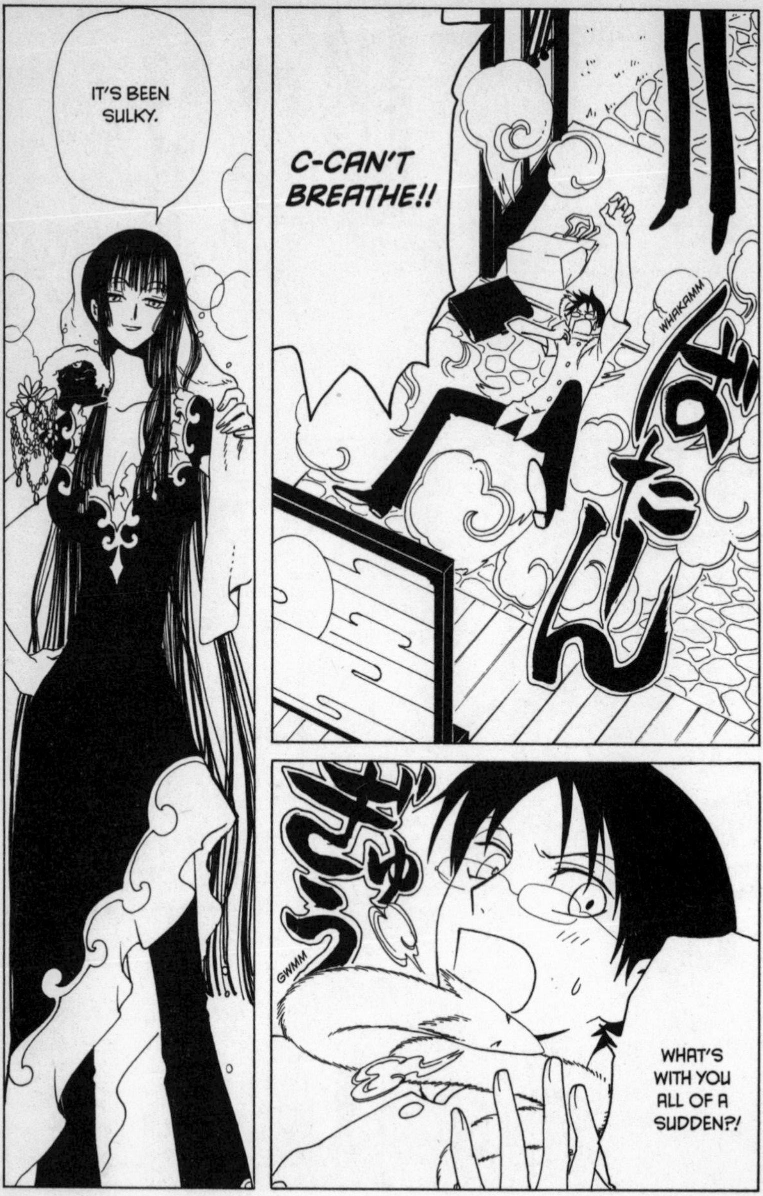
C-CAN'T BREATHE!!
WHAKAMM
GWMM
WHAT'S WITH YOU ALL OF A SUDDEN?!
IT'S BEEN SULKY.

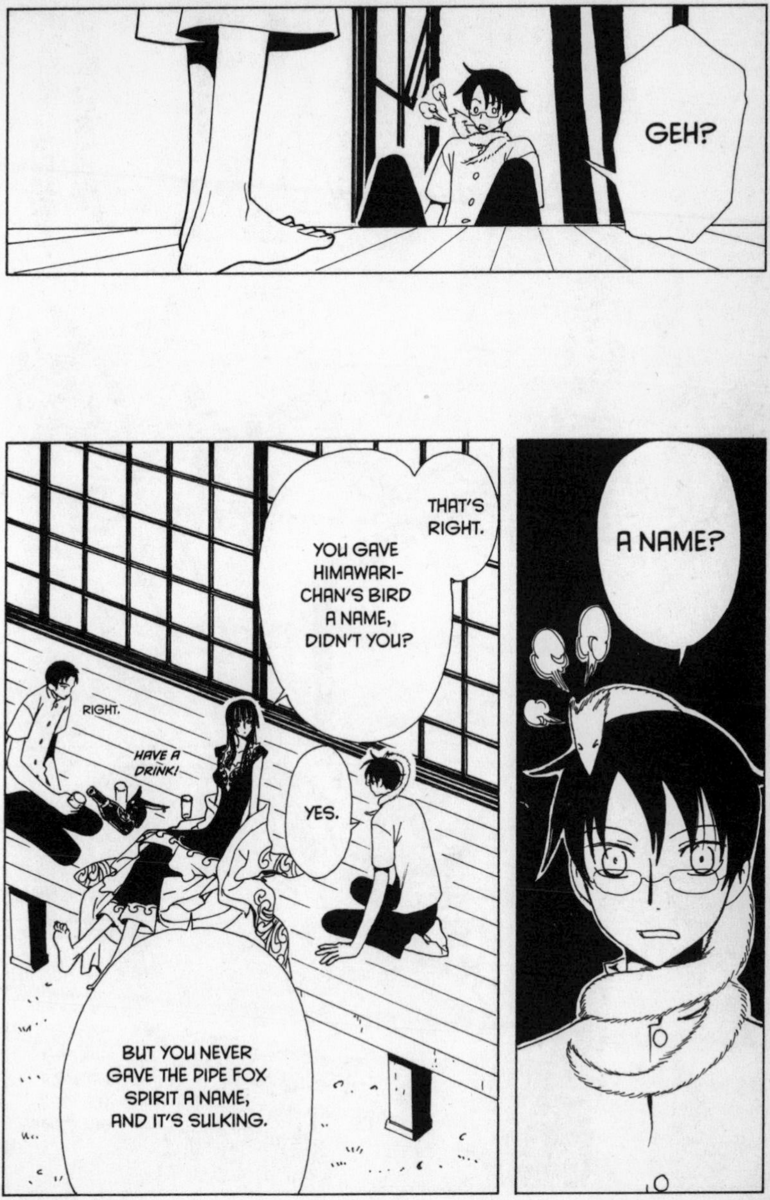
GEH?
A NAME?
THAT'S RIGHT.
YOU GAVE HIMAWARI-CHAN'S BIRD A NAME, DIDN'T YOU?
YES.
RIGHT.
HAVE A DRINK!
BUT YOU NEVER GAVE THE PIPE FOX SPIRIT A NAME, AND IT'S SULKING.

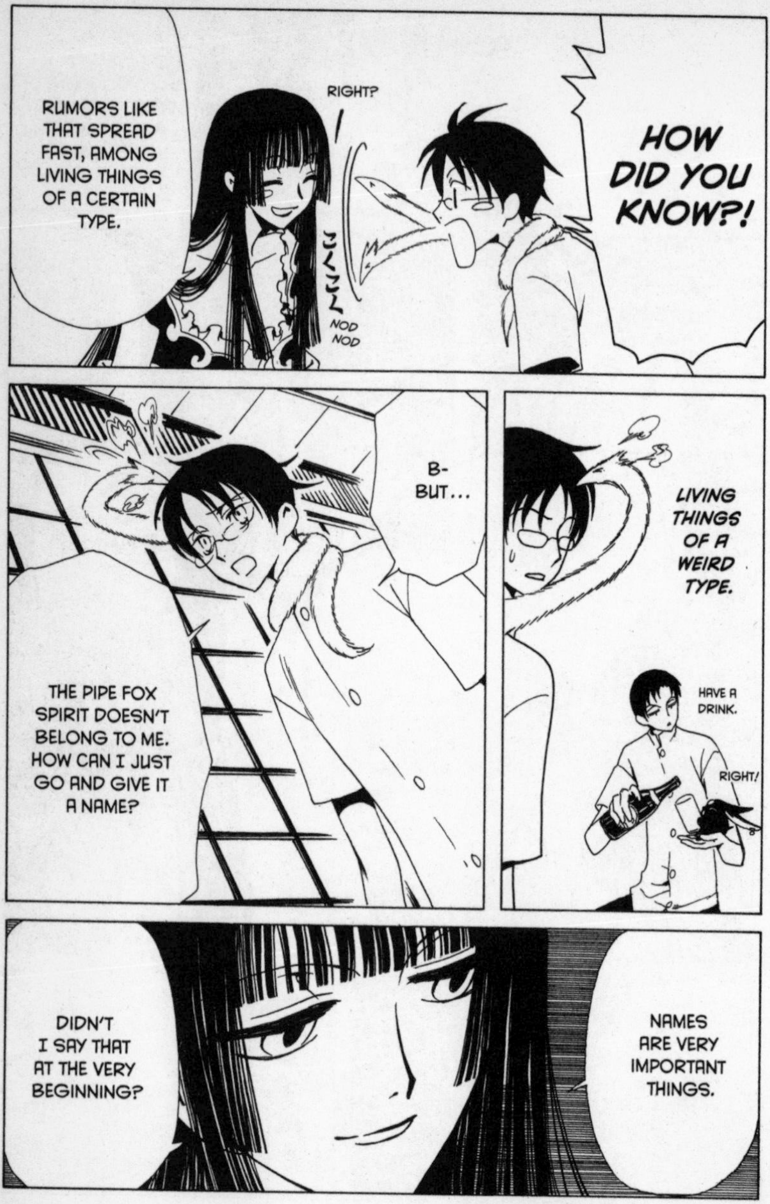
HOW DID YOU KNOW?!
RIGHT?
こくこく
NOD NOD
RUMORS LIKE THAT SPREAD FAST, AMONG LIVING THINGS OF A CERTAIN TYPE.
LIVING THINGS OF A WEIRD TYPE.
HAVE A DRINK.
RIGHT!
B- BUT...
THE PIPE FOX SPIRIT DOESN'T BELONG TO ME. HOW CAN I JUST GO AND GIVE IT A NAME?
NAMES ARE VERY IMPORTANT THINGS.
DIDN'T I SAY THAT AT THE VERY BEGINNING?

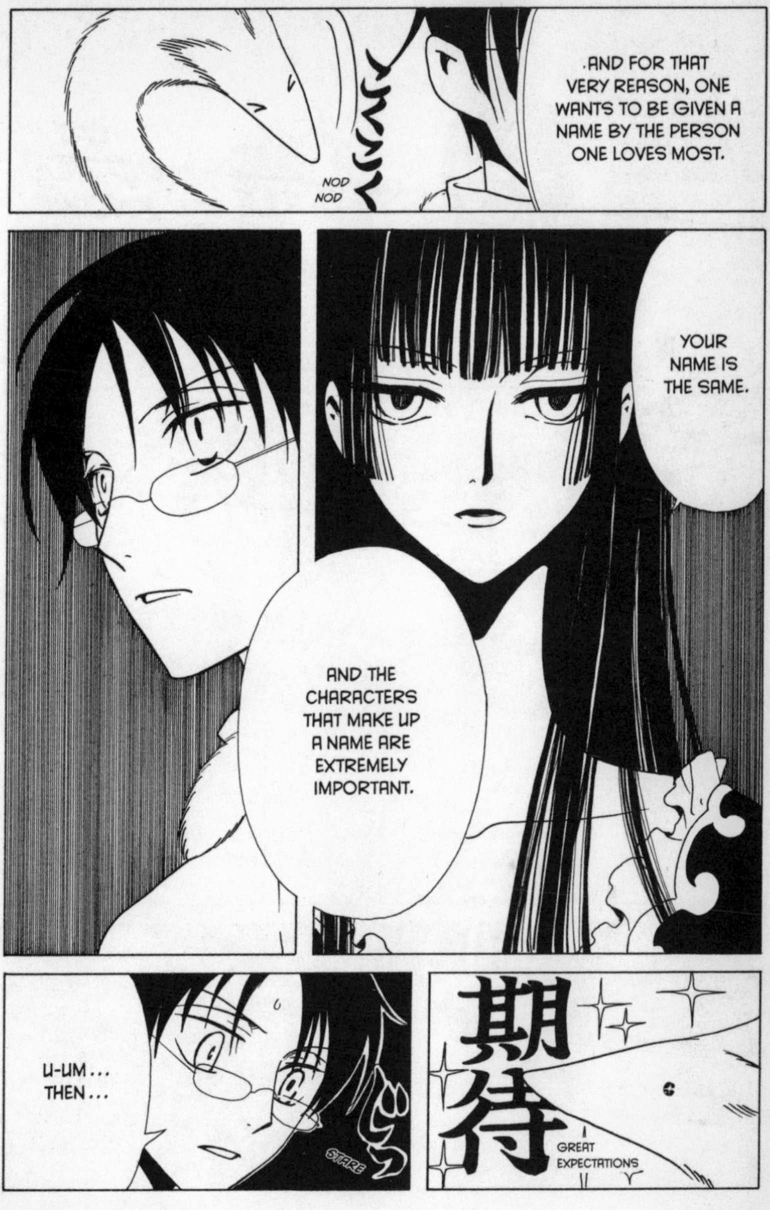
.AND FOR THAT VERY REASON, ONE WANTS TO BE GIVEN A NAME BY THE PERSON ONE LOVES MOST.
NOD NOD
YOUR NAME IS THE SAME.
AND THE CHARACTERS THAT MAKE UP A NAME ARE EXTREMELY IMPORTANT.
期待
GREAT EXPECTATIONS
STARE
U-UM... THEN...

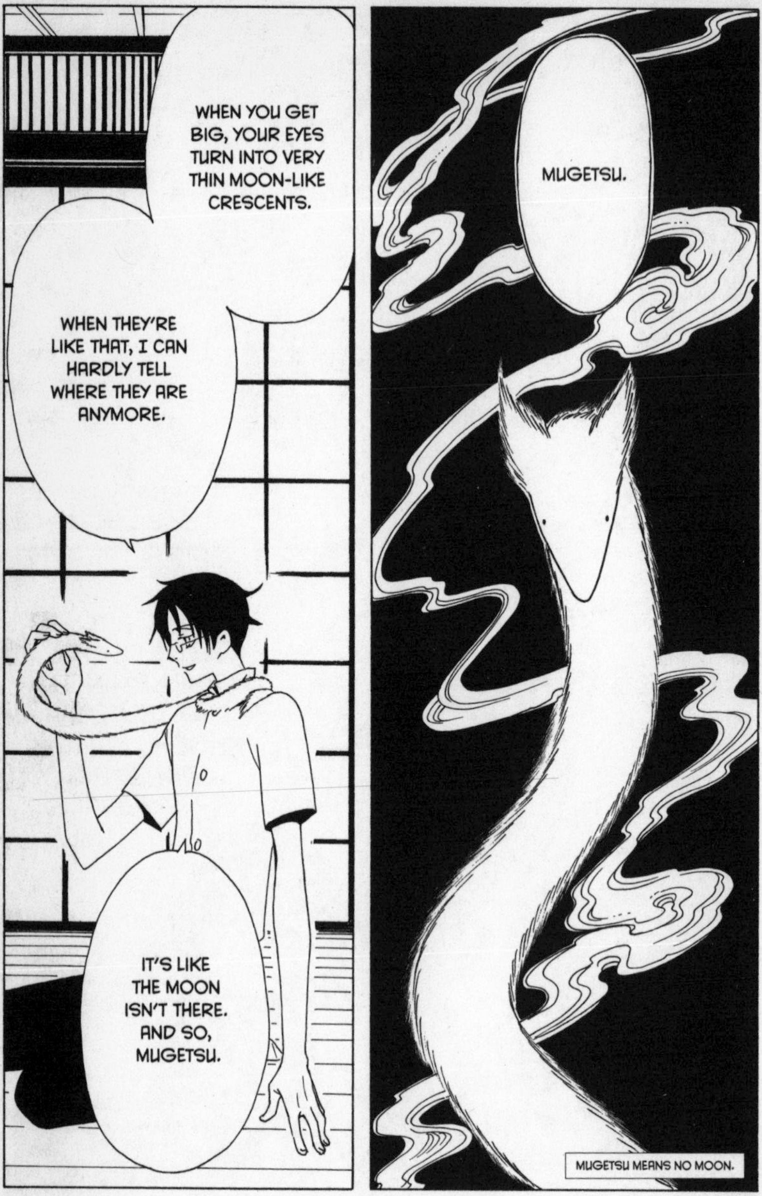
MUGETSU.
MUGETSU MEANS NO MOON.
WHEN YOU GET BIG, YOUR EYES TURN INTO VERY THIN MOON-LIKE CRESCENTS.
WHEN THEY'RE LIKE THAT, I CAN HARDLY TELL WHERE THEY ARE ANYMORE.
IT'S LIKE THE MOON ISN'T THERE. AND SO, MUGETSU.

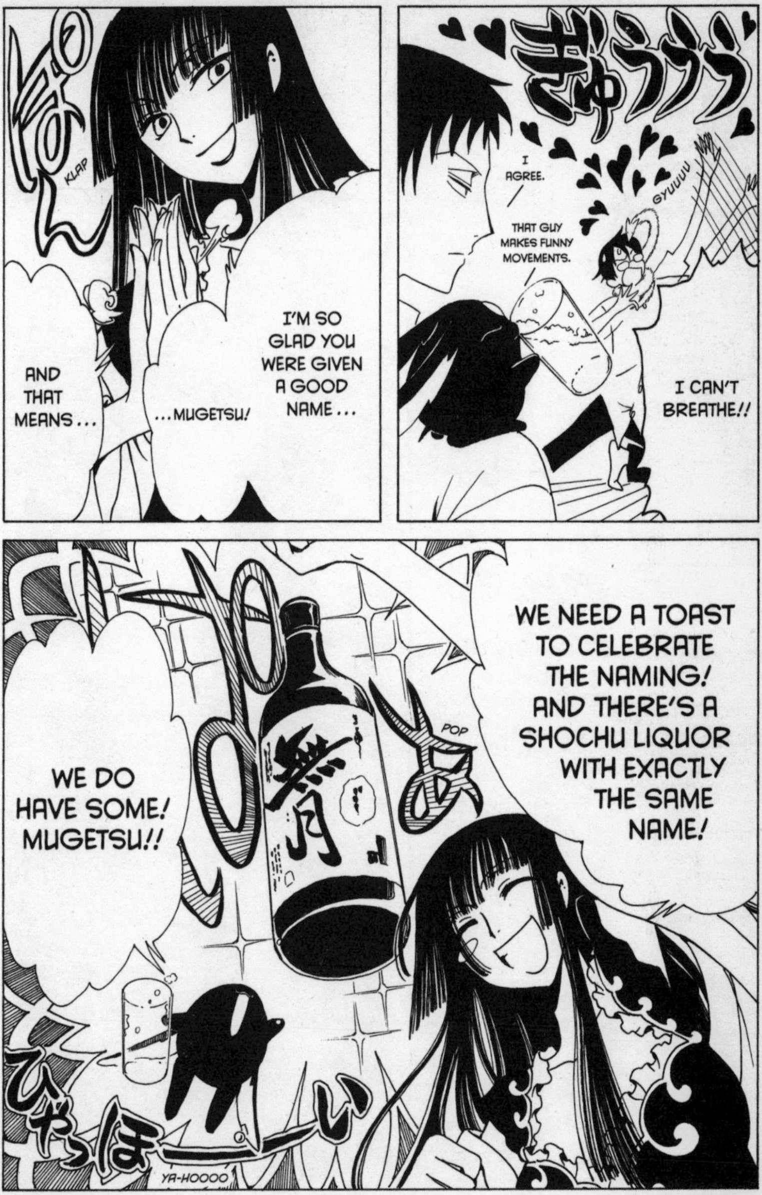
ぎゅううう
GYUUUU
I AGREE.
THAT GUY MAKES FUNNY MOVEMENTS.
I CAN'T BREATHE!!
ぽん
KLAP
I'M SO GLAD YOU WERE GIVEN A GOOD NAME . . .
. . . MUGETSU!
AND THAT MEANS . . .
WE NEED A TOAST TO CELEBRATE THE NAMING! AND THERE'S A SHOCHU LIQUOR WITH EXACTLY THE SAME NAME!
POP
WE DO HAVE SOME! MUGETSU!!
ひゃっほーーい
YA-HOOOO

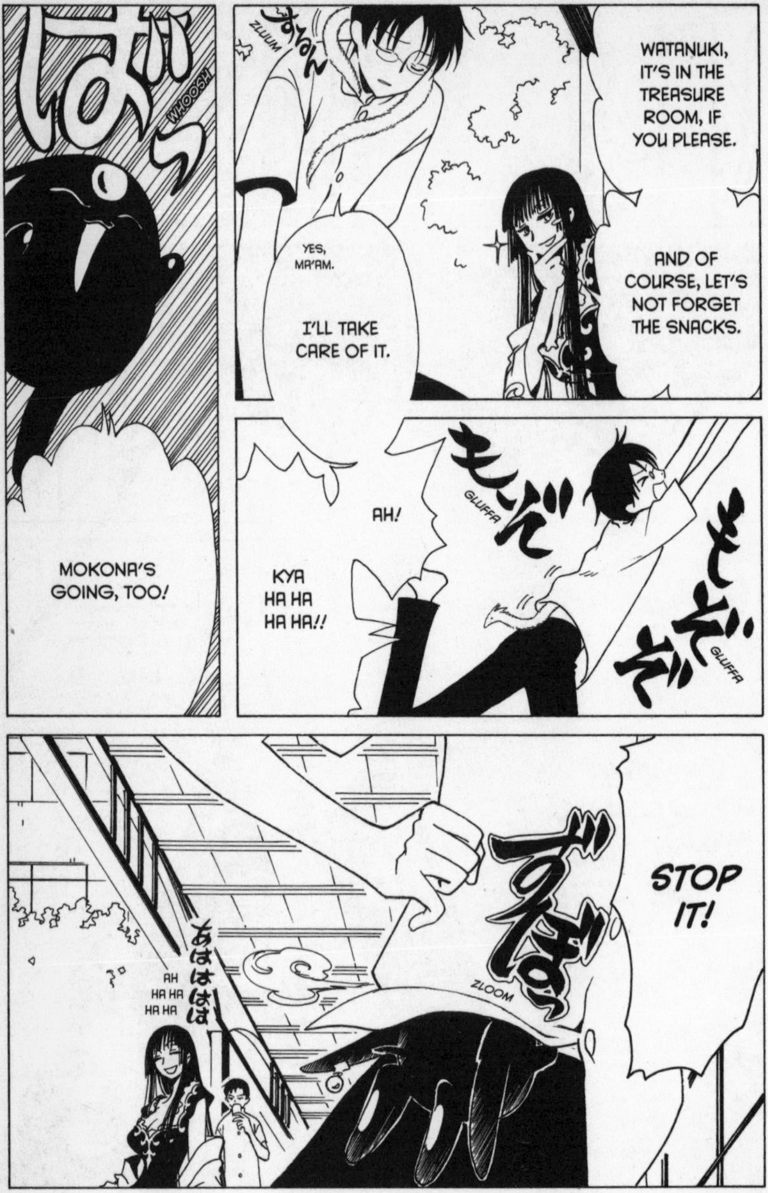
WATANUKI, IT'S IN THE TREASURE ROOM, IF YOU PLEASE.
AND OF COURSE, LET'S NOT FORGET THE SNACKS.
ZLUUM
YES, MA'AM.
I'LL TAKE CARE OF IT.
GLUFFA
GLUFFA
AH!
KYA HA HA HA HA!!
WHOOSH
MOKONA'S GOING, TOO!
STOP IT!
ZLOOM
AH HA HA HA HA

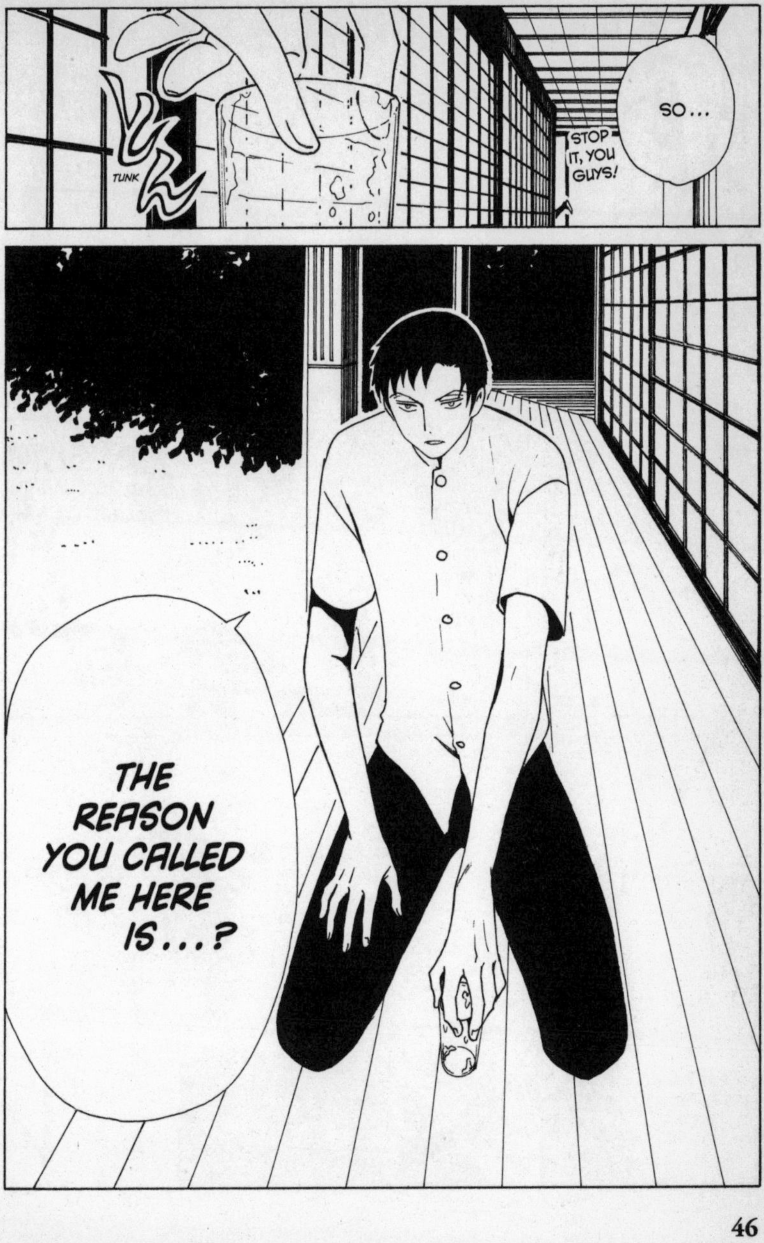
SO...
STOP IT, YOU GUYS!
TUNK
THE REASON YOU CALLED ME HERE IS...?

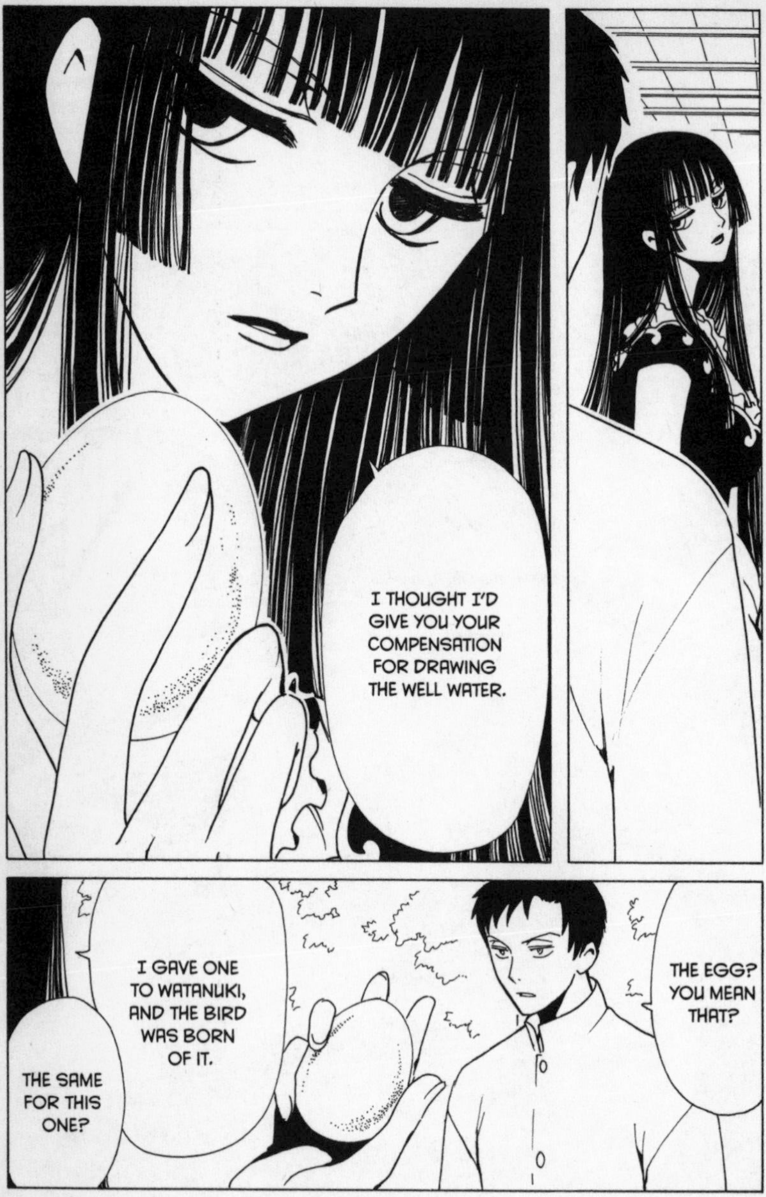
I THOUGHT I'D GIVE YOU YOUR COMPENSATION FOR DRAWING THE WELL WATER.
THE EGG? YOU MEAN THAT?
I GAVE ONE TO WATANUKI, AND THE BIRD WAS BORN OF IT.
THE SAME FOR THIS ONE?

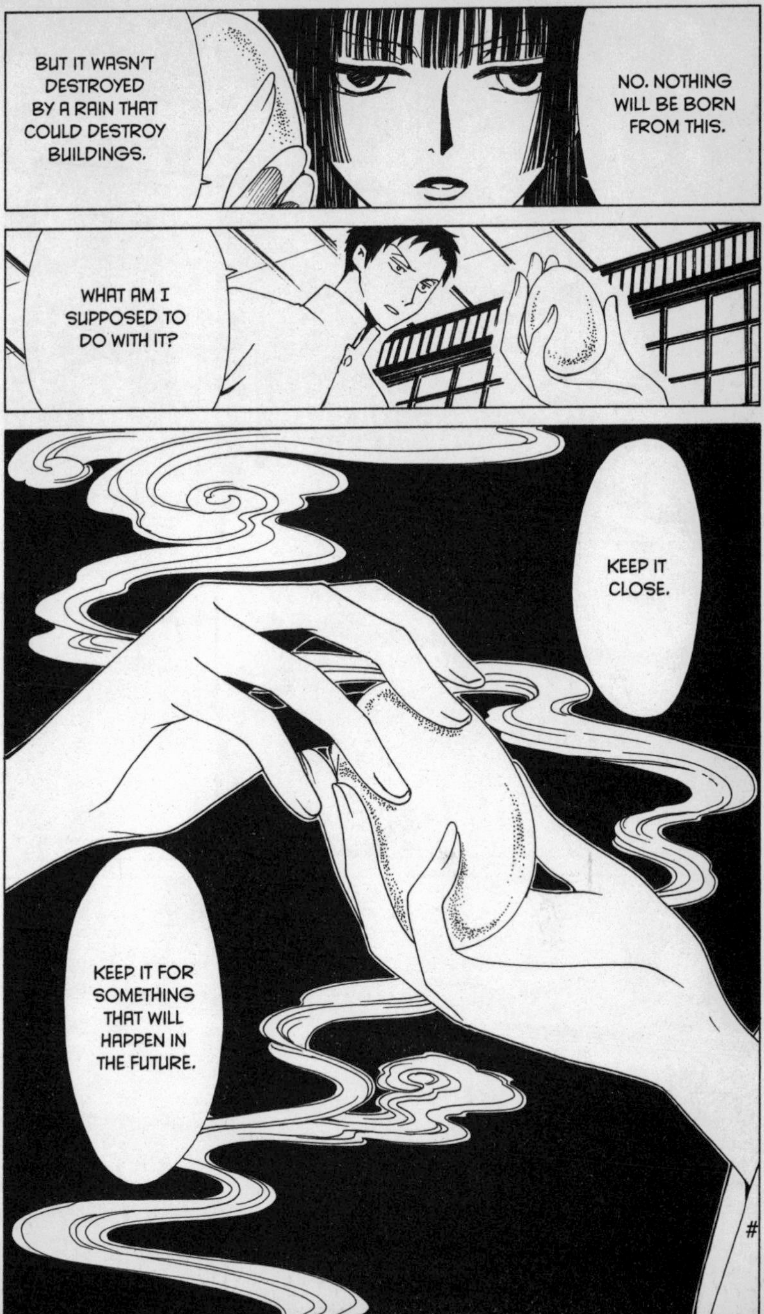
NO. NOTHING WILL BE BORN FROM THIS.
BUT IT WASN'T DESTROYED BY A RAIN THAT COULD DESTROY BUILDINGS.
WHAT AM I SUPPOSED TO DO WITH IT?
KEEP IT CLOSE.
KEEP IT FOR SOMETHING THAT WILL HAPPEN IN THE FUTURE.

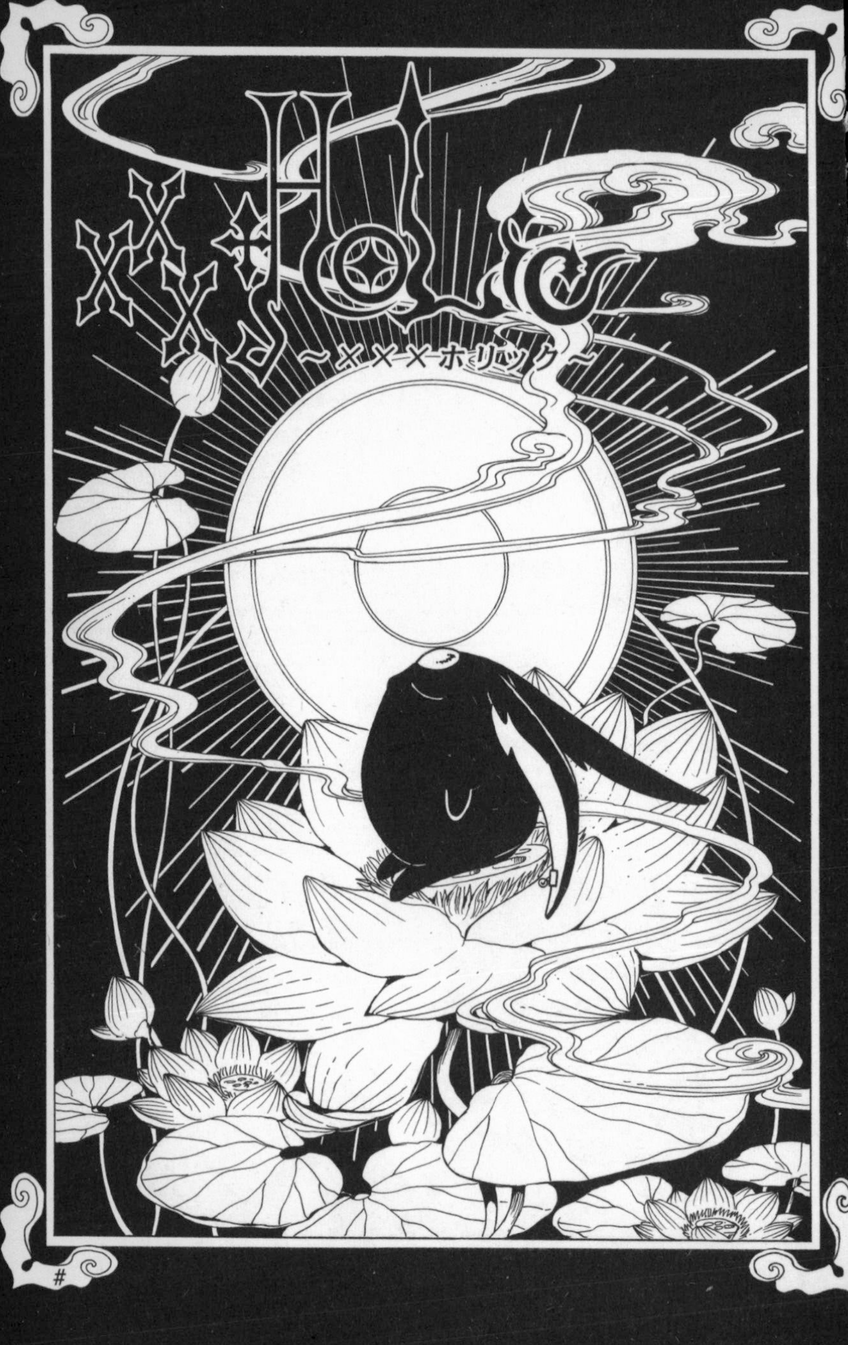
xxxHOLiC
~×××ホリック~
#

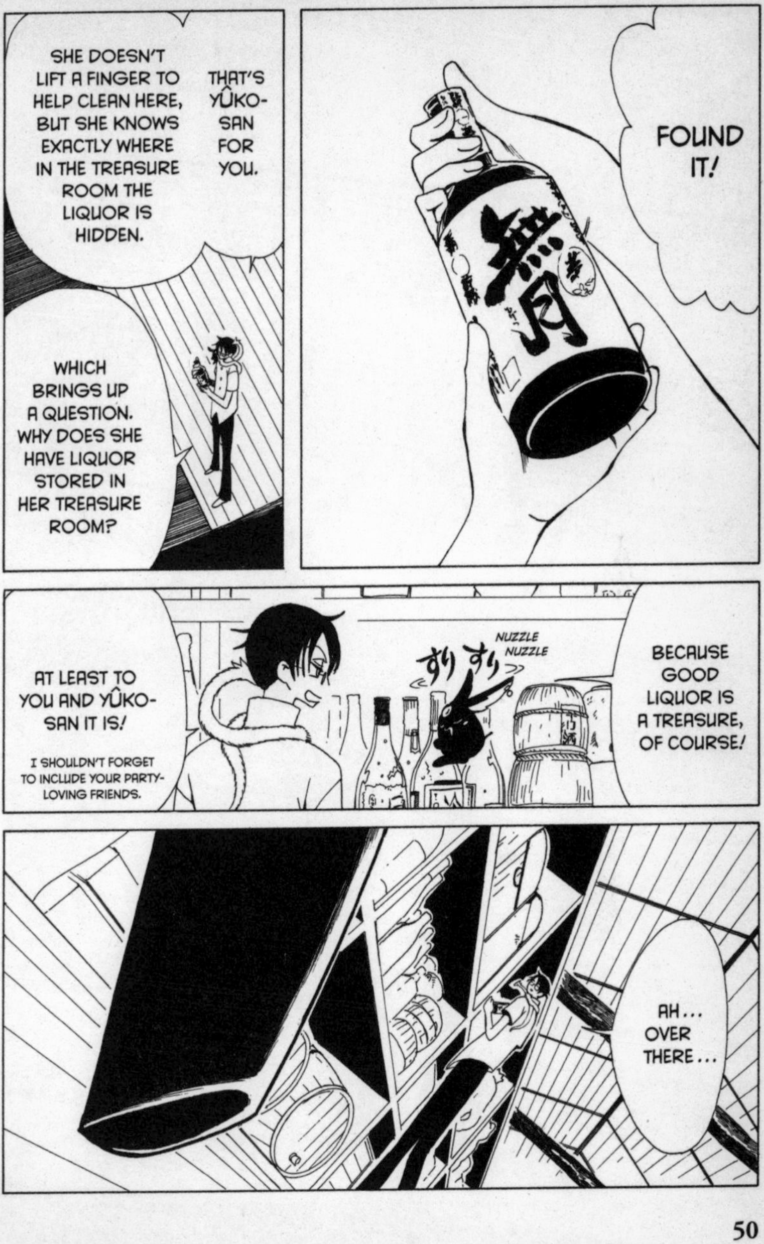
FOUND IT!
SHE DOESN'T LIFT A FINGER TO HELP CLEAN HERE, BUT SHE KNOWS EXACTLY WHERE IN THE TREASURE ROOM THE LIQUOR IS HIDDEN.
THAT'S YÛKO-SAN FOR YOU.
WHICH BRINGS UP A QUESTION. WHY DOES SHE HAVE LIQUOR STORED IN HER TREASURE ROOM?
BECAUSE GOOD LIQUOR IS A TREASURE, OF COURSE!
すり すり
NUZZLE NUZZLE
AT LEAST TO YOU AND YÛKO-SAN IT IS!
I SHOULDN'T FORGET TO INCLUDE YOUR PARTY-LOVING FRIENDS.
AH... OVER THERE...

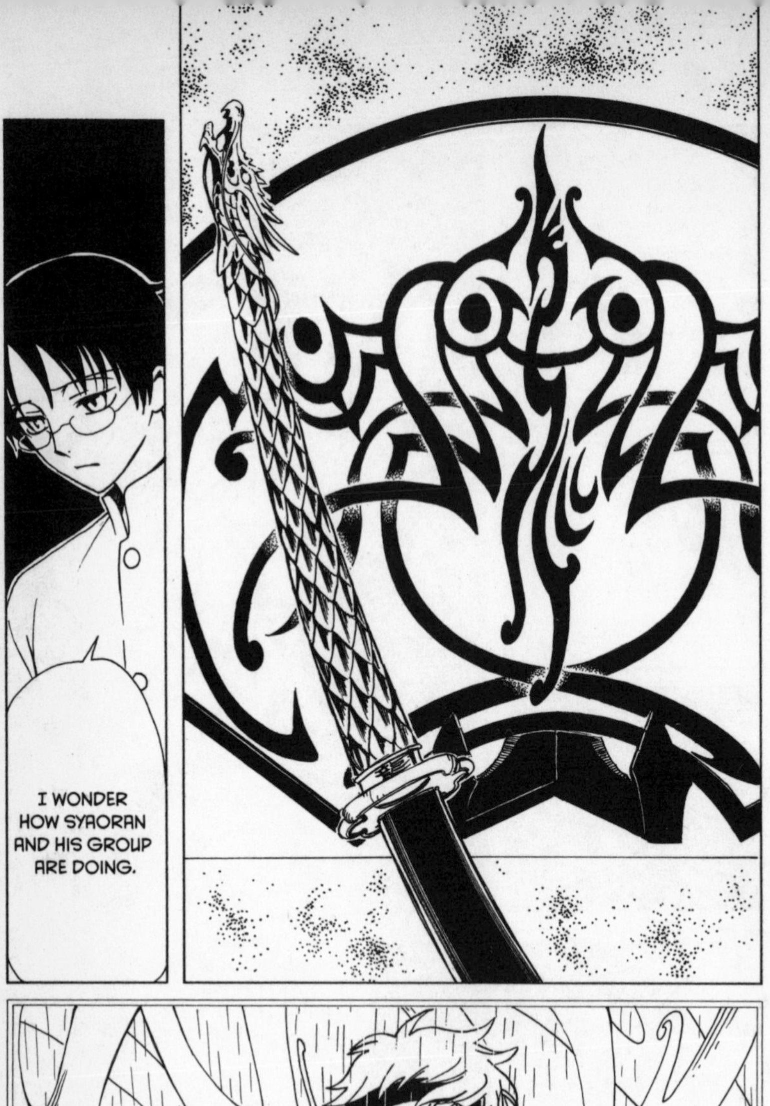
I WONDER HOW SYAORAN AND HIS GROUP ARE DOING.

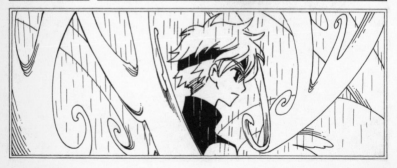

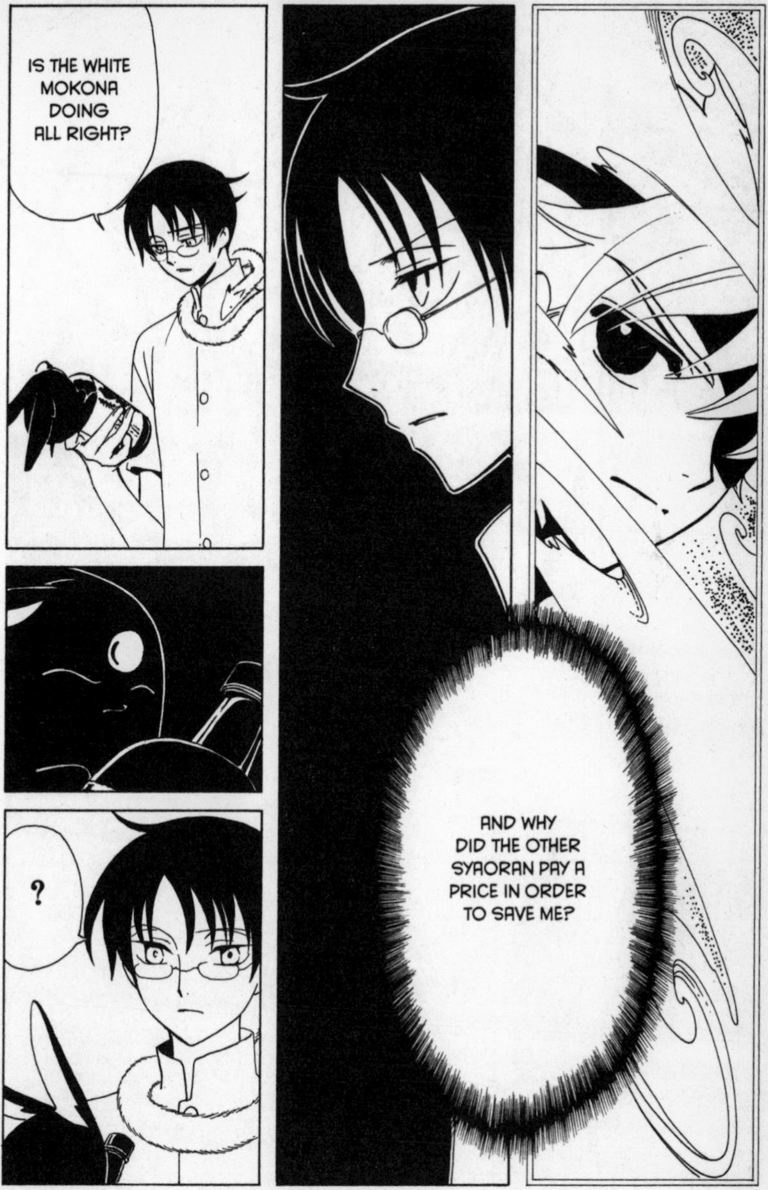
AND WHY DID THE OTHER SYAORAN PAY A PRICE IN ORDER TO SAVE ME?
IS THE WHITE MOKONA DOING ALL RIGHT?
?

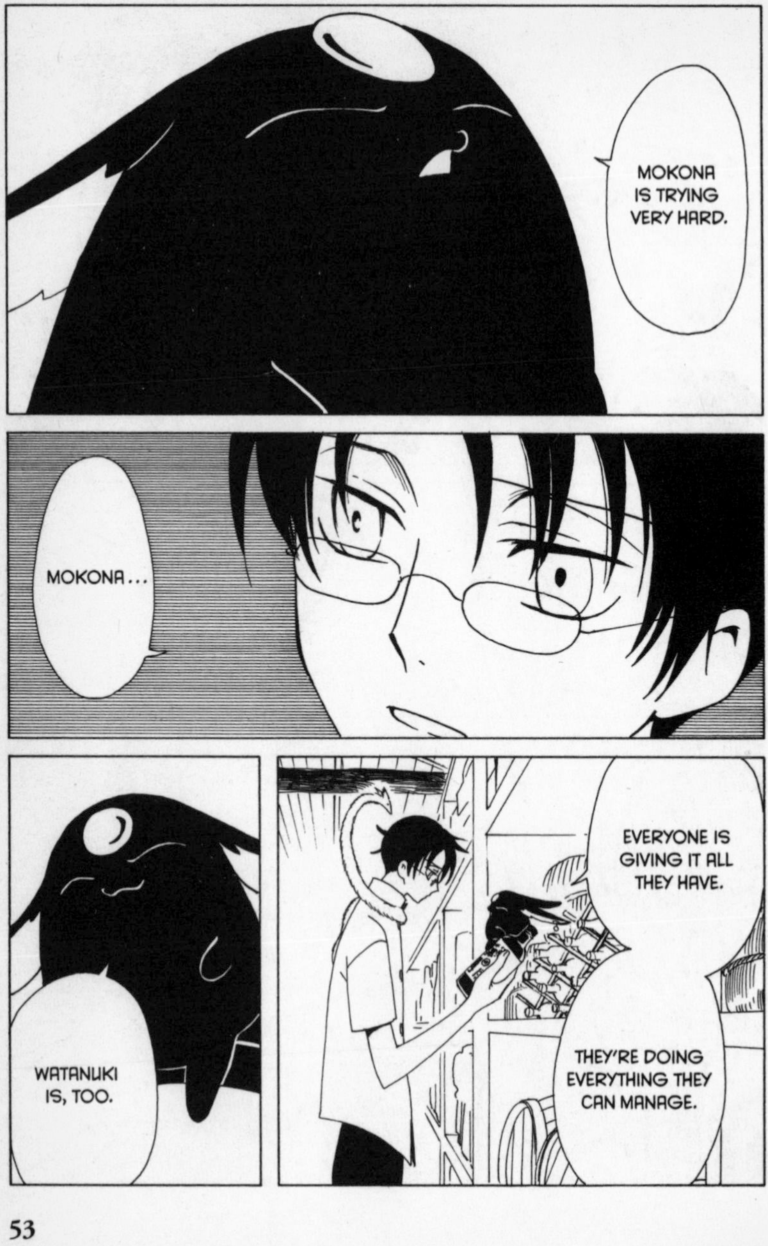
MOKONA IS TRYING VERY HARD.
MOKONA...
EVERYONE IS GIVING IT ALL THEY HAVE.
THEY'RE DOING EVERYTHING THEY CAN MANAGE.
WATANUKI IS, TOO.

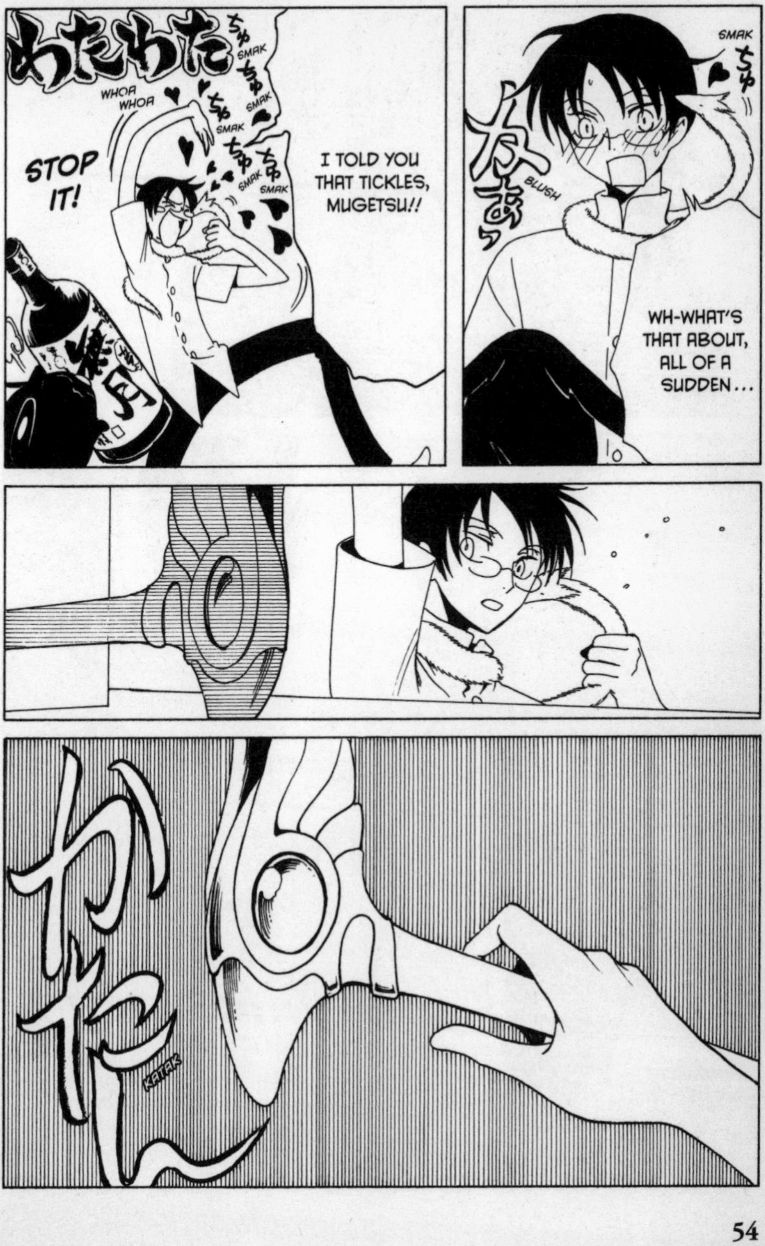
SMAK
BLUSH
WH-WHAT'S THAT ABOUT, ALL OF A SUDDEN...
WHOA WHOA
SMAK
SMAK
SMAK
SMAK
SMAK
STOP IT!
I TOLD YOU THAT TICKLES, MUGETSU!!
KATAK

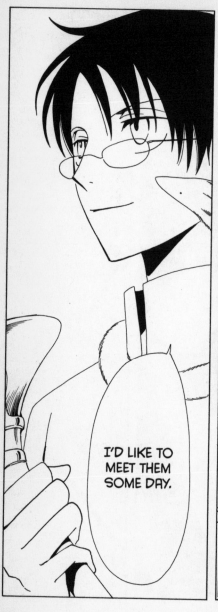
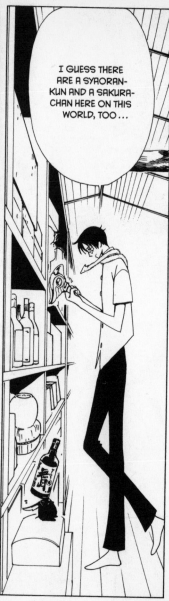

I GUESS THERE ARE A SYAORAN-KUN AND A SAKURA-CHAN HERE ON THIS WORLD, TOO...

I'D LIKE TO MEET THEM SOME DAY.

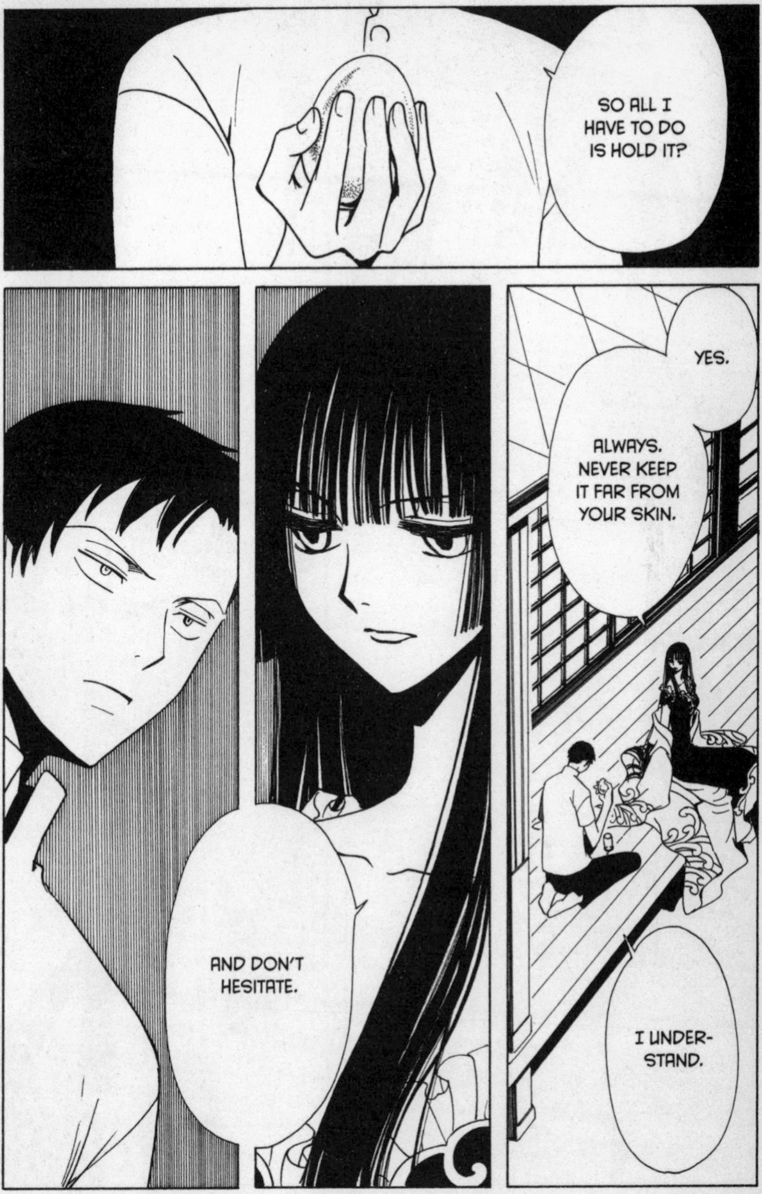
SO ALL I HAVE TO DO IS HOLD IT?
YES.
ALWAYS. NEVER KEEP IT FAR FROM YOUR SKIN.
I UNDER-STAND.
AND DON'T HESITATE.

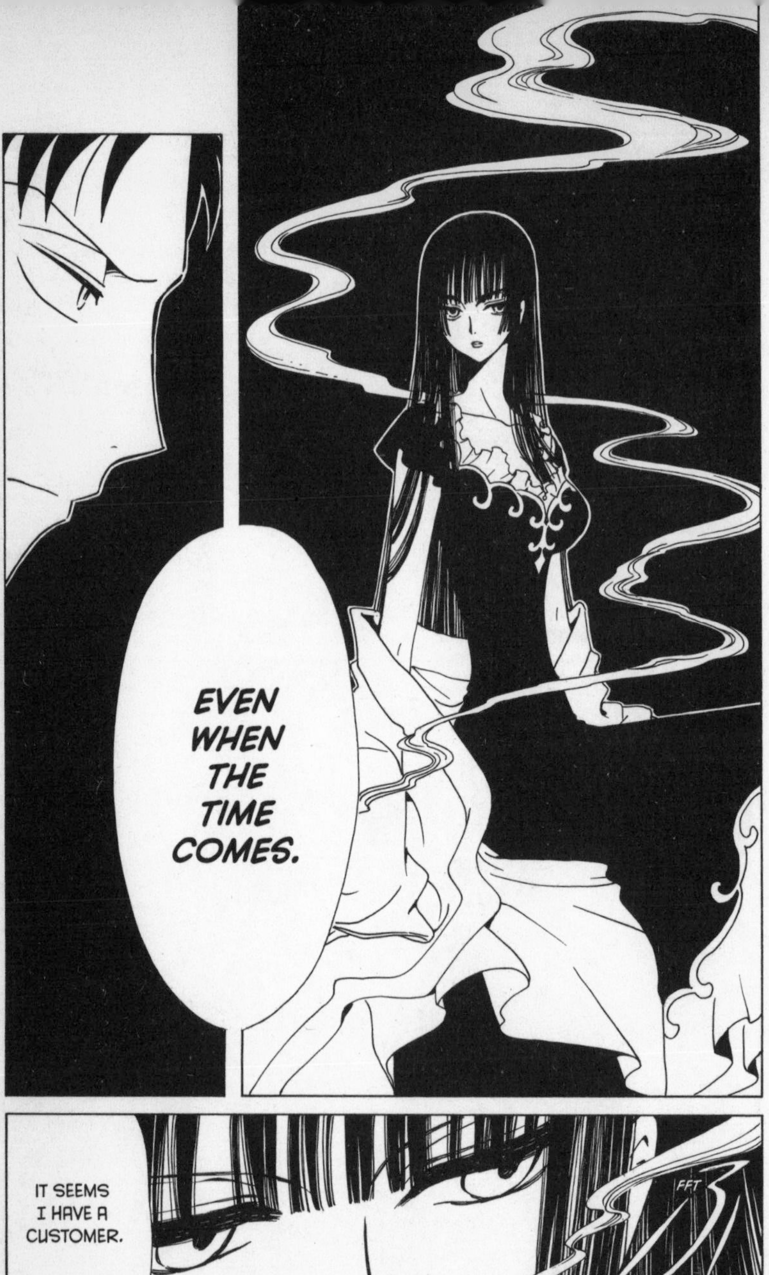
EVEN WHEN THE TIME COMES.
IT SEEMS I HAVE A CUSTOMER.
FFT

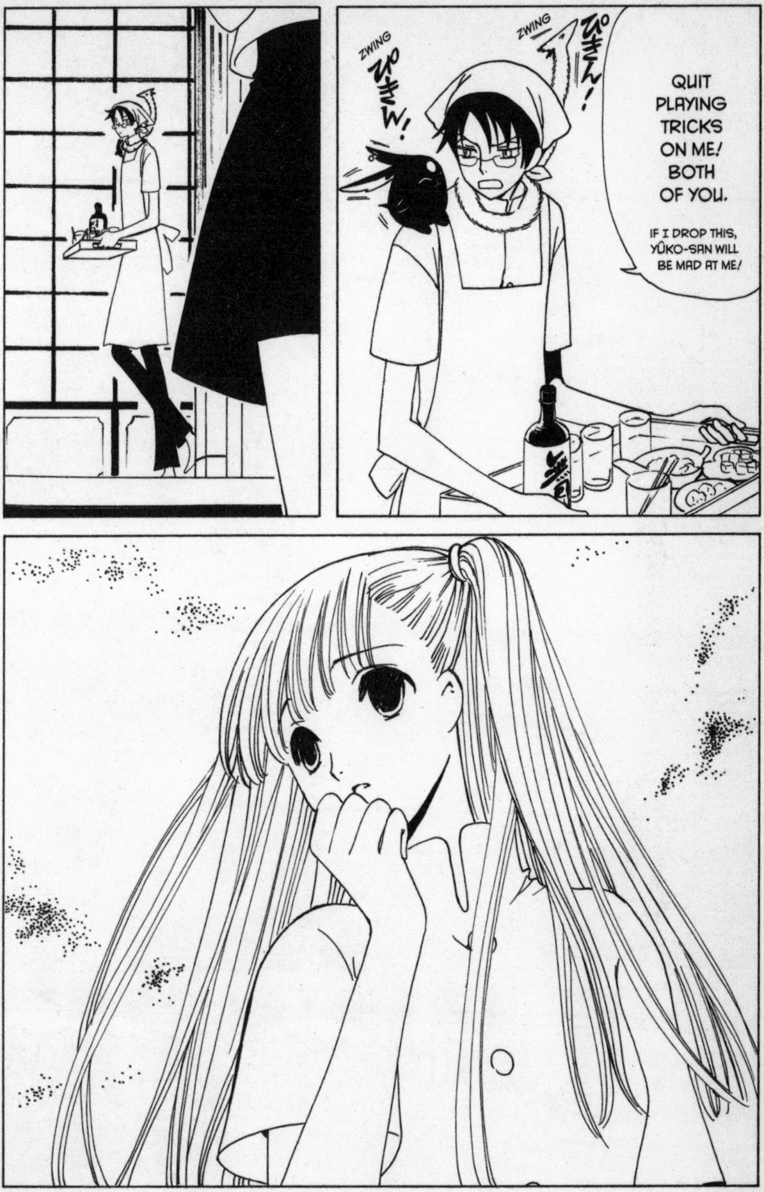

QUIT PLAYING TRICKS ON ME! BOTH OF YOU.
IF I DROP THIS, YÛKO-SAN WILL BE MAD AT ME!
ぴきん!
ZWING
ぴきん!
ZWING

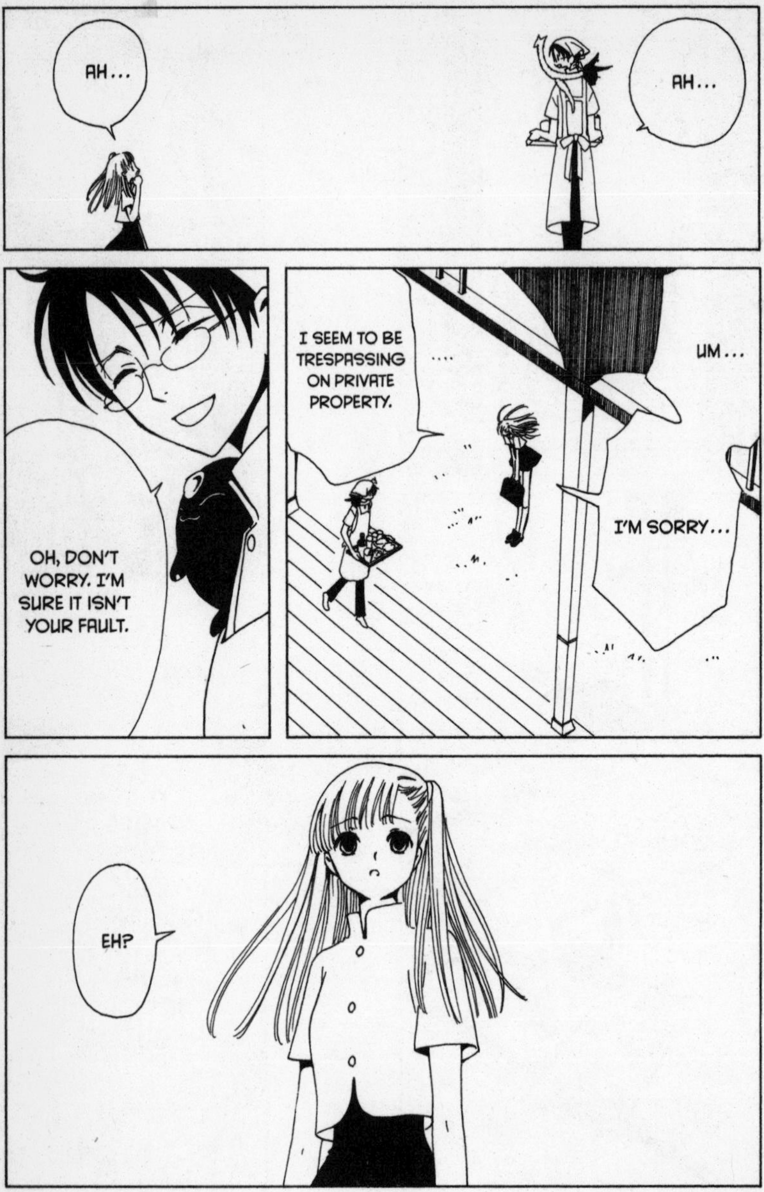
AH...
AH...
UM...
I'M SORRY...
....
I SEEM TO BE TRESPASSING ON PRIVATE PROPERTY.
OH, DON'T WORRY. I'M SURE IT ISN'T YOUR FAULT.
EH?

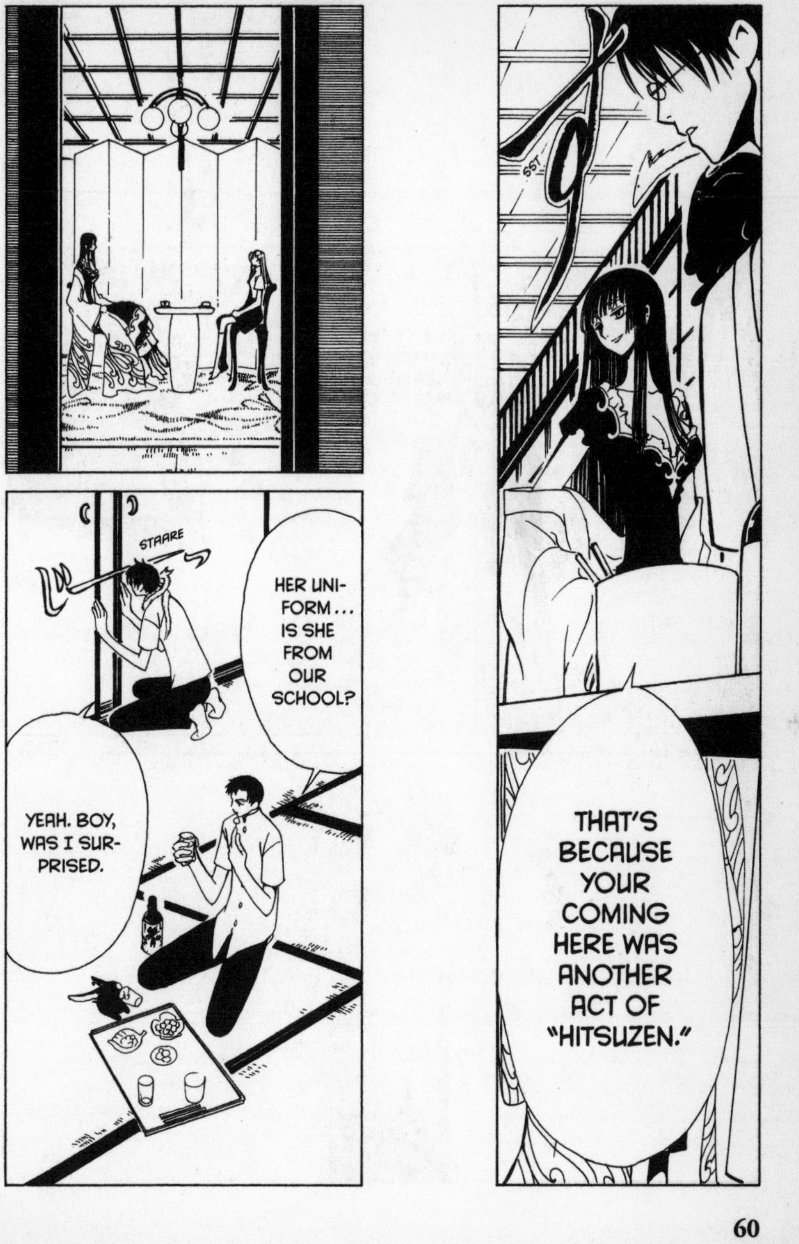
SST
THAT'S BECAUSE YOUR COMING HERE WAS ANOTHER ACT OF "HITSUZEN."
STAARE
HER UNIFORM... IS SHE FROM OUR SCHOOL?
YEAH. BOY, WAS I SURPRISED.

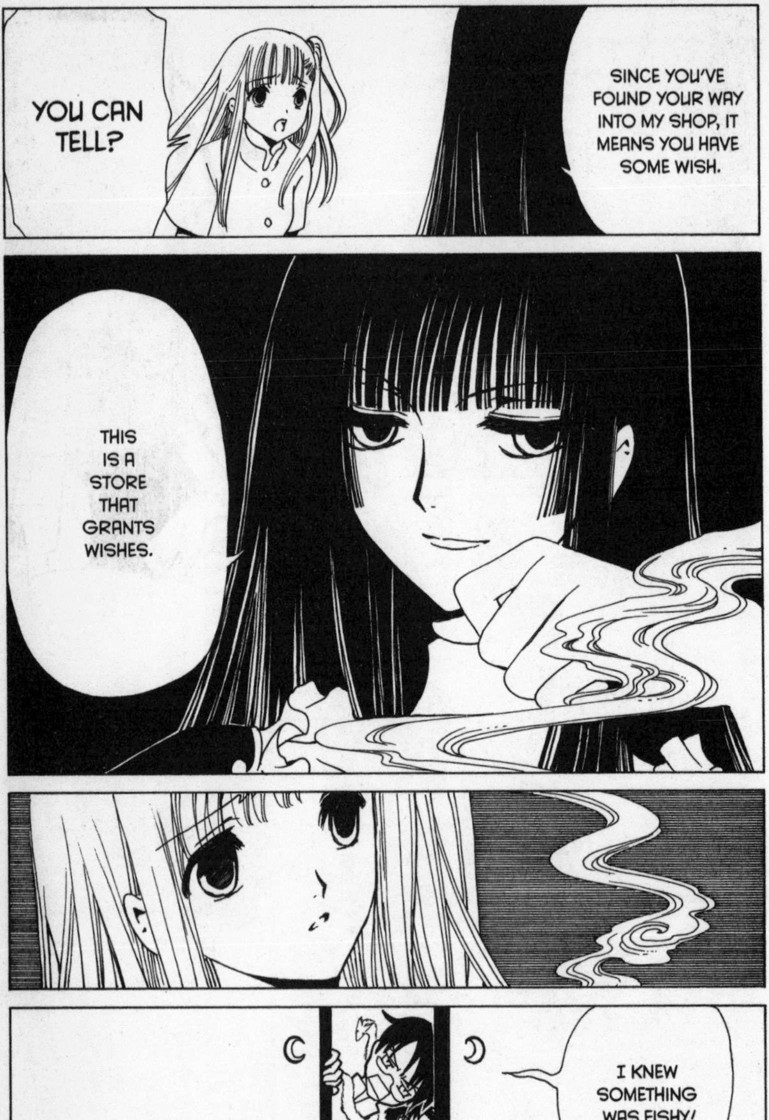
SINCE YOU'VE FOUND YOUR WAY INTO MY SHOP, IT MEANS YOU HAVE SOME WISH.
YOU CAN TELL?
THIS IS A STORE THAT GRANTS WISHES.
I KNEW SOMETHING WAS FISHY!

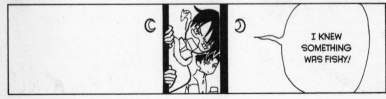

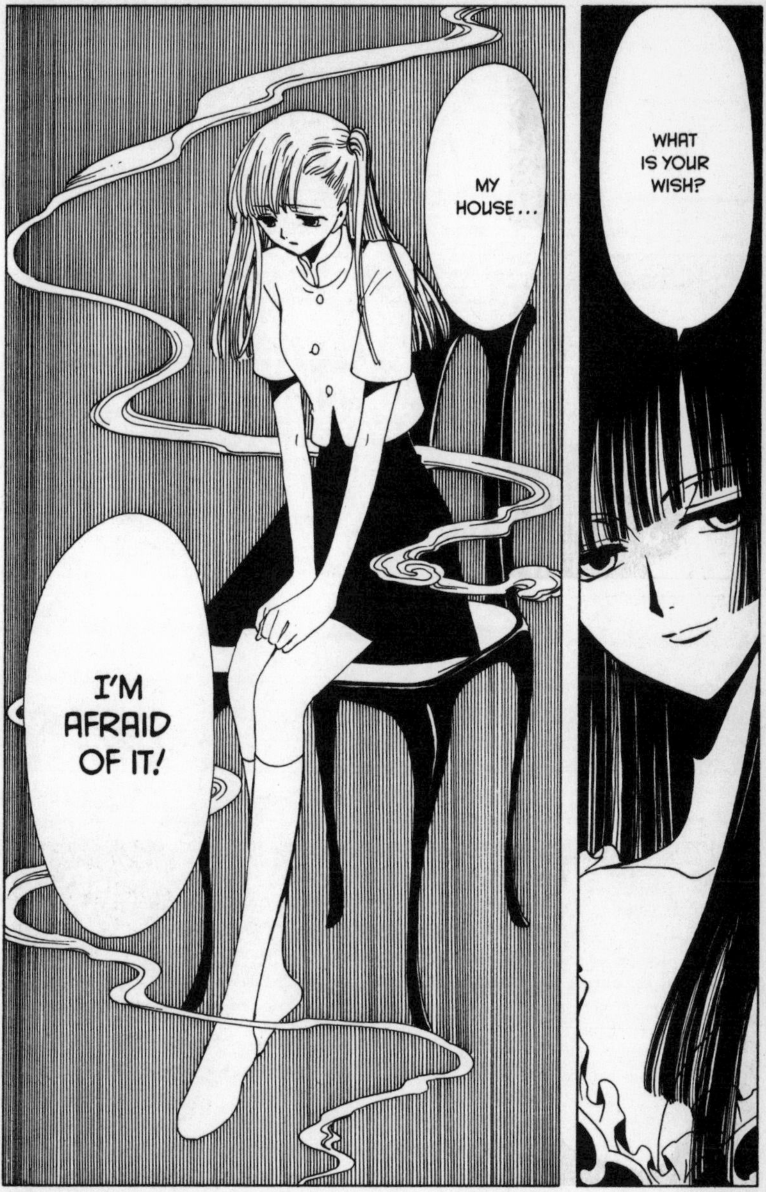
WHAT IS YOUR WISH?
MY HOUSE...
I'M AFRAID OF IT!

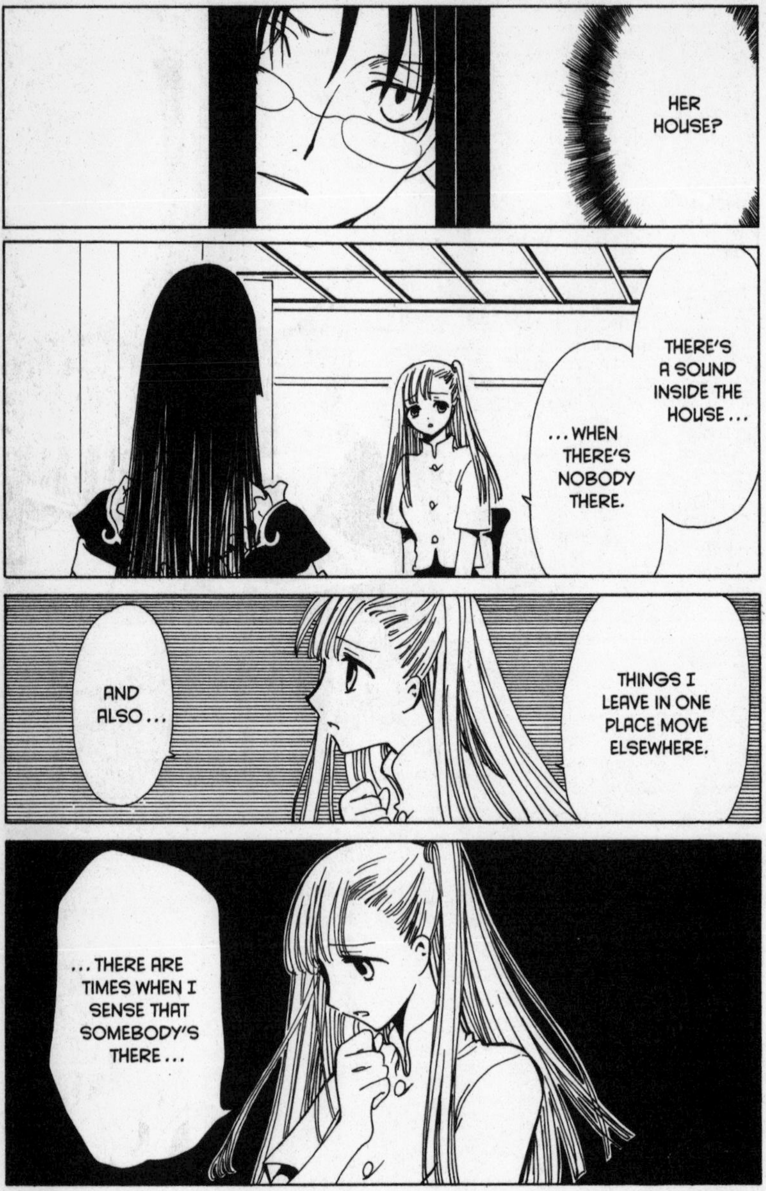
HER HOUSE?
THERE'S A SOUND INSIDE THE HOUSE...
...WHEN THERE'S NOBODY THERE.
THINGS I LEAVE IN ONE PLACE MOVE ELSEWHERE.
AND ALSO...
...THERE ARE TIMES WHEN I SENSE THAT SOMEBODY'S THERE...

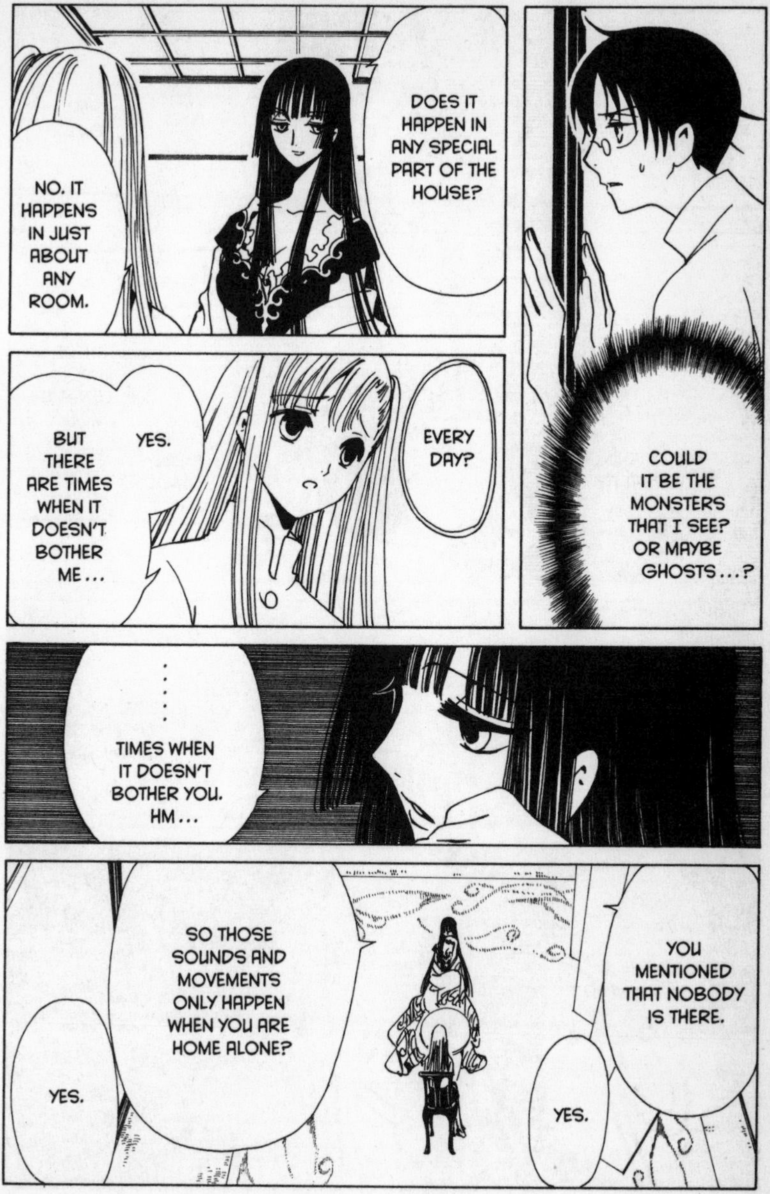
COULD IT BE THE MONSTERS THAT I SEE? OR MAYBE GHOSTS...?
DOES IT HAPPEN IN ANY SPECIAL PART OF THE HOUSE?
NO. IT HAPPENS IN JUST ABOUT ANY ROOM.
EVERY DAY?
YES.
BUT THERE ARE TIMES WHEN IT DOESN'T BOTHER ME...
......
TIMES WHEN IT DOESN'T BOTHER YOU. HM...
YOU MENTIONED THAT NOBODY IS THERE.
YES.
SO THOSE SOUNDS AND MOVEMENTS ONLY HAPPEN WHEN YOU ARE HOME ALONE?
YES.

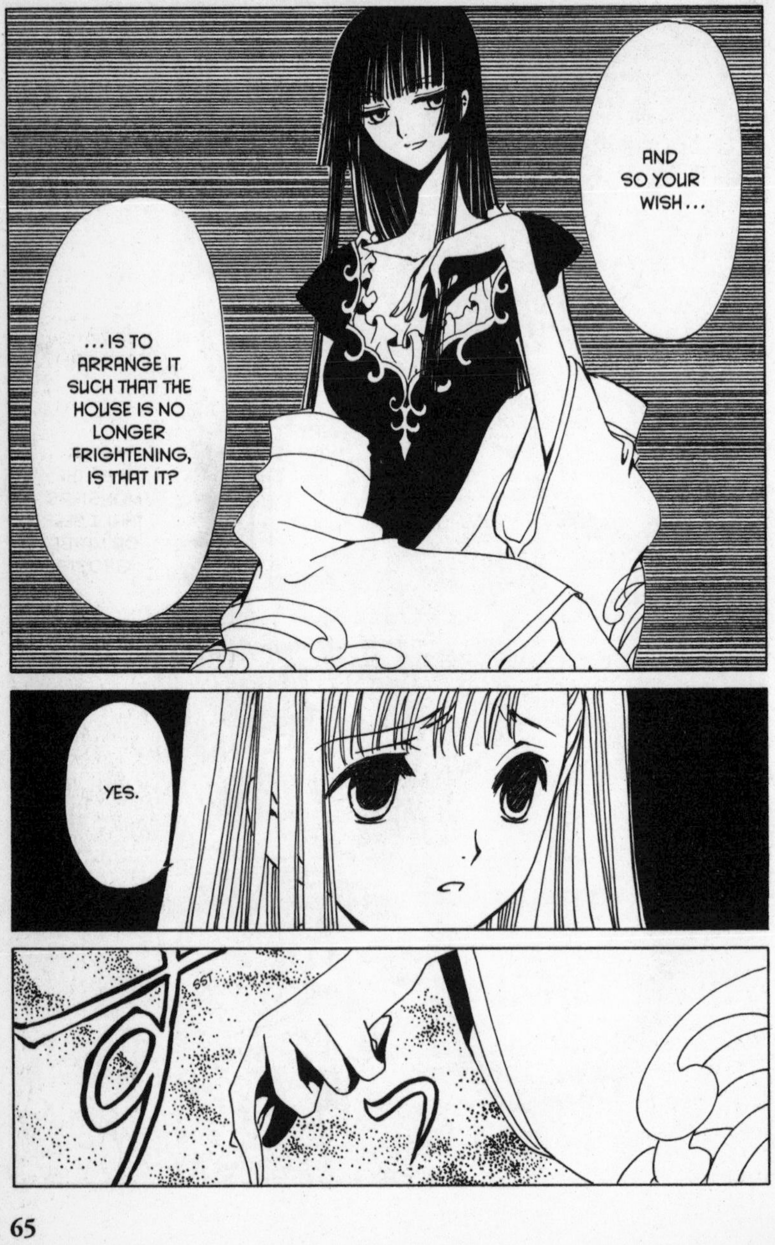
AND SO YOUR WISH...
...IS TO ARRANGE IT SUCH THAT THE HOUSE IS NO LONGER FRIGHTENING, IS THAT IT?
YES.
SST

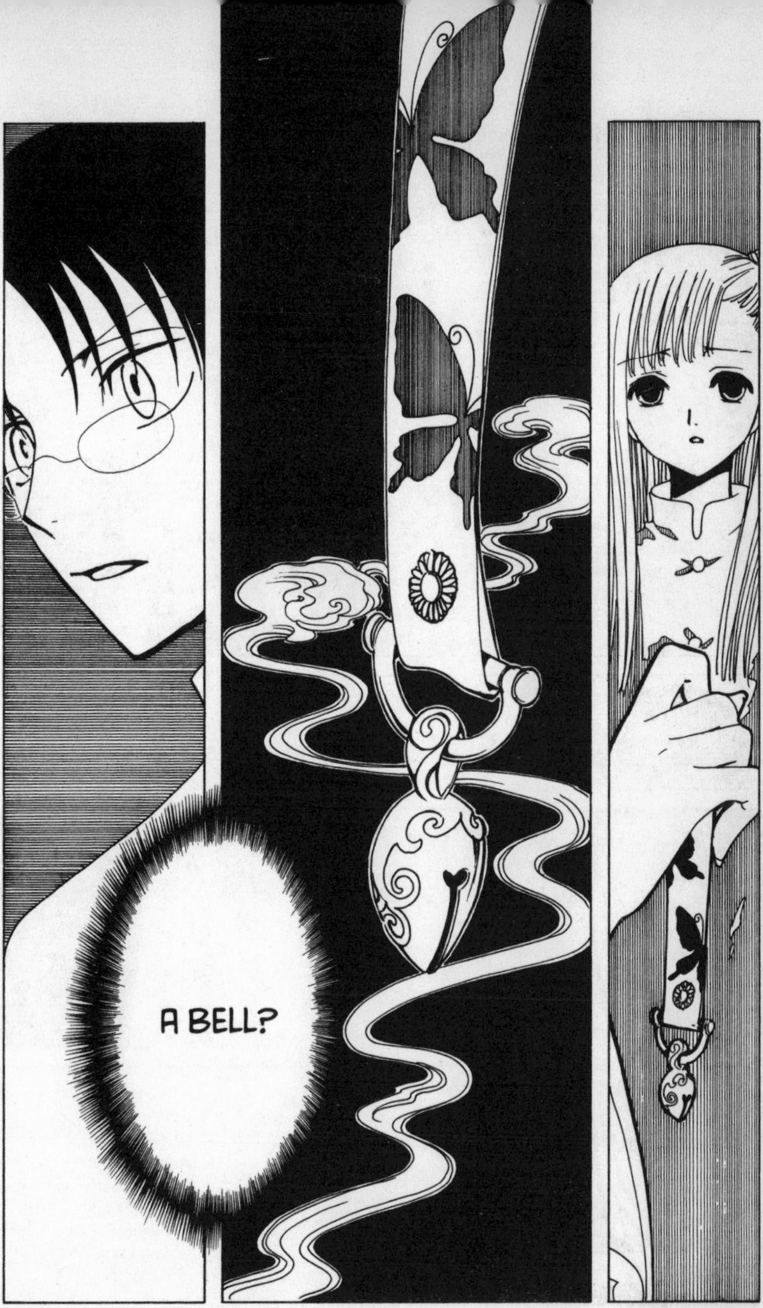
A BELL?

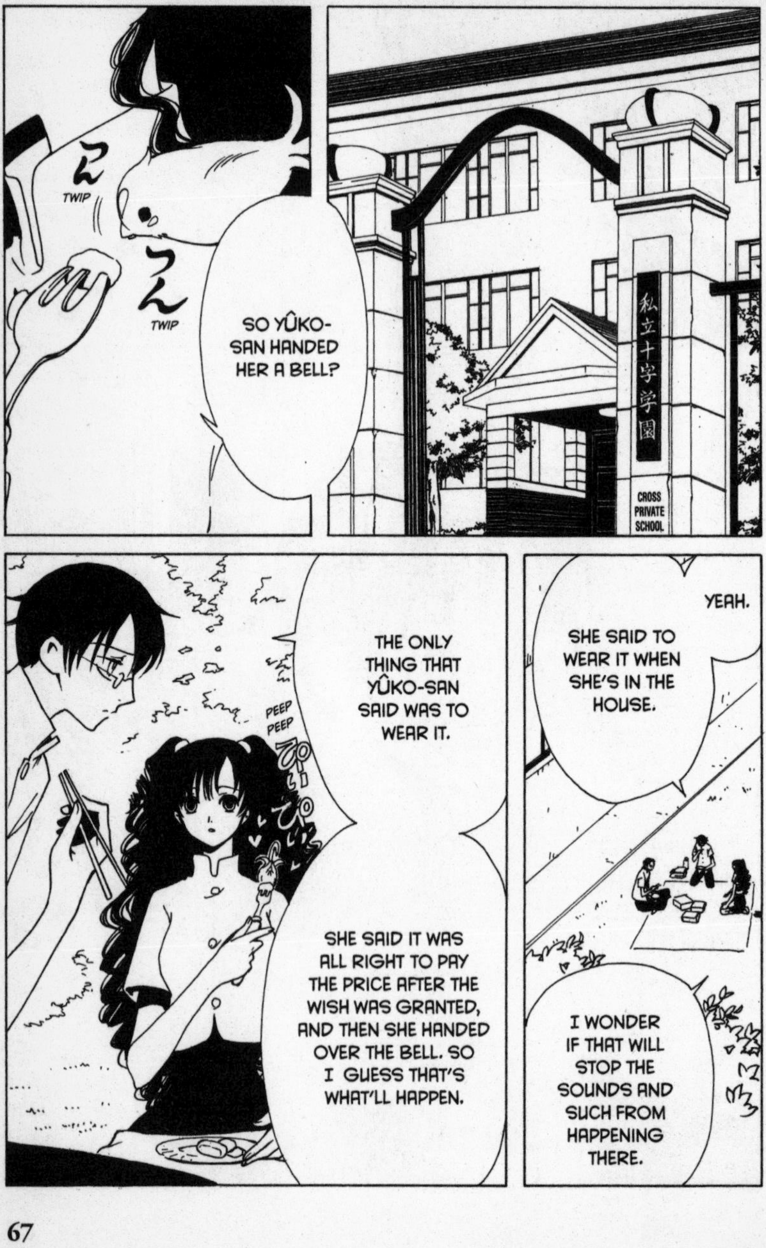
私立十字学園
CROSS PRIVATE SCHOOL
TWIP
TWIP
SO YÛKO-SAN HANDED HER A BELL?
YEAH.
SHE SAID TO WEAR IT WHEN SHE'S IN THE HOUSE.
I WONDER IF THAT WILL STOP THE SOUNDS AND SUCH FROM HAPPENING THERE.
THE ONLY THING THAT YÛKO-SAN SAID WAS TO WEAR IT.
PEEP PEEP
SHE SAID IT WAS ALL RIGHT TO PAY THE PRICE AFTER THE WISH WAS GRANTED, AND THEN SHE HANDED OVER THE BELL. SO I GUESS THAT'S WHAT'LL HAPPEN.

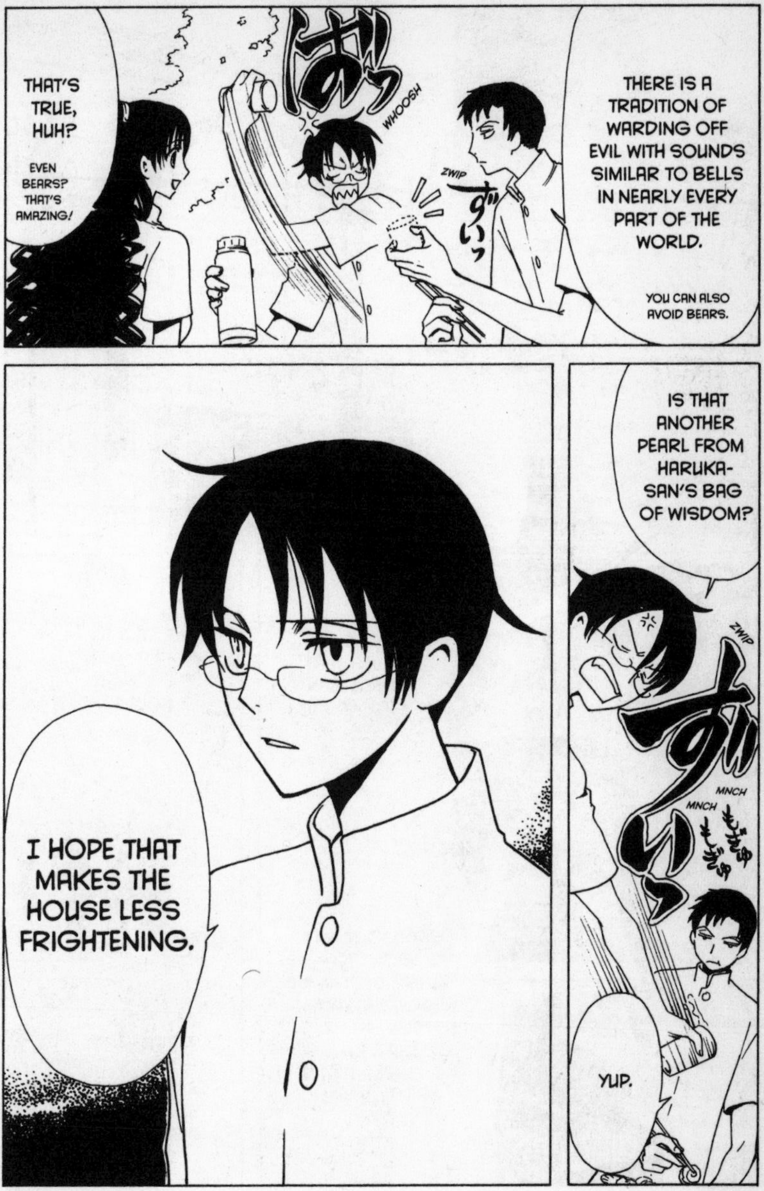
THERE IS A TRADITION OF WARDING OFF EVIL WITH SOUNDS SIMILAR TO BELLS IN NEARLY EVERY PART OF THE WORLD.
YOU CAN ALSO AVOID BEARS.
ZWIP
WHOOSH
THAT'S TRUE, HUH?
EVEN BEARS? THAT'S AMAZING!
IS THAT ANOTHER PEARL FROM HARUKA-SAN'S BAG OF WISDOM?
ZWIP
MNCH
MNCH
YUP.
I HOPE THAT MAKES THE HOUSE LESS FRIGHTENING.

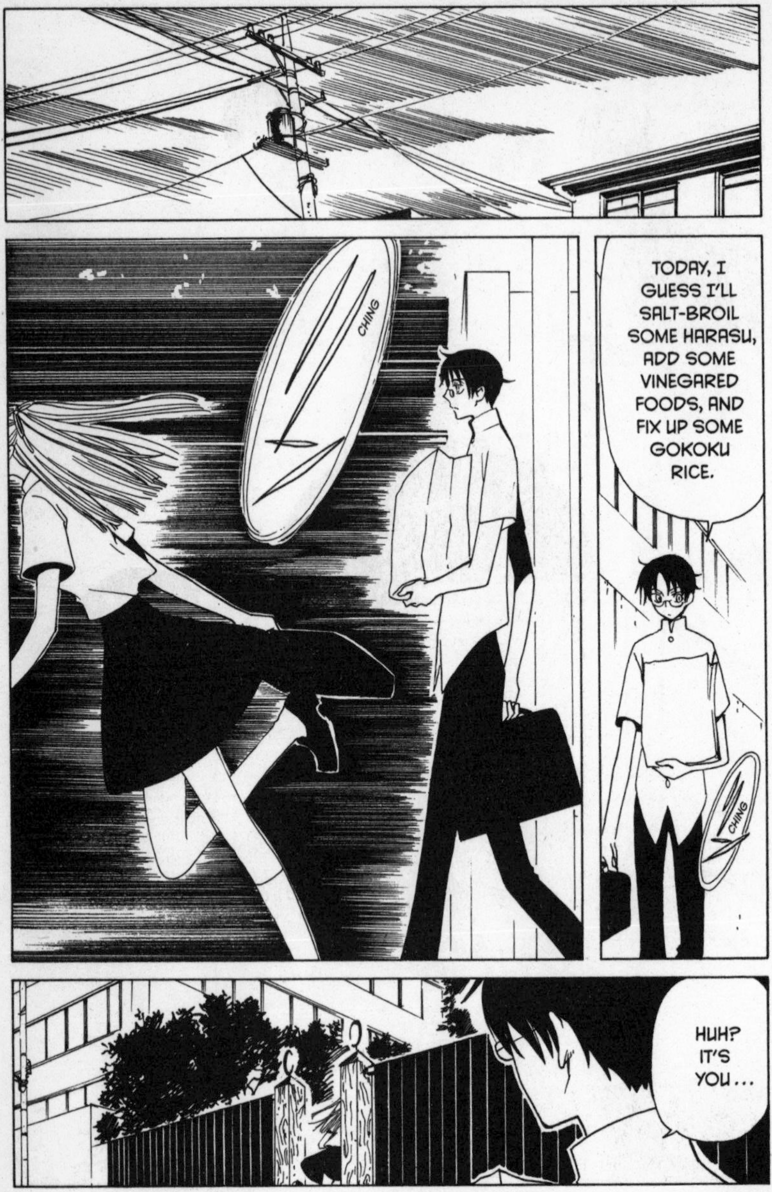
TODAY, I GUESS I'LL SALT-BROIL SOME HARASU, ADD SOME VINEGARED FOODS, AND FIX UP SOME GOKOKU RICE.
CHING
CHING
HUH? IT'S YOU...

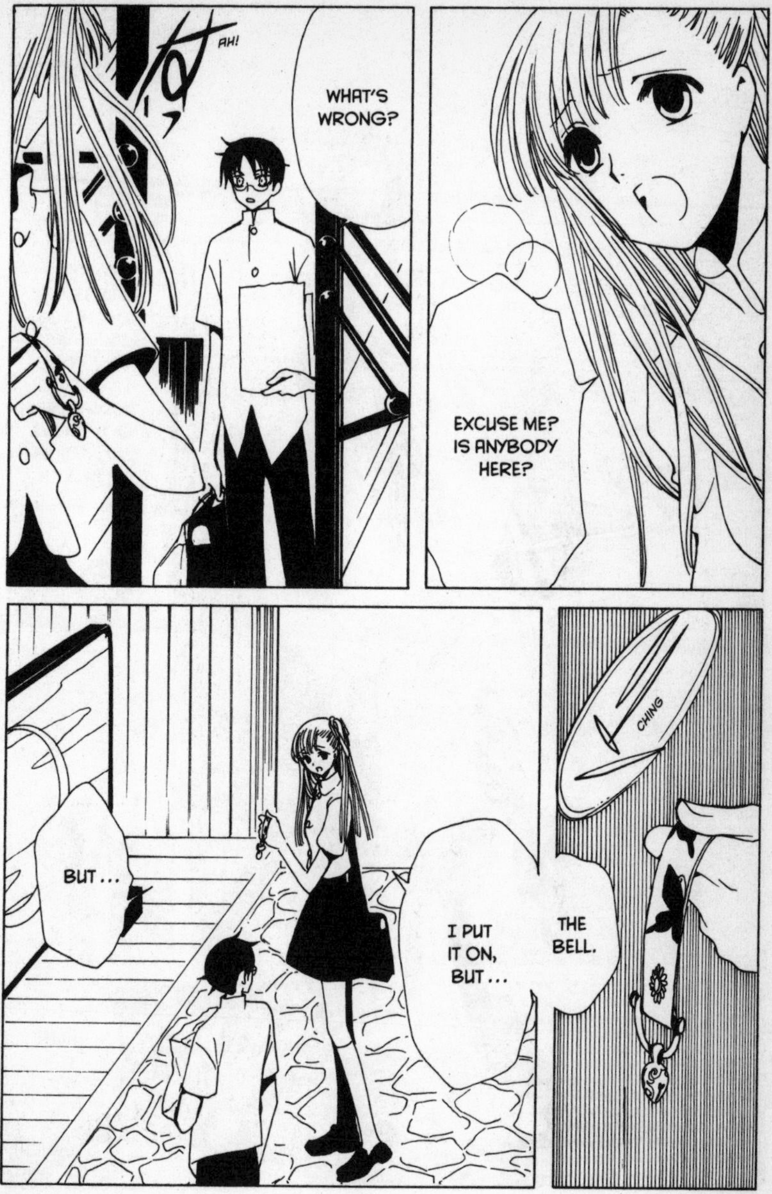
EXCUSE ME? IS ANYBODY HERE?
AH!
WHAT'S WRONG?
CHING
THE BELL.
I PUT IT ON, BUT...
BUT...

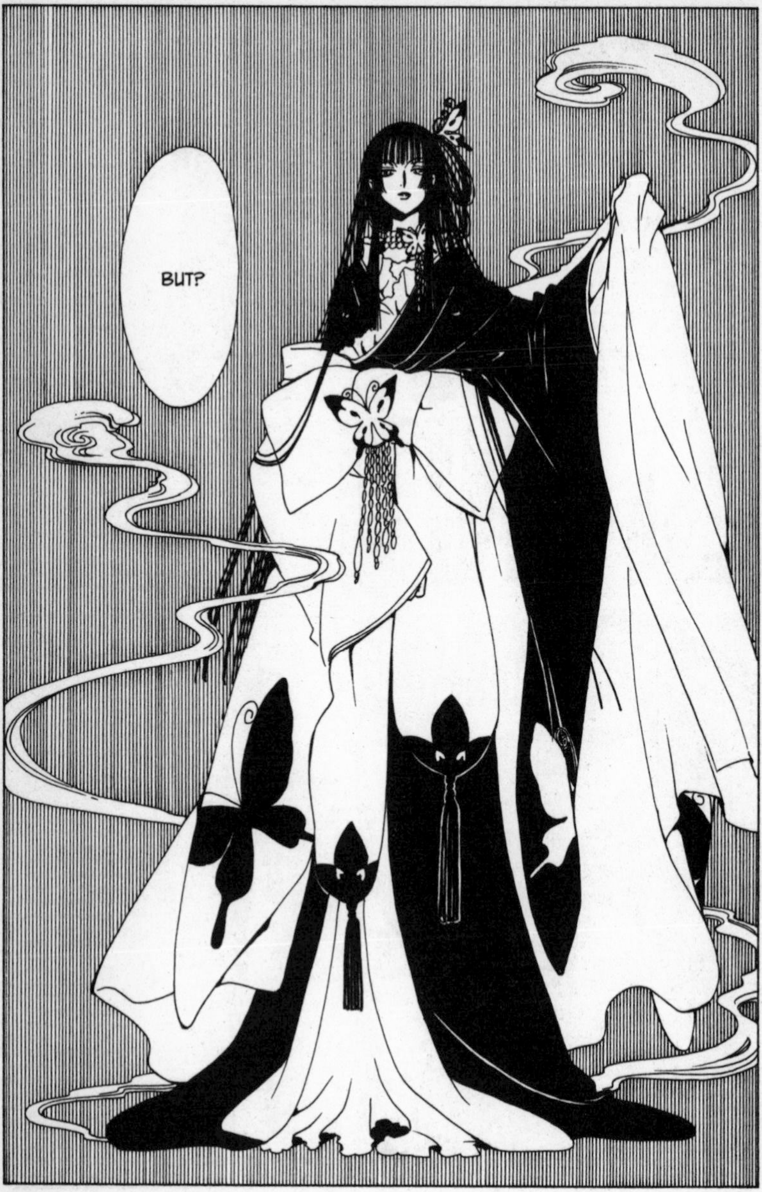
BUT?

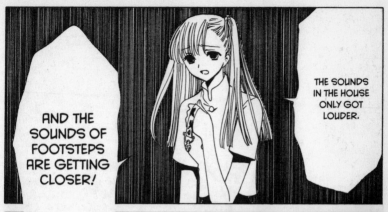

THE SOUNDS IN THE HOUSE ONLY GOT LOUDER.

AND THE SOUNDS OF FOOTSTEPS ARE GETTING CLOSER!

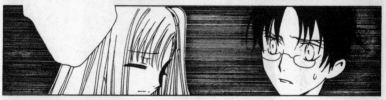

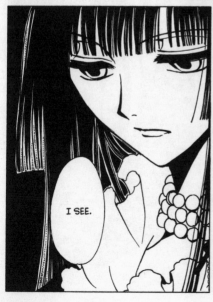

I SEE.

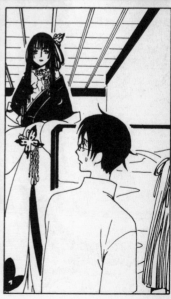

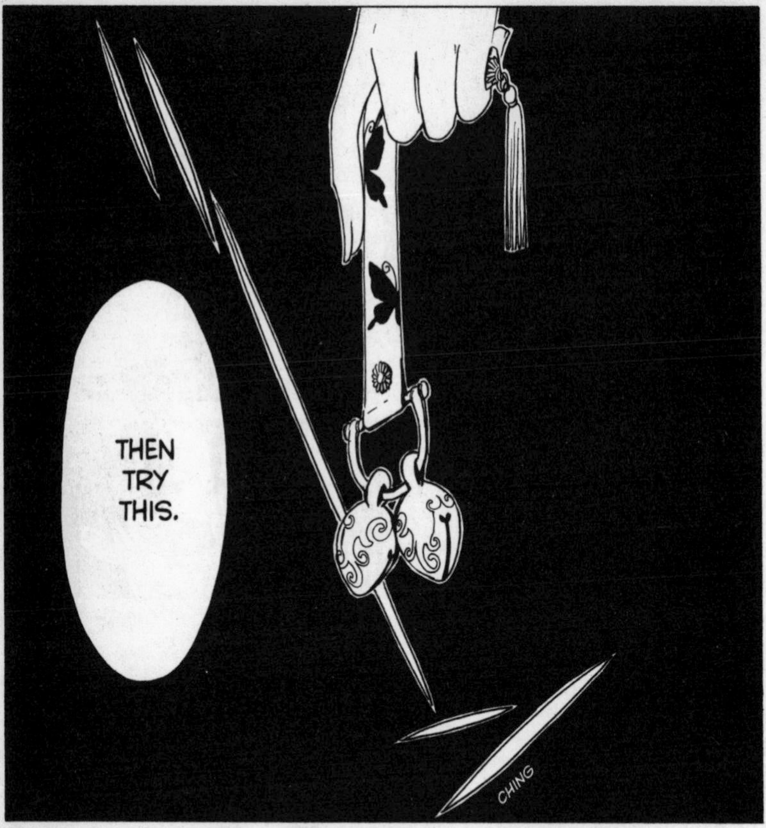
THEN TRY THIS.
CHING

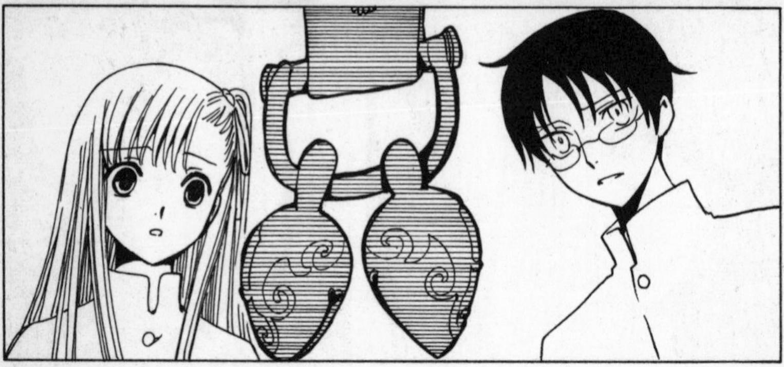

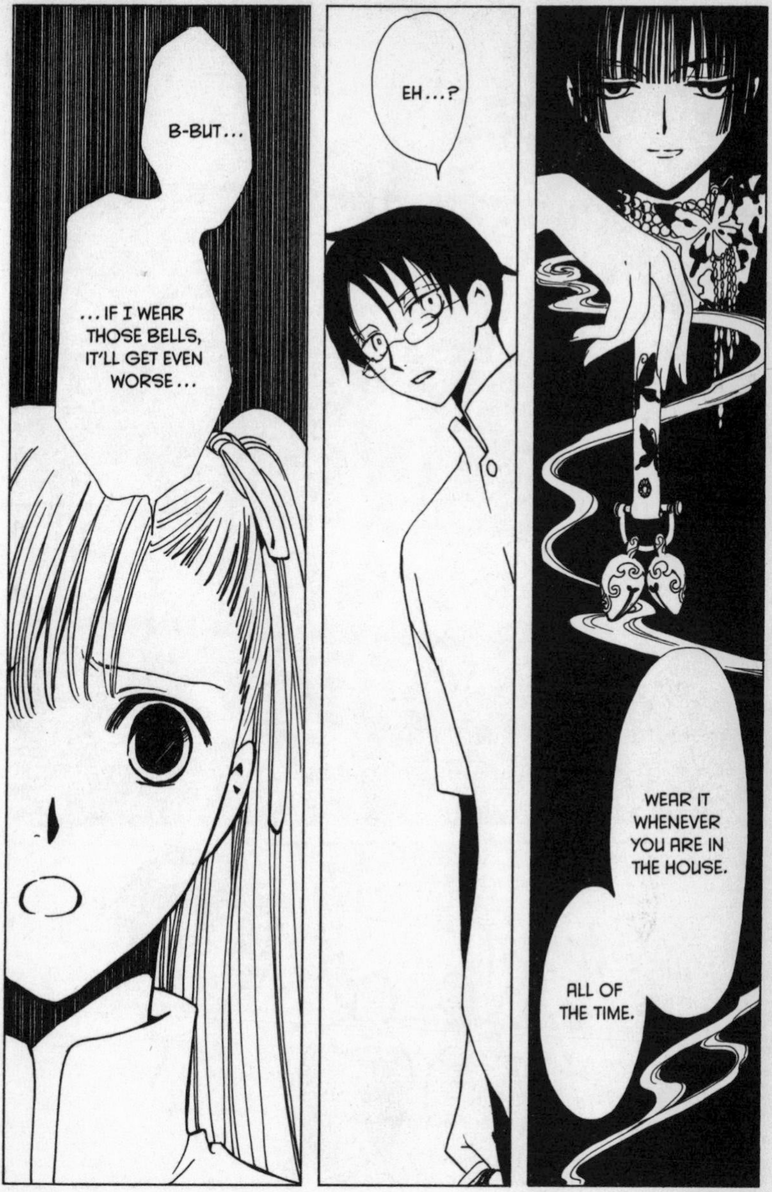
WEAR IT WHENEVER YOU ARE IN THE HOUSE.
ALL OF THE TIME.
EH...?
B-BUT...
...IF I WEAR THOSE BELLS, IT'LL GET EVEN WORSE...

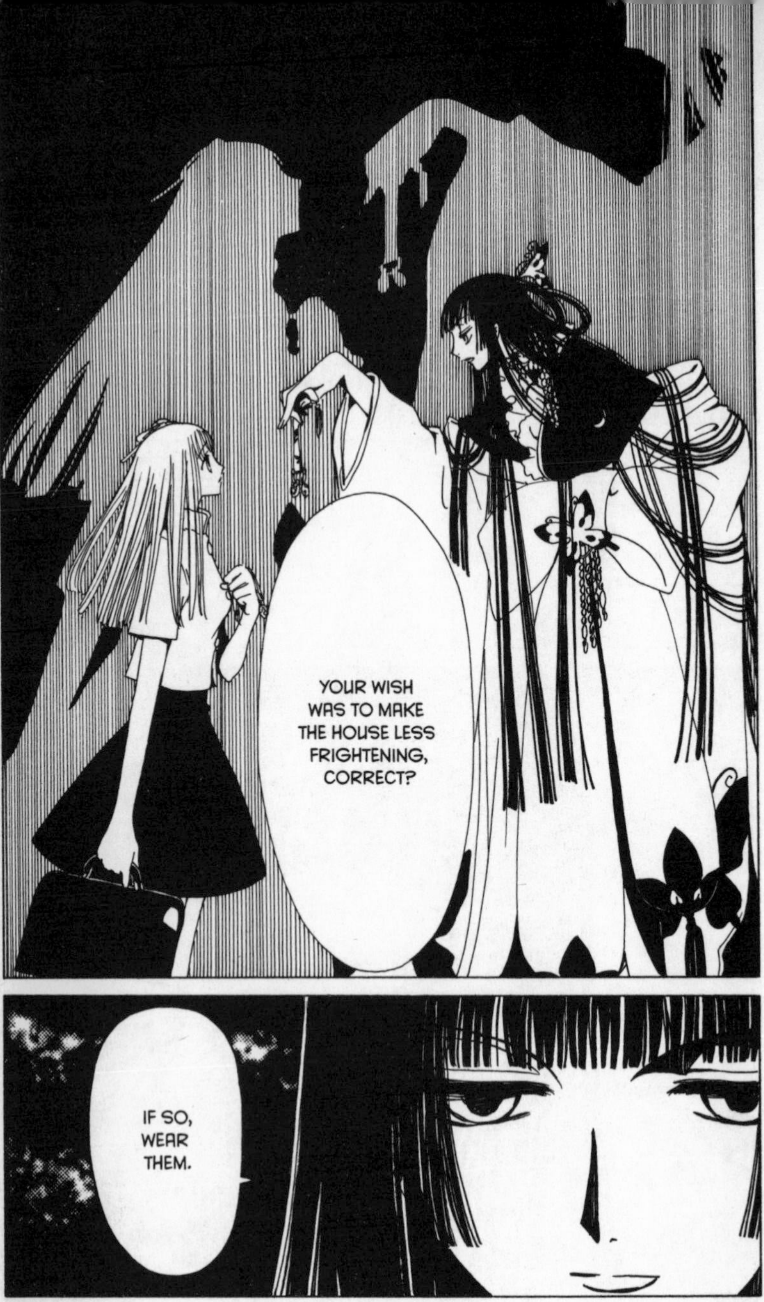
YOUR WISH WAS TO MAKE THE HOUSE LESS FRIGHTENING, CORRECT?
IF SO, WEAR THEM.

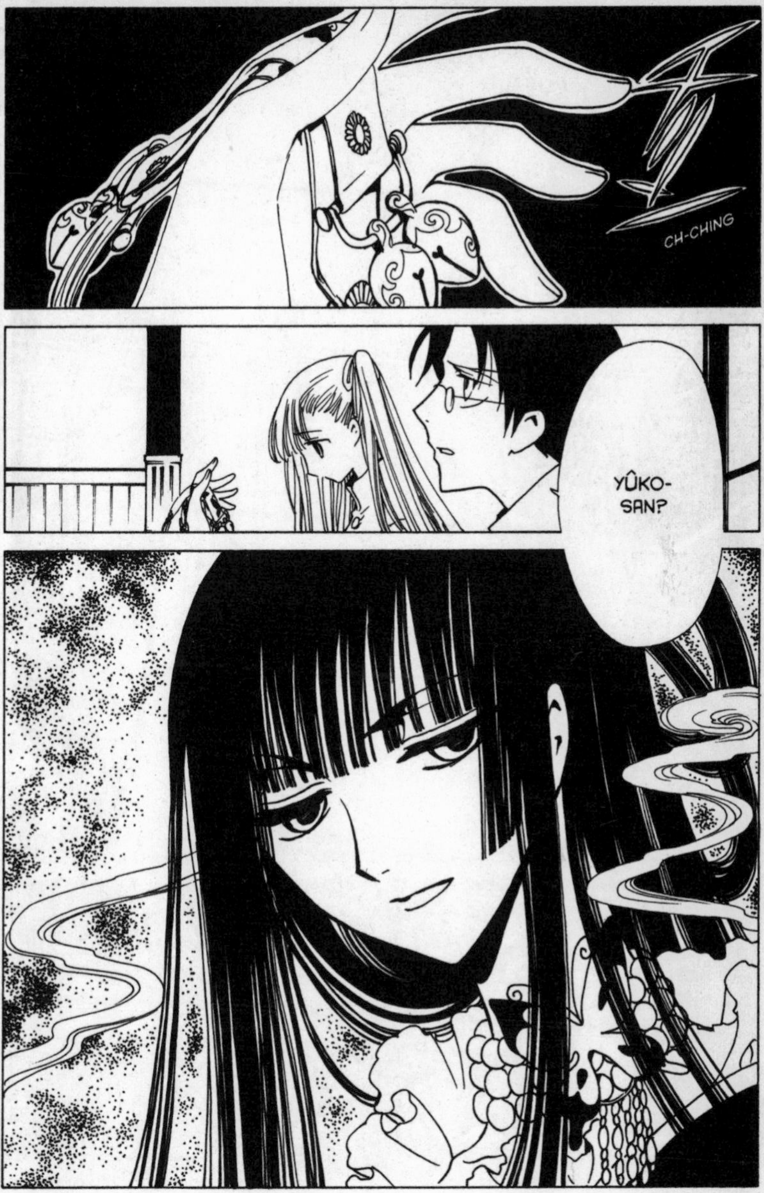
CH-CHING
YÛKO-SAN?

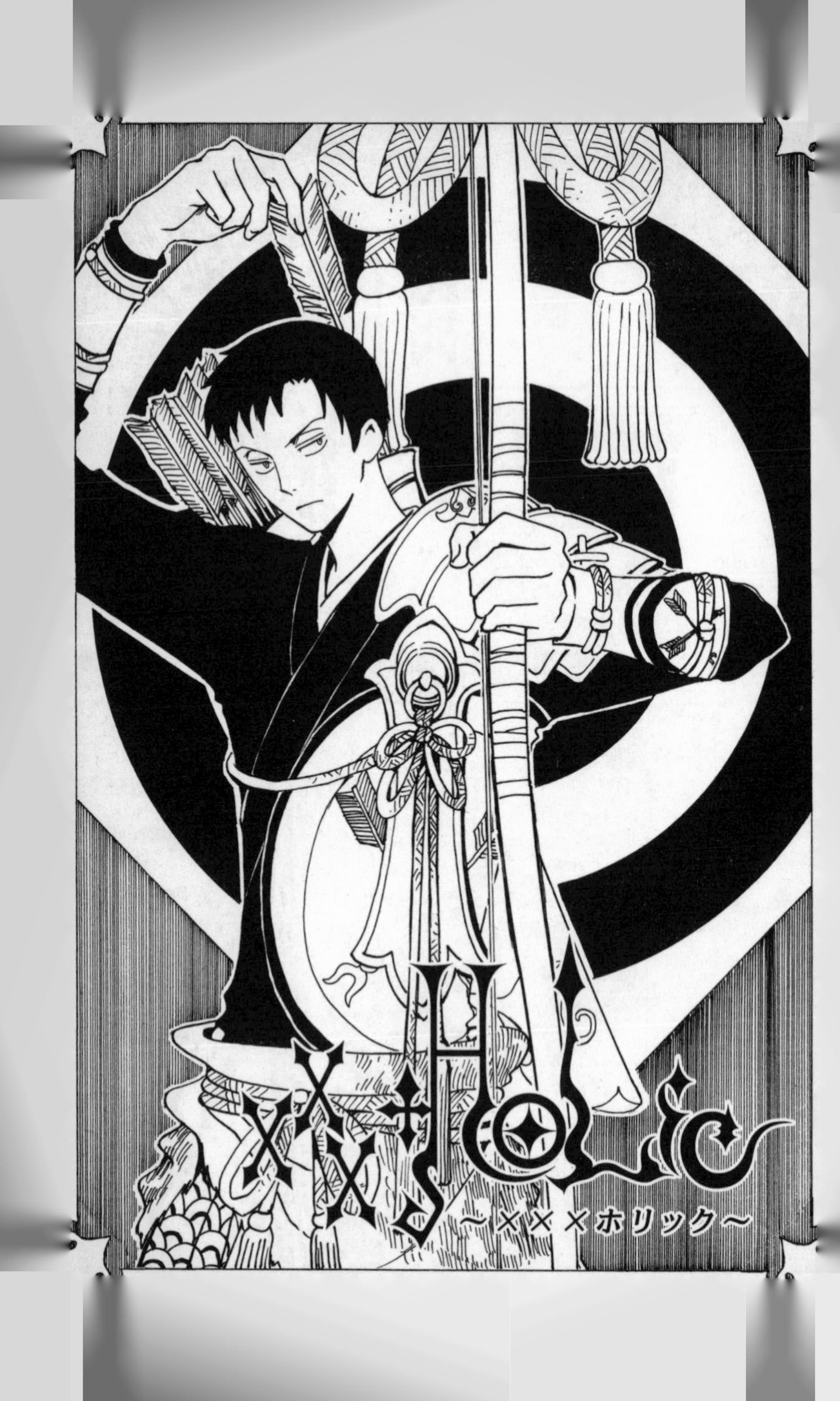
xxxHOLiC
～×××ホリック～

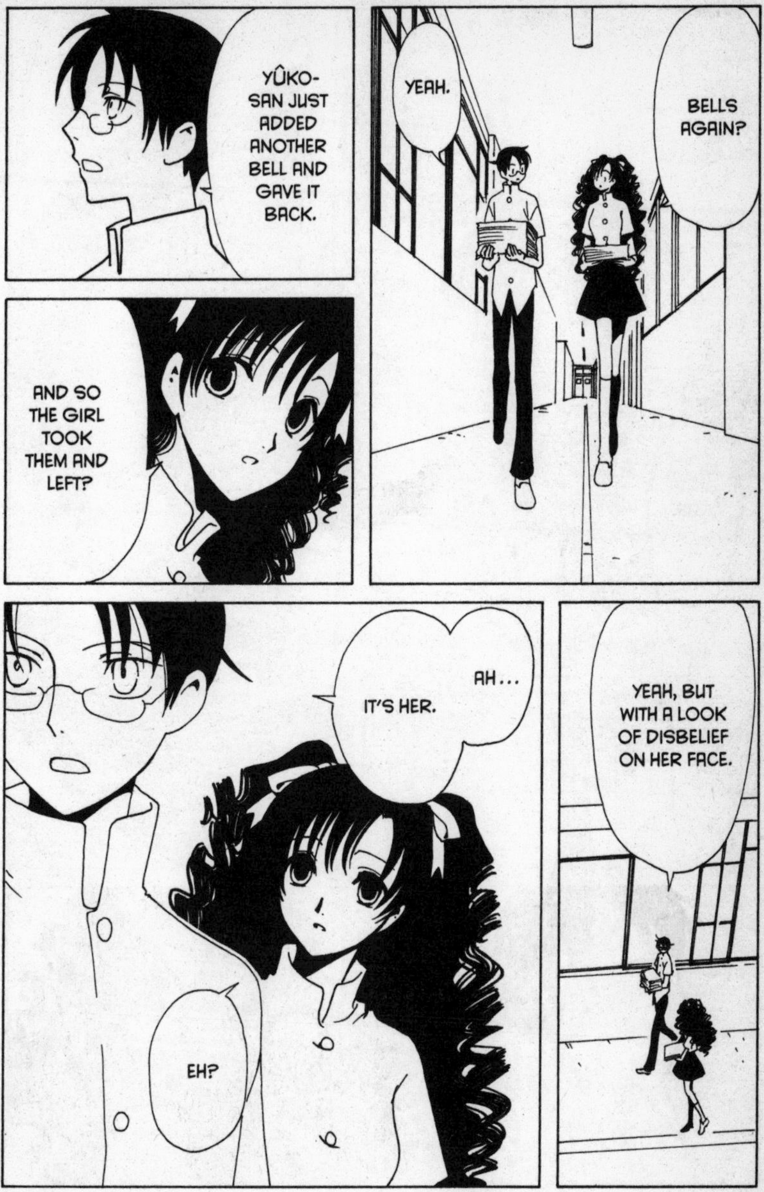
BELLS AGAIN?
YEAH.
YÛKO-SAN JUST ADDED ANOTHER BELL AND GAVE IT BACK.
AND SO THE GIRL TOOK THEM AND LEFT?
YEAH, BUT WITH A LOOK OF DISBELIEF ON HER FACE.
AH... IT'S HER.
EH?

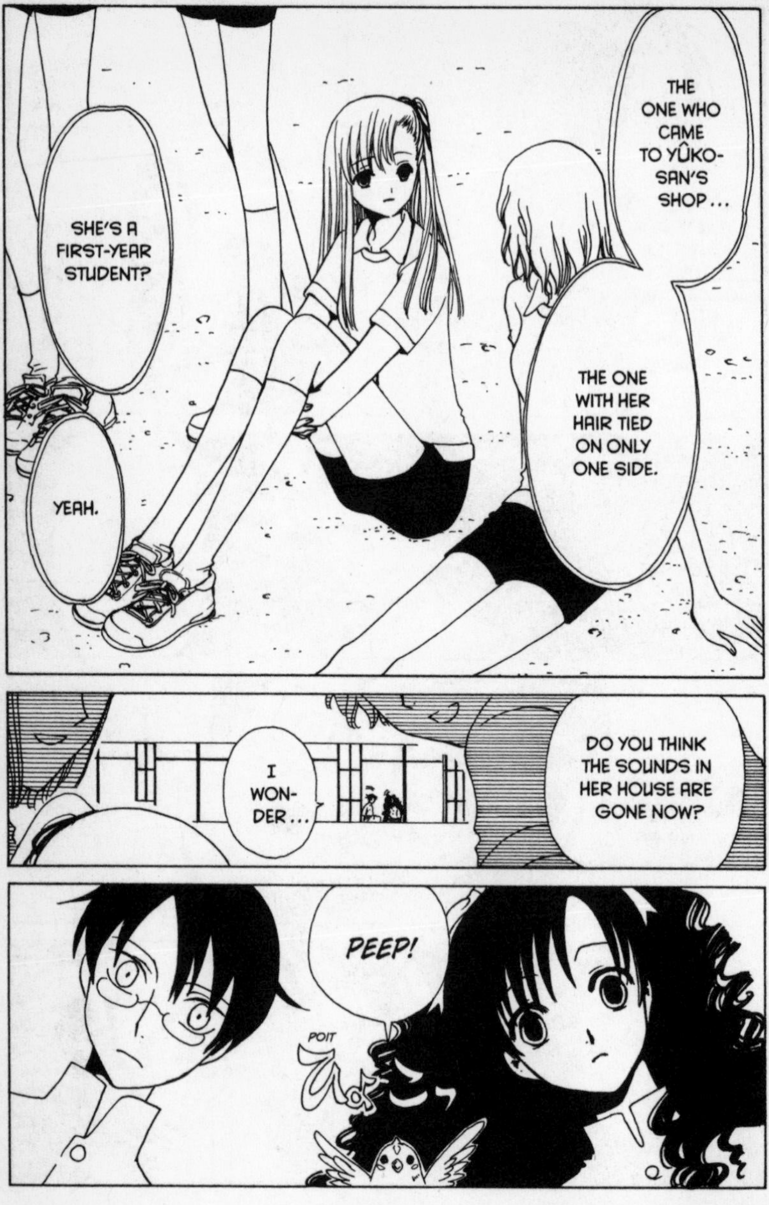
THE ONE WHO CAME TO YÛKO-SAN'S SHOP...
THE ONE WITH HER HAIR TIED ON ONLY ONE SIDE.
SHE'S A FIRST-YEAR STUDENT?
YEAH.
DO YOU THINK THE SOUNDS IN HER HOUSE ARE GONE NOW?
I WONDER...
PEEP!
POIT

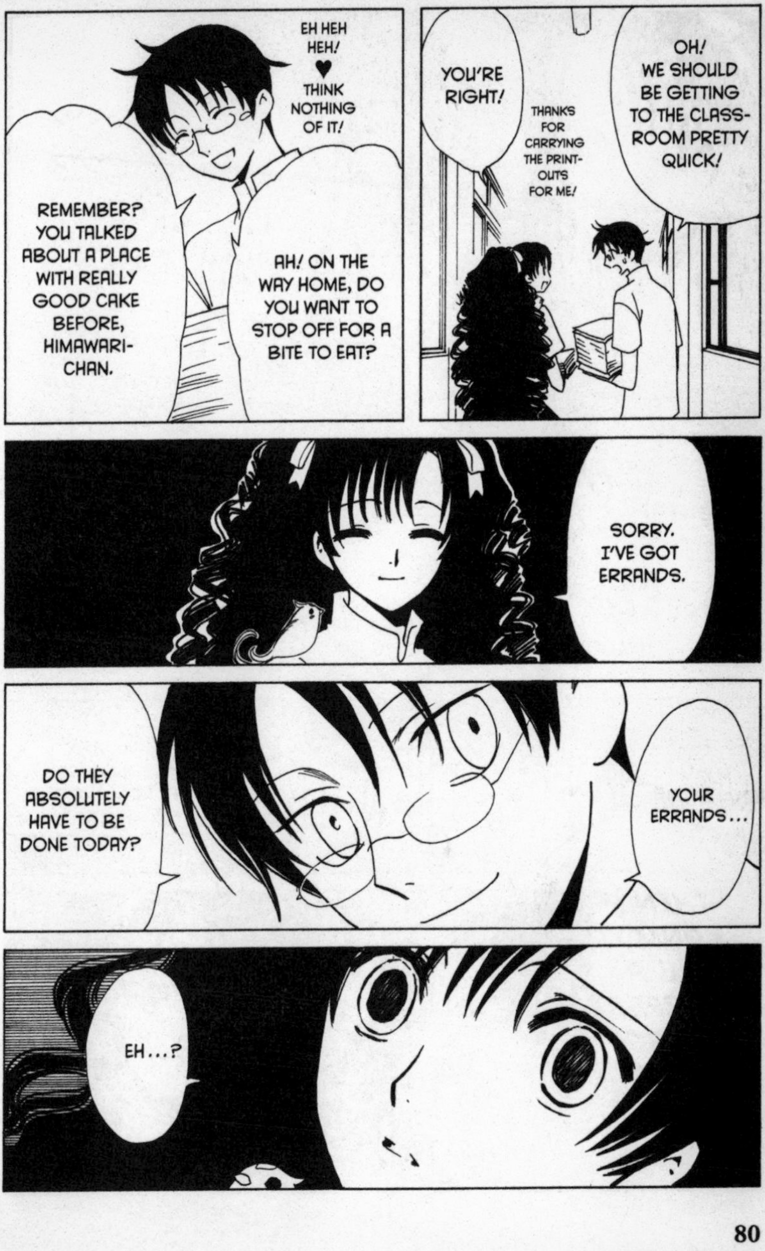

OH! WE SHOULD BE GETTING TO THE CLASS-ROOM PRETTY QUICK!
THANKS FOR CARRYING THE PRINT-OUTS FOR ME!
YOU'RE RIGHT!
EH HEH HEH! ♥ THINK NOTHING OF IT!
AH! ON THE WAY HOME, DO YOU WANT TO STOP OFF FOR A BITE TO EAT?
REMEMBER? YOU TALKED ABOUT A PLACE WITH REALLY GOOD CAKE BEFORE, HIMAWARI-CHAN.
SORRY. I'VE GOT ERRANDS.
YOUR ERRANDS...
DO THEY ABSOLUTELY HAVE TO BE DONE TODAY?
EH...?

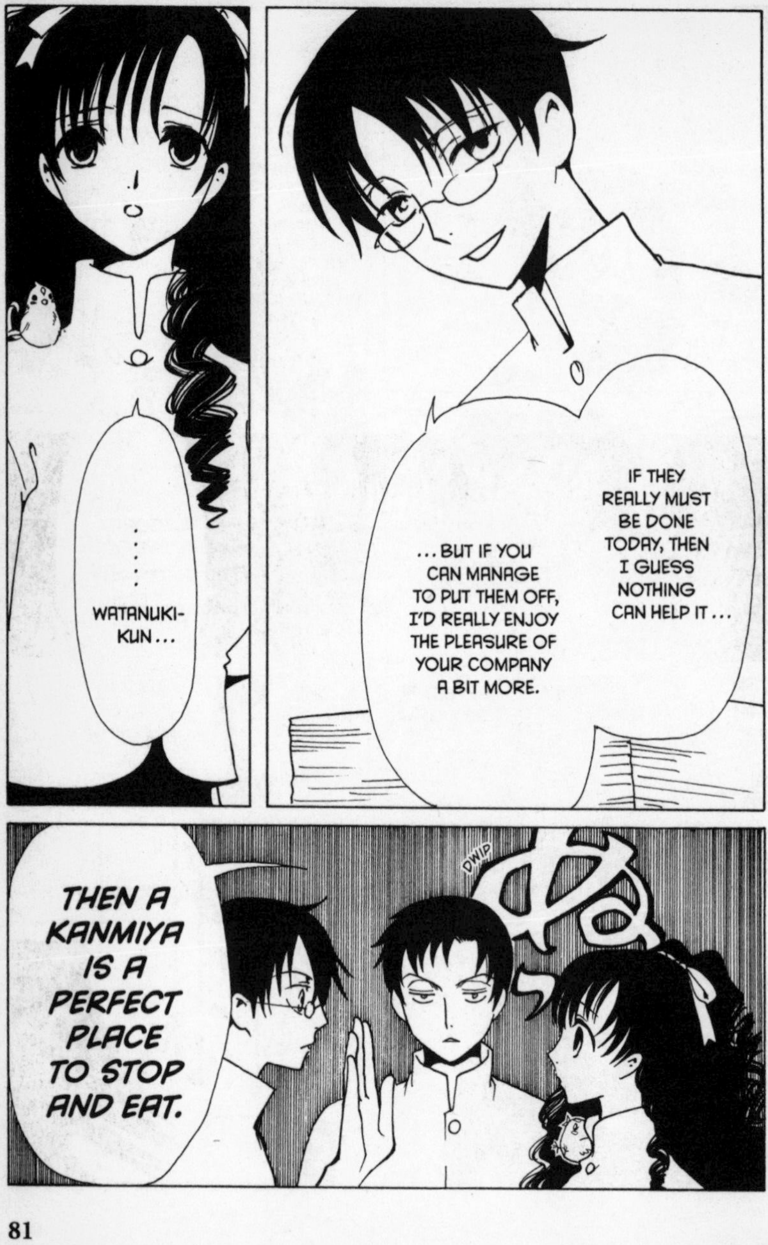
IF THEY REALLY MUST BE DONE TODAY, THEN I GUESS NOTHING CAN HELP IT...
...BUT IF YOU CAN MANAGE TO PUT THEM OFF, I'D REALLY ENJOY THE PLEASURE OF YOUR COMPANY A BIT MORE.
...... WATANUKI-KUN...
DWIP
THEN A KANMIYA IS A PERFECT PLACE TO STOP AND EAT.

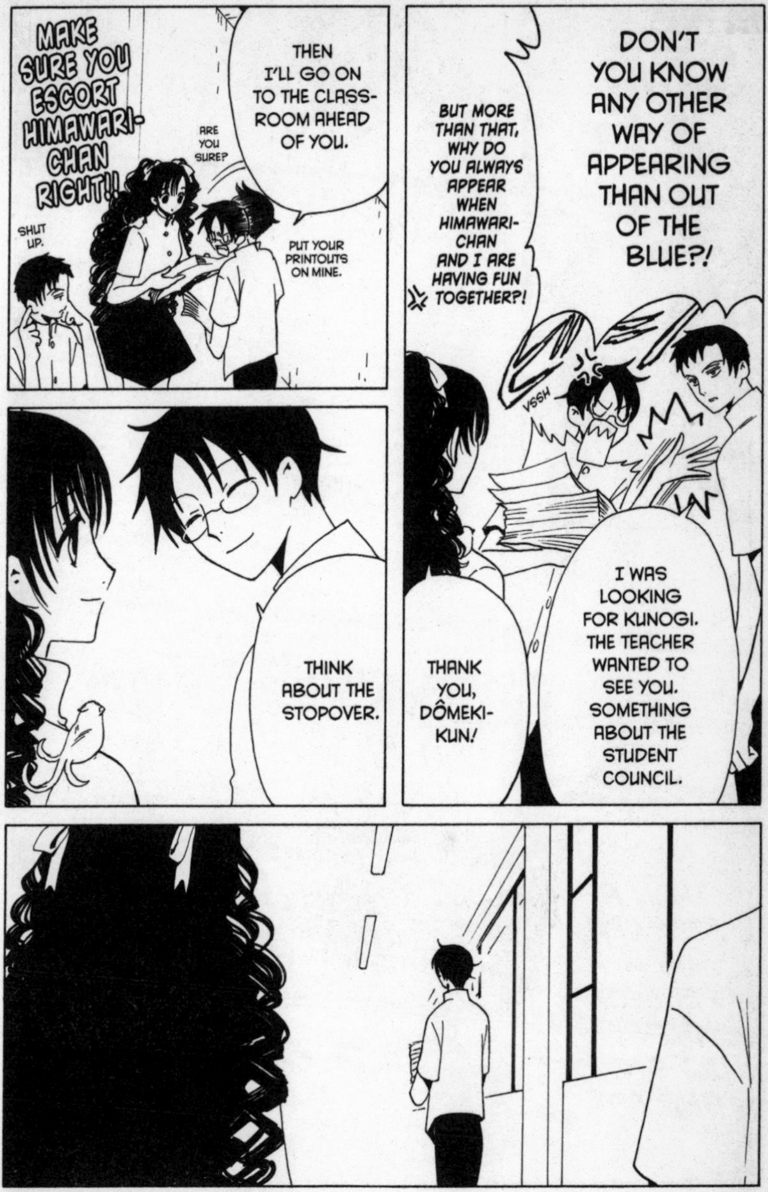
DON'T YOU KNOW ANY OTHER WAY OF APPEARING THAN OUT OF THE BLUE?!
BUT MORE THAN THAT, WHY DO YOU ALWAYS APPEAR WHEN HIMAWARI-CHAN AND I ARE HAVING FUN TOGETHER?!
VSSH
I WAS LOOKING FOR KUNOGI. THE TEACHER WANTED TO SEE YOU. SOMETHING ABOUT THE STUDENT COUNCIL.
THANK YOU, DÔMEKI-KUN!
THEN I'LL GO ON TO THE CLASS-ROOM AHEAD OF YOU.
ARE YOU SURE?
PUT YOUR PRINTOUTS ON MINE.
MAKE SURE YOU ESCORT HIMAWARI-CHAN RIGHT!!
SHUT UP.
THINK ABOUT THE STOPOVER.

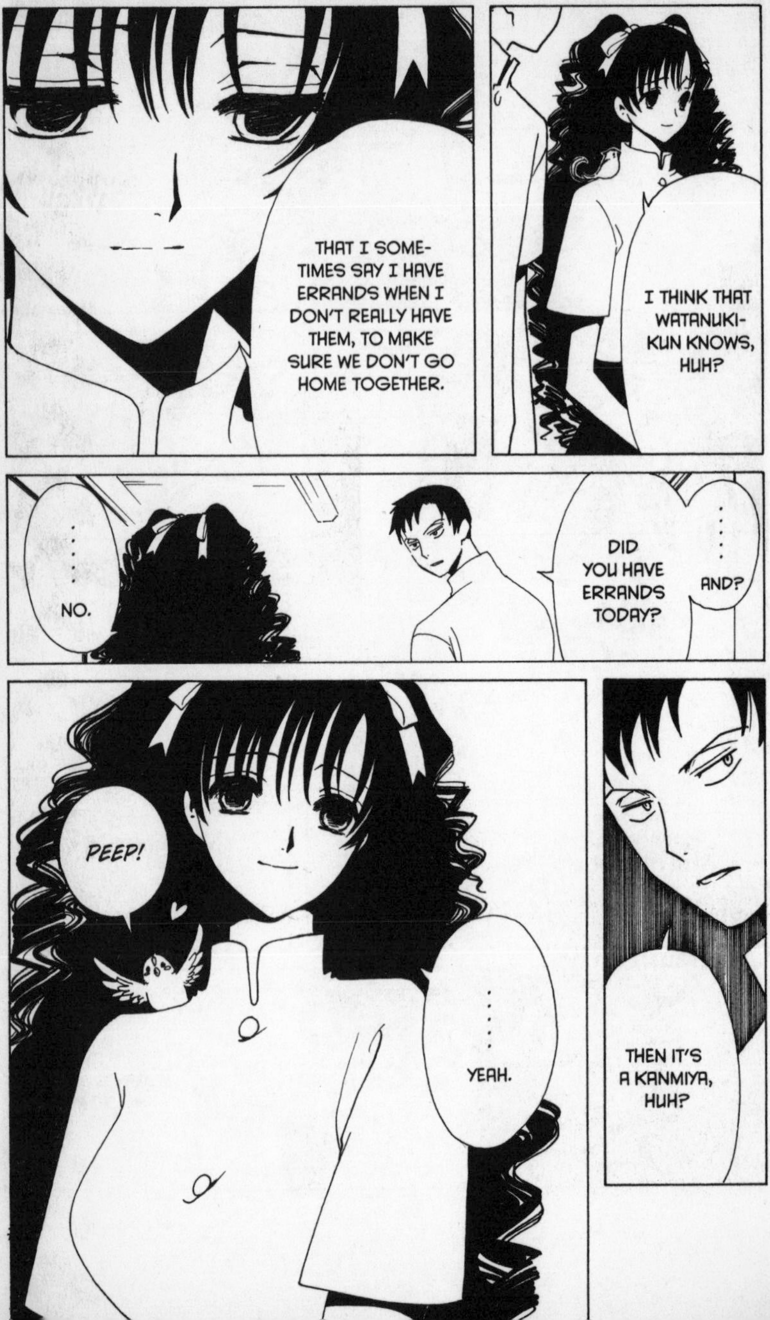
I THINK THAT WATANUKI-KUN KNOWS, HUH?
THAT I SOMETIMES SAY I HAVE ERRANDS WHEN I DON'T REALLY HAVE THEM, TO MAKE SURE WE DON'T GO HOME TOGETHER.
...... AND?
DID YOU HAVE ERRANDS TODAY?
...... NO.
THEN IT'S A KANMIYA, HUH?
...... YEAH.
PEEP!

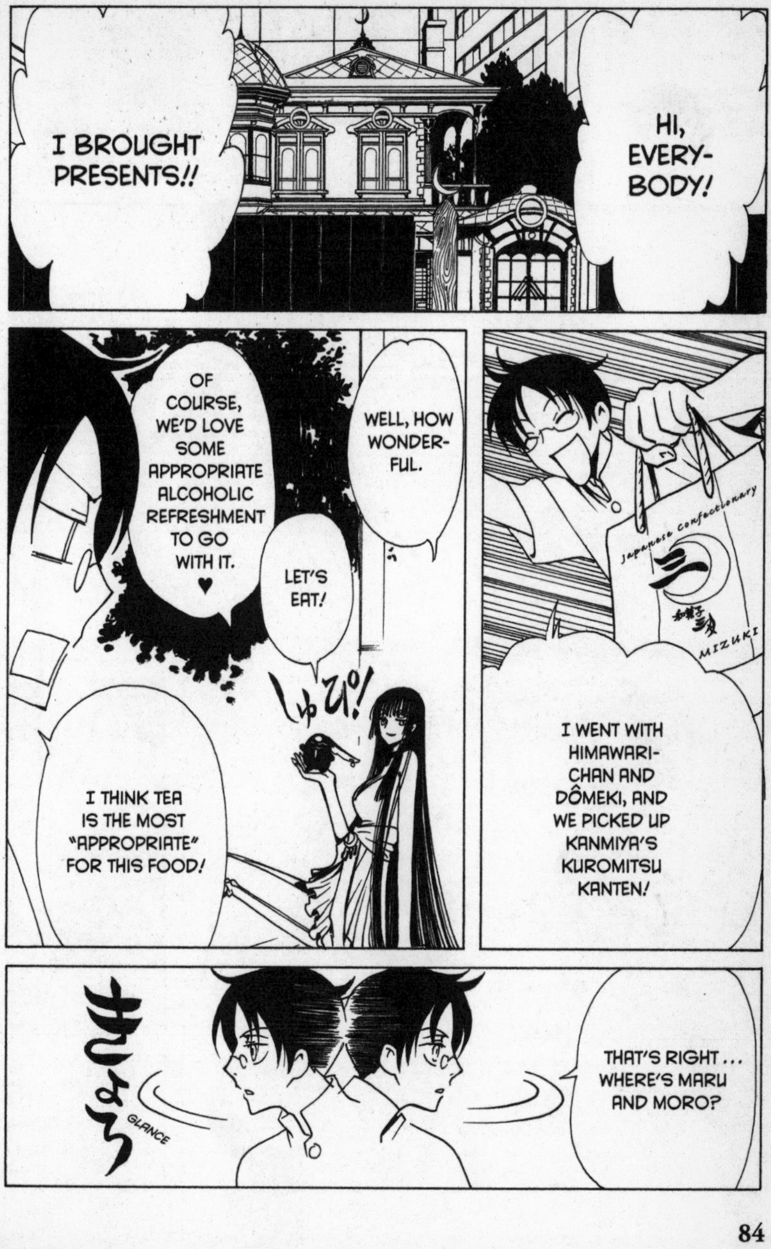
HI, EVERY-BODY!
I BROUGHT PRESENTS!!
Japanese confectionary
MIZUKI
I WENT WITH HIMAWARI-CHAN AND DÔMEKI, AND WE PICKED UP KANMIYA'S KUROMITSU KANTEN!
WELL, HOW WONDERFUL.
OF COURSE, WE'D LOVE SOME APPROPRIATE ALCOHOLIC REFRESHMENT TO GO WITH IT. ♥
LET'S EAT!
しゅぴ!
I THINK TEA IS THE MOST "APPROPRIATE" FOR THIS FOOD!
THAT'S RIGHT... WHERE'S MARU AND MORO?
きょろ
GLANCE

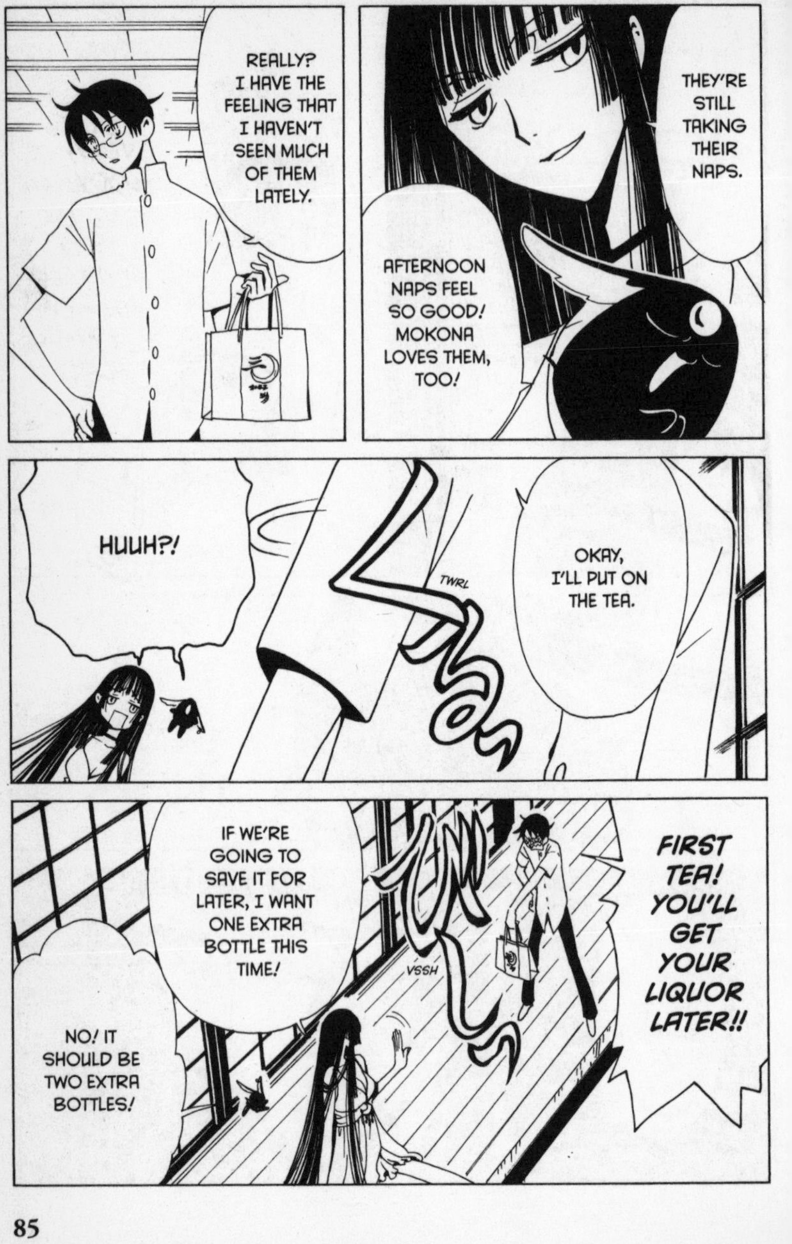
THEY'RE STILL TAKING THEIR NAPS.
AFTERNOON NAPS FEEL SO GOOD! MOKONA LOVES THEM, TOO!
REALLY? I HAVE THE FEELING THAT I HAVEN'T SEEN MUCH OF THEM LATELY.
OKAY, I'LL PUT ON THE TEA.
TWRL
HUUH?!
FIRST TEA! YOU'LL GET YOUR LIQUOR LATER!!
VSSH
IF WE'RE GOING TO SAVE IT FOR LATER, I WANT ONE EXTRA BOTTLE THIS TIME!
NO! IT SHOULD BE TWO EXTRA BOTTLES!

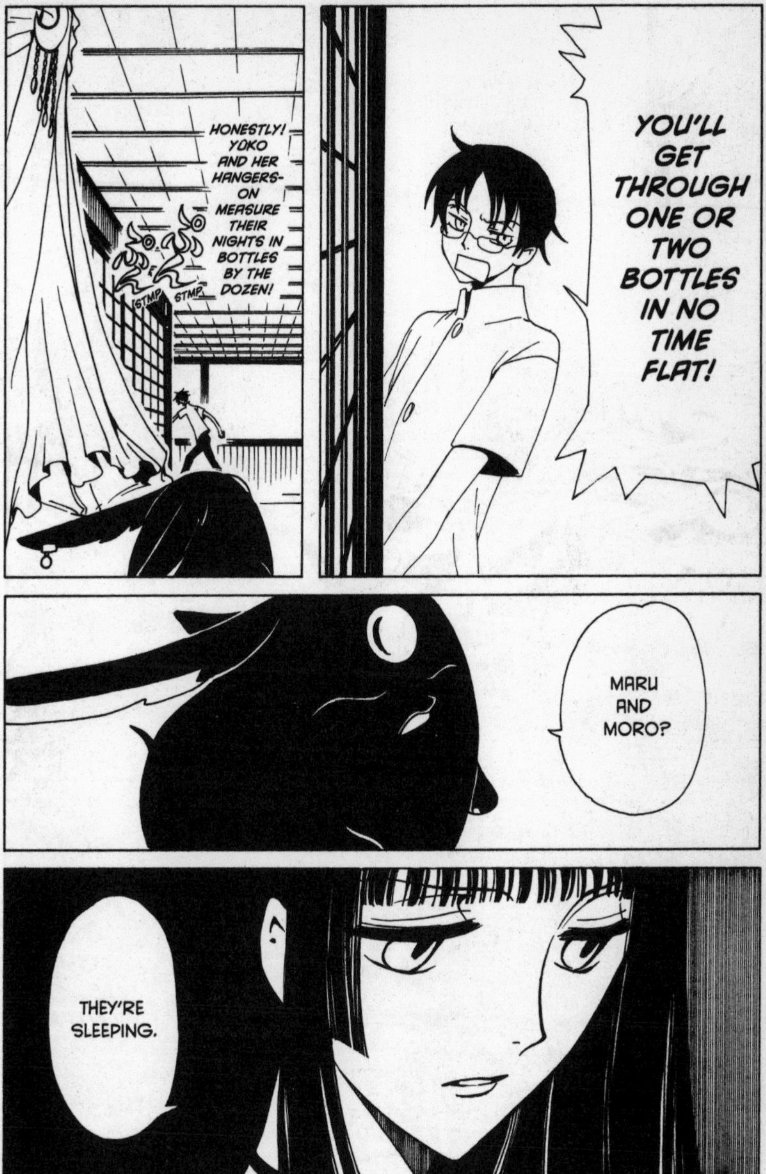
YOU'LL GET THROUGH ONE OR TWO BOTTLES IN NO TIME FLAT!
HONESTLY! YŪKO AND HER HANGERS-ON MEASURE THEIR NIGHTS IN BOTTLES BY THE DOZEN!
STMP STMP
MARU AND MORO?
THEY'RE SLEEPING.

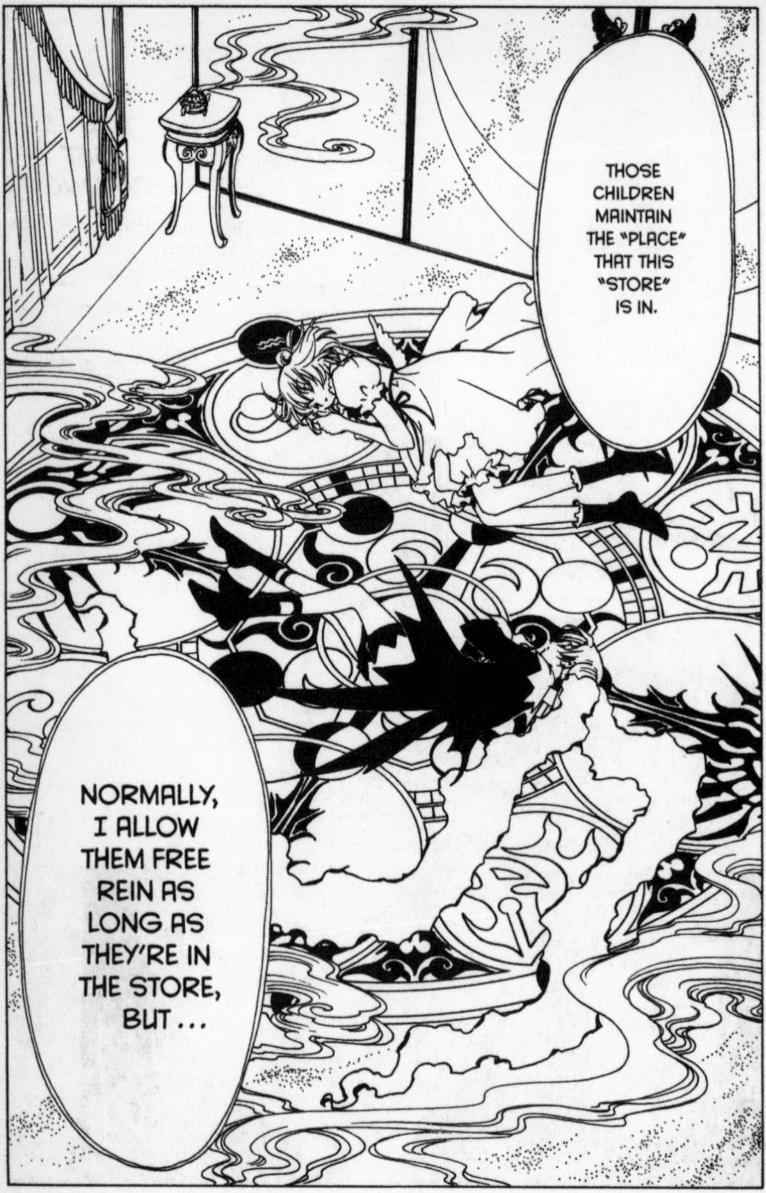
THOSE CHILDREN MAINTAIN THE "PLACE" THAT THIS "STORE" IS IN.
NORMALLY, I ALLOW THEM FREE REIN AS LONG AS THEY'RE IN THE STORE, BUT . . .

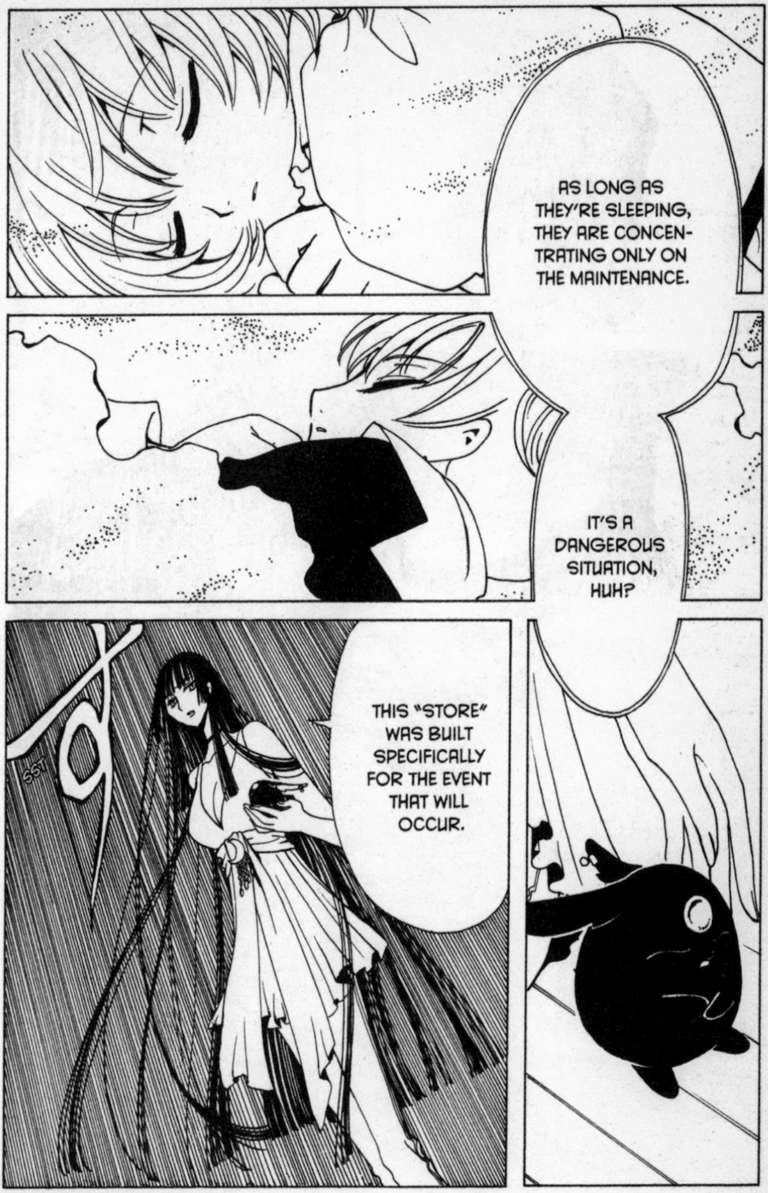
AS LONG AS THEY'RE SLEEPING, THEY ARE CONCEN-TRATING ONLY ON THE MAINTENANCE.
IT'S A DANGEROUS SITUATION, HUH?
THIS "STORE" WAS BUILT SPECIFICALLY FOR THE EVENT THAT WILL OCCUR.
SST

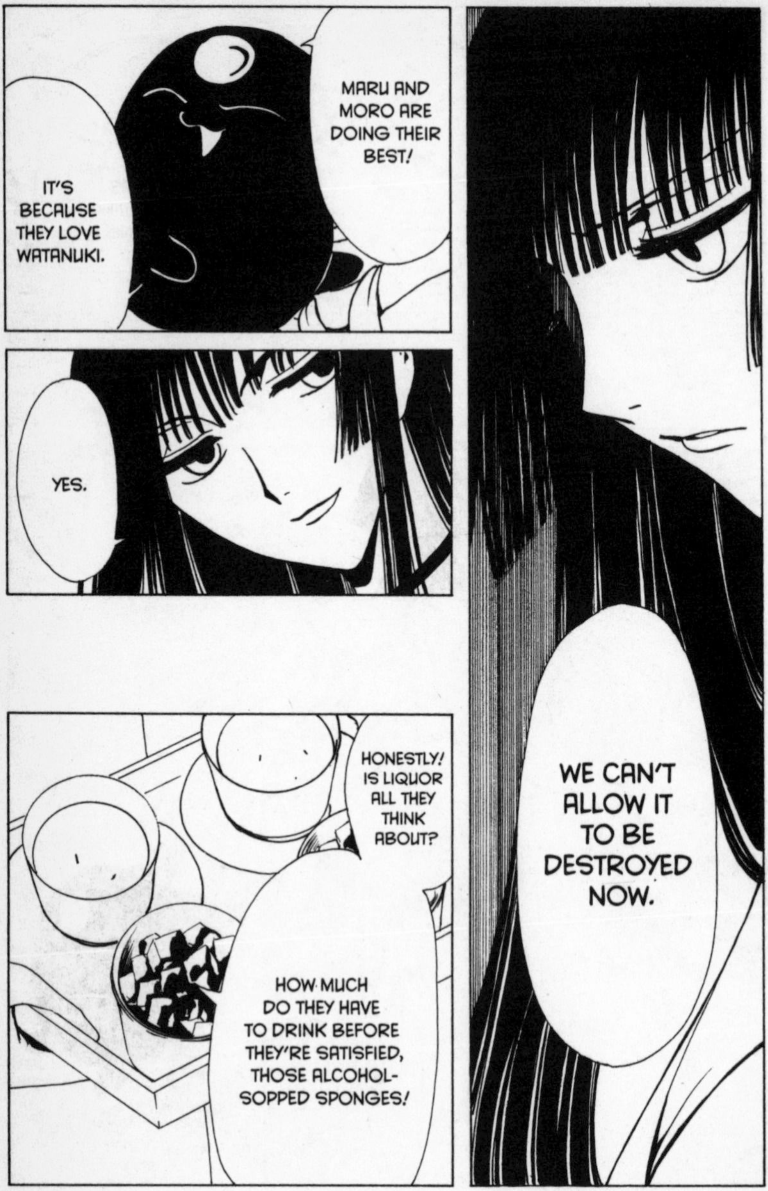
WE CAN'T ALLOW IT TO BE DESTROYED NOW.
MARU AND MORO ARE DOING THEIR BEST!
IT'S BECAUSE THEY LOVE WATANUKI.
YES.
HONESTLY! IS LIQUOR ALL THEY THINK ABOUT?
HOW MUCH DO THEY HAVE TO DRINK BEFORE THEY'RE SATISFIED, THOSE ALCOHOL-SOPPED SPONGES!

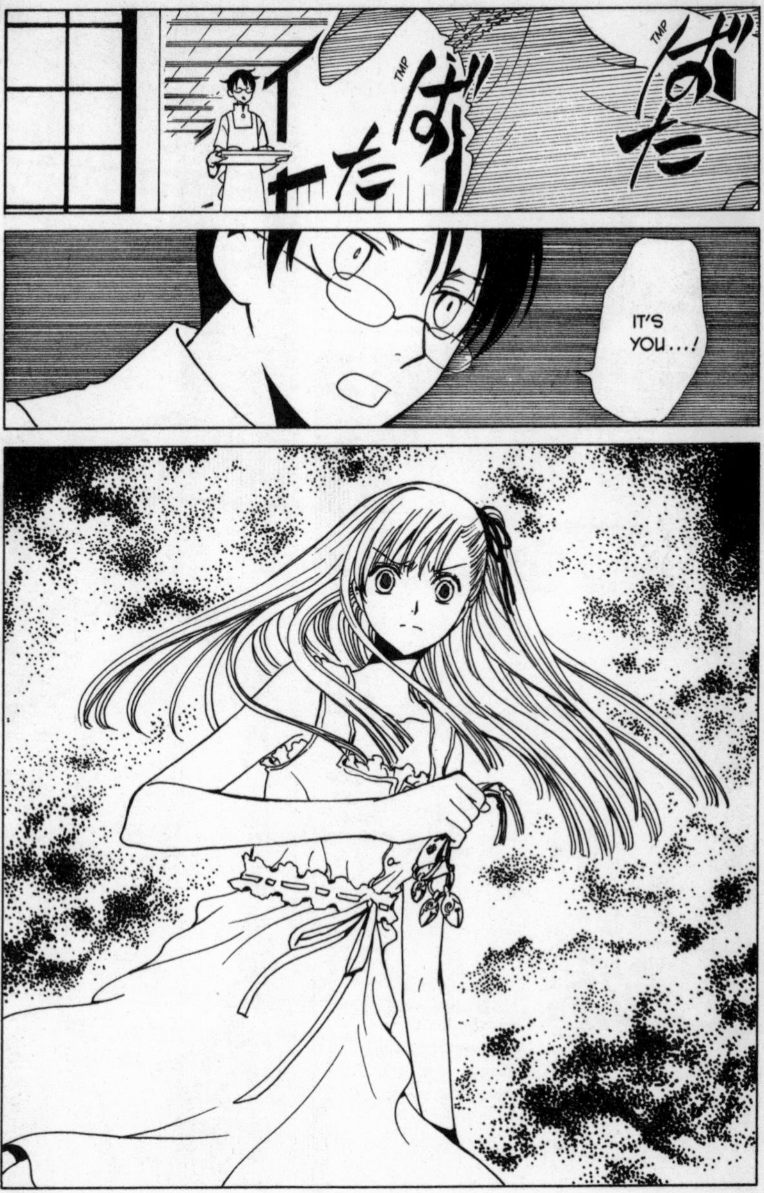
TMP
ばた
TMP
ばた
IT'S YOU...!

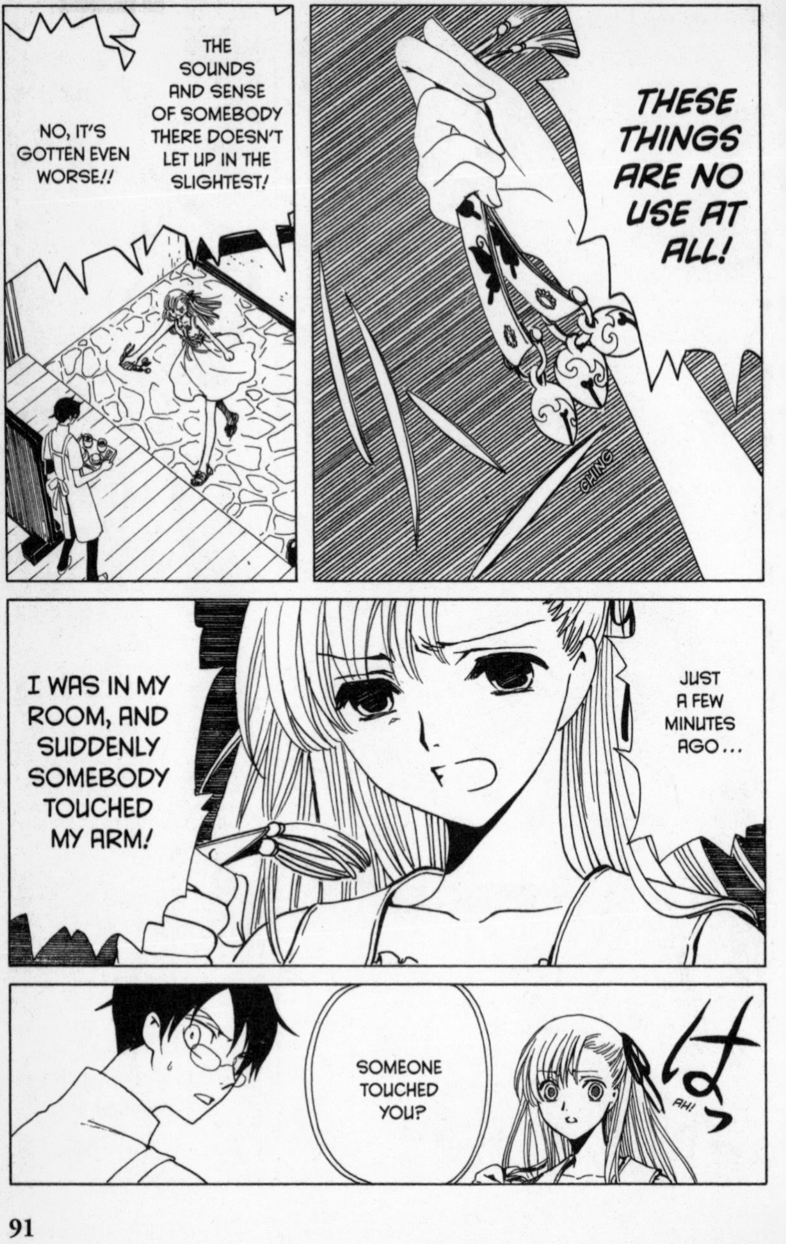
THESE THINGS ARE NO USE AT ALL!
CHING
THE SOUNDS AND SENSE OF SOMEBODY THERE DOESN'T LET UP IN THE SLIGHTEST!
NO, IT'S GOTTEN EVEN WORSE!!
JUST A FEW MINUTES AGO...
I WAS IN MY ROOM, AND SUDDENLY SOMEBODY TOUCHED MY ARM!
はっ
AH!
SOMEONE TOUCHED YOU?

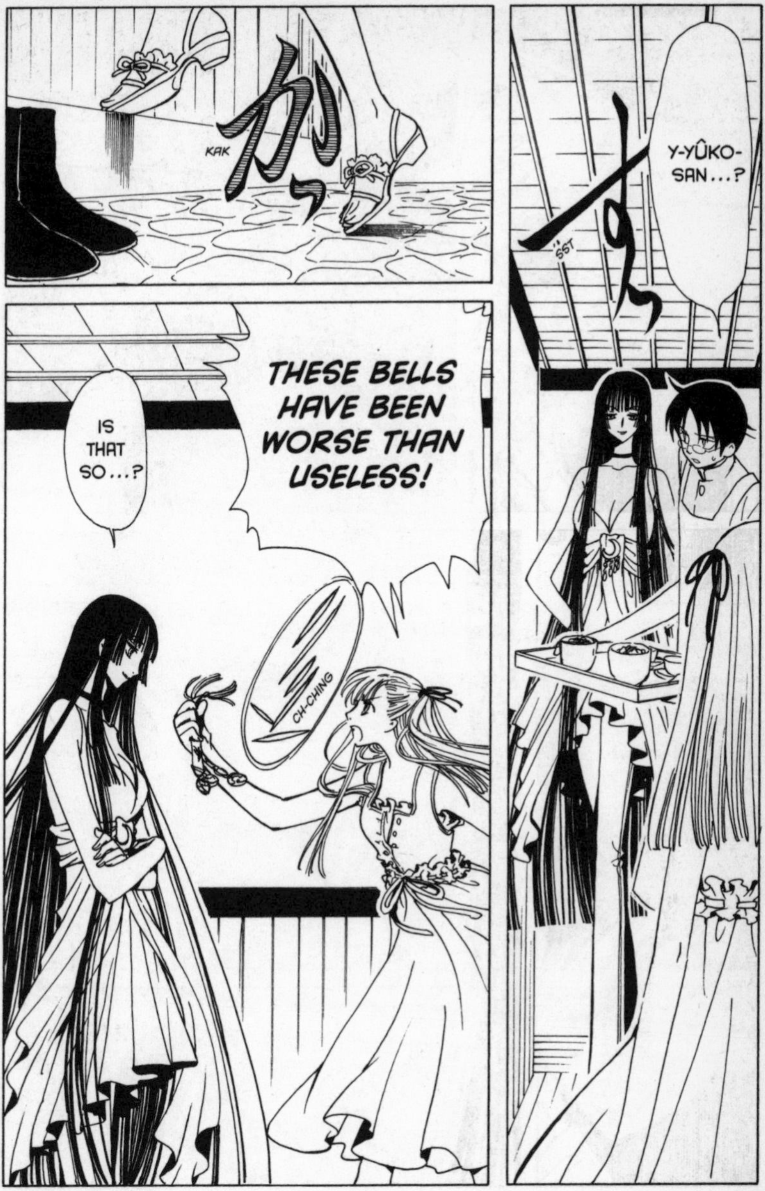
Y-YÛKO-SAN...?
SST
KAK
THESE BELLS HAVE BEEN WORSE THAN USELESS!
IS THAT SO...?
CH-CHING

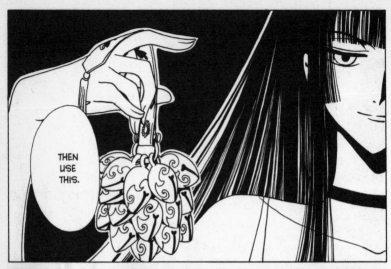

THEN USE THIS.

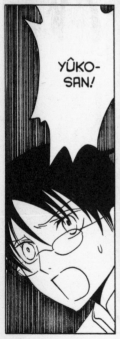

YÛKO-SAN!

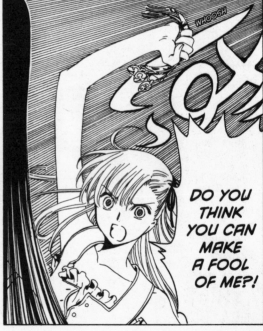

WHOOSH

DO YOU THINK YOU CAN MAKE A FOOL OF ME?!

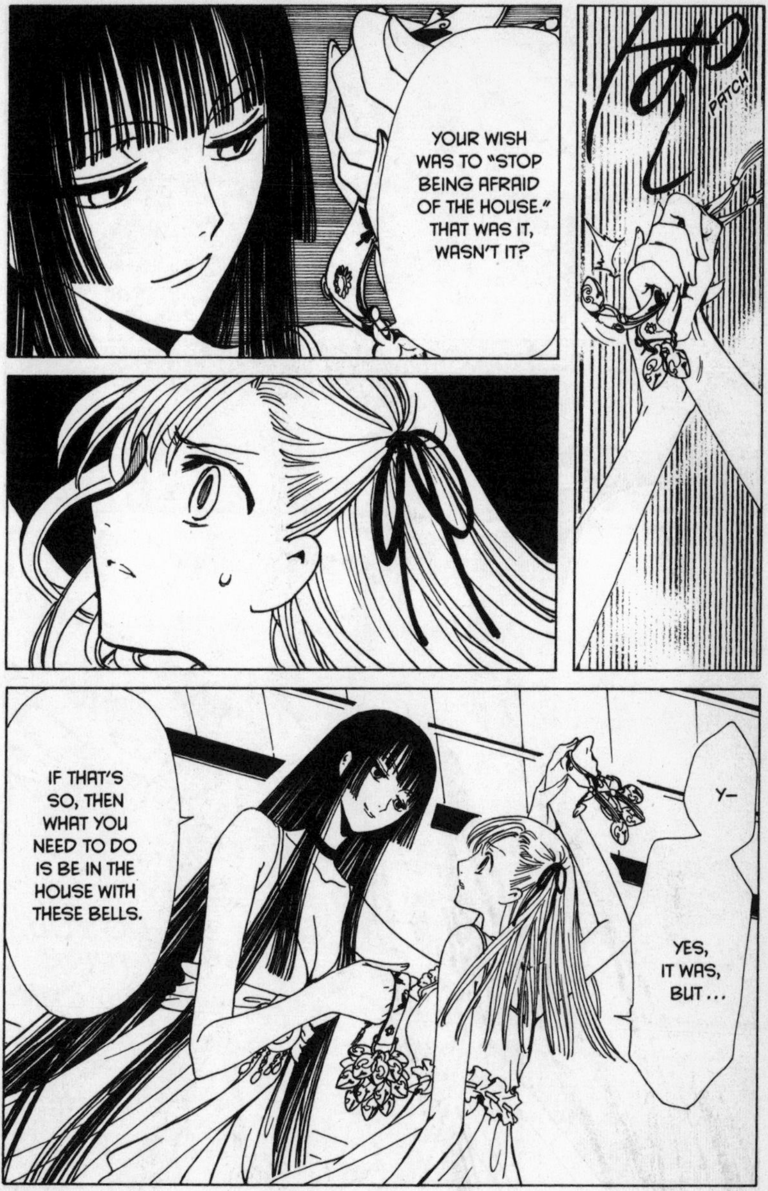
PATCH
YOUR WISH WAS TO "STOP BEING AFRAID OF THE HOUSE." THAT WAS IT, WASN'T IT?
Y—
YES, IT WAS, BUT . . .
IF THAT'S SO, THEN WHAT YOU NEED TO DO IS BE IN THE HOUSE WITH THESE BELLS.

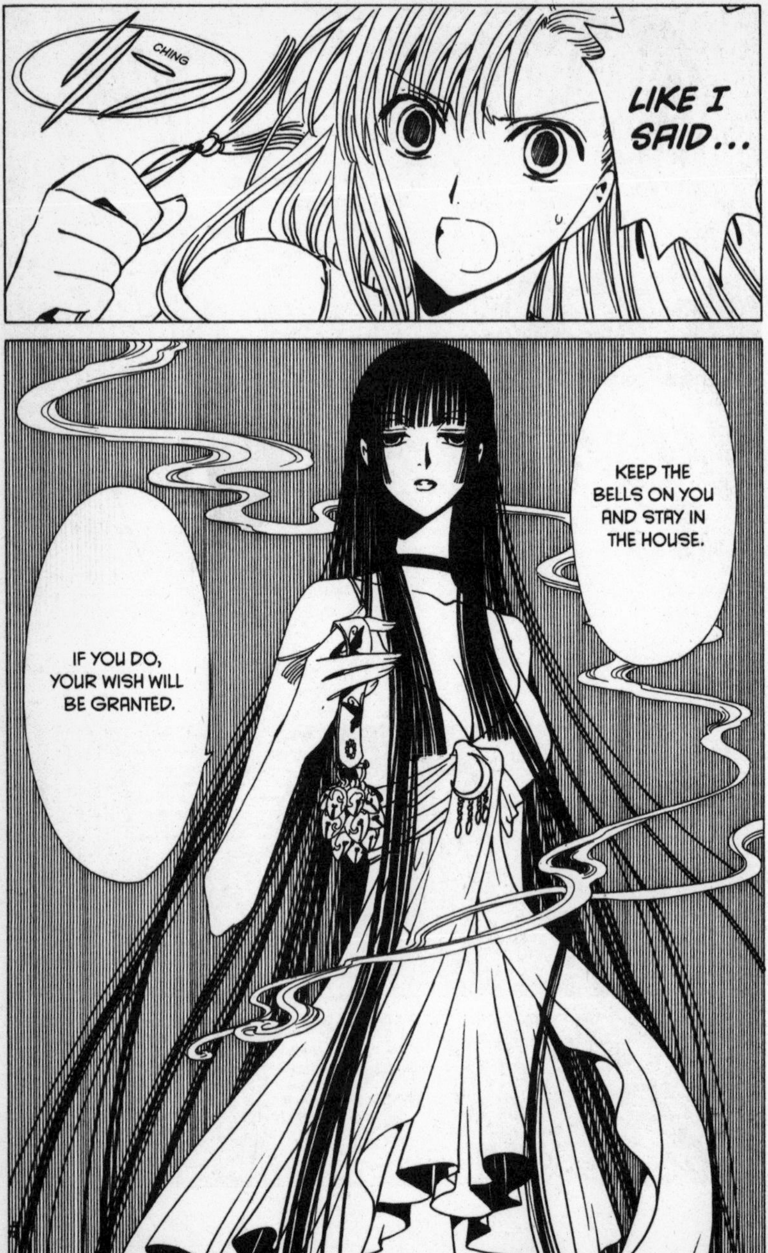
LIKE I SAID...
CHING
KEEP THE BELLS ON YOU AND STAY IN THE HOUSE.
IF YOU DO, YOUR WISH WILL BE GRANTED.

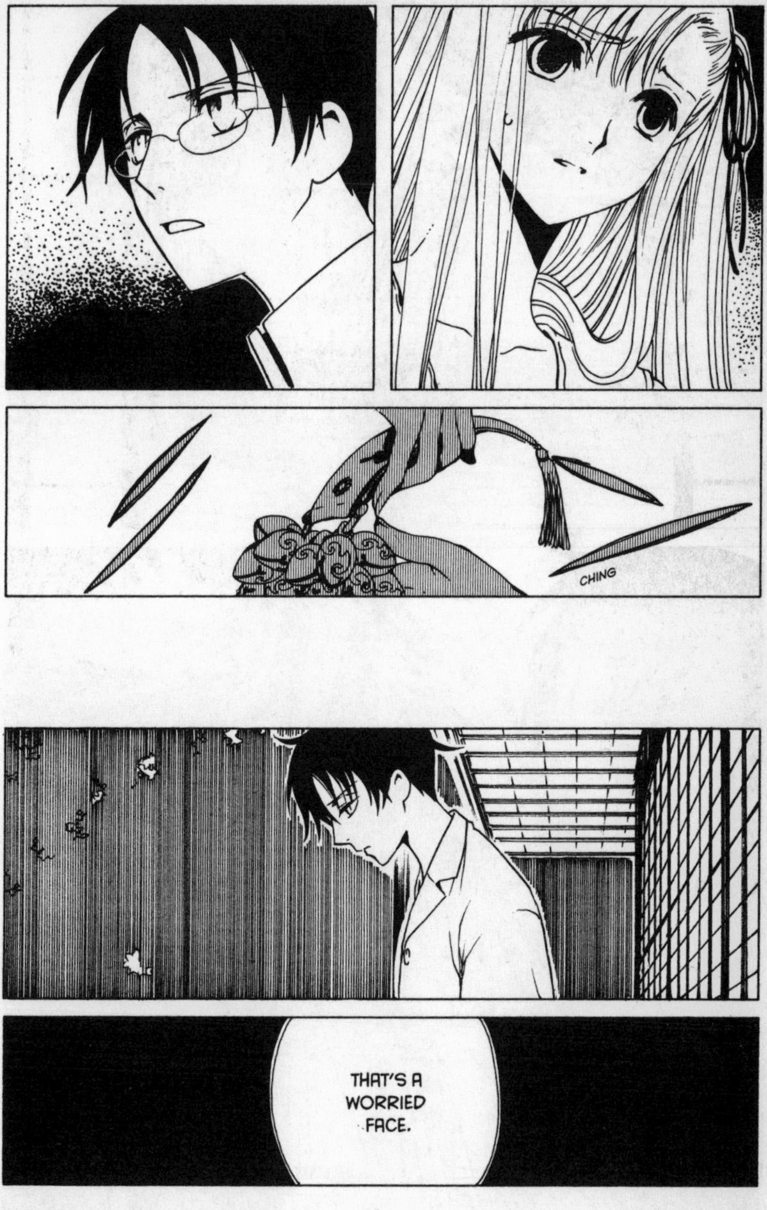
CHING
THAT'S A WORRIED FACE.

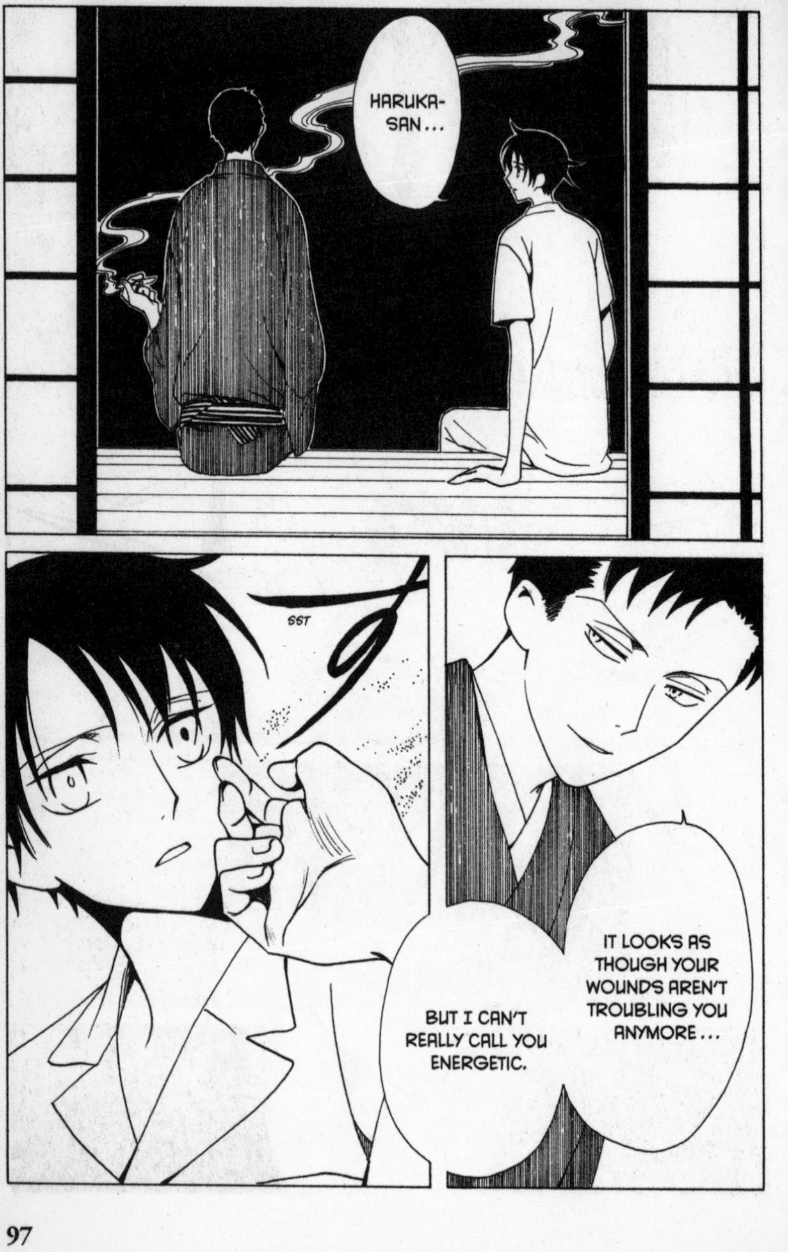
HARUKA-SAN...
IT LOOKS AS THOUGH YOUR WOUNDS AREN'T TROUBLING YOU ANYMORE...
BUT I CAN'T REALLY CALL YOU ENERGETIC.
SST

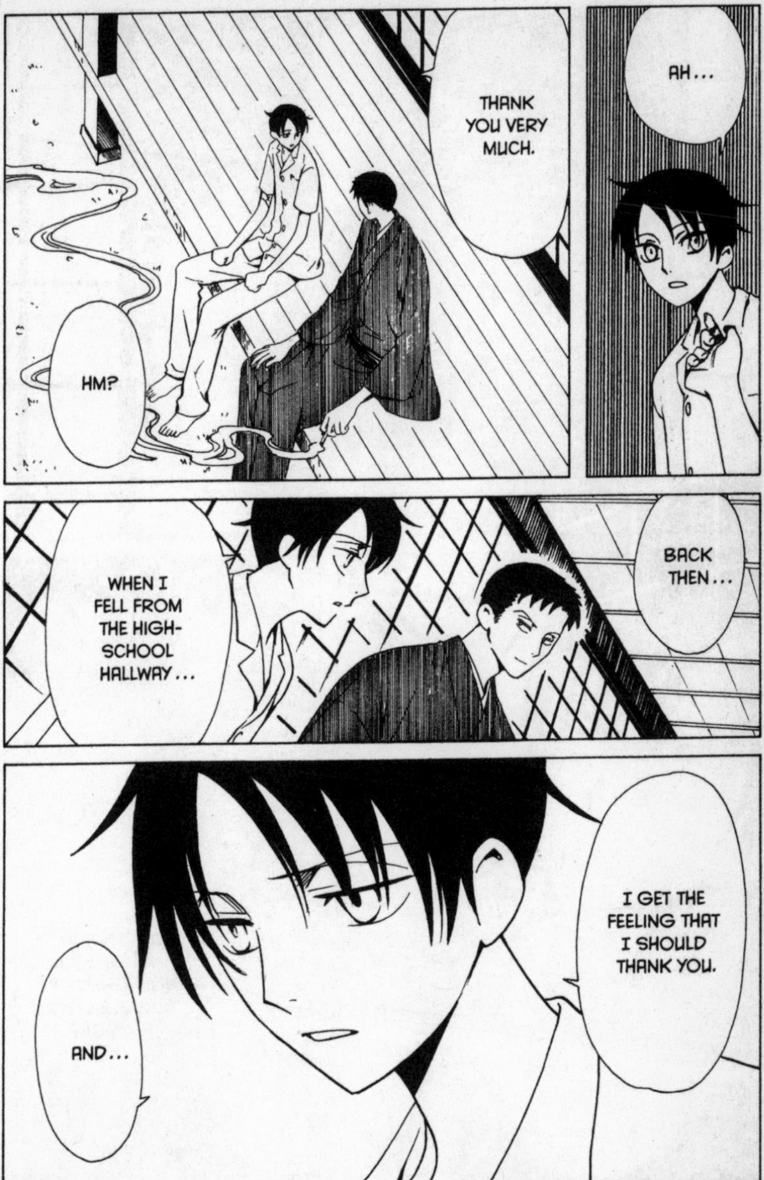
AH...
THANK YOU VERY MUCH.
HM?
BACK THEN...
WHEN I FELL FROM THE HIGH-SCHOOL HALLWAY...
I GET THE FEELING THAT I SHOULD THANK YOU.
AND...

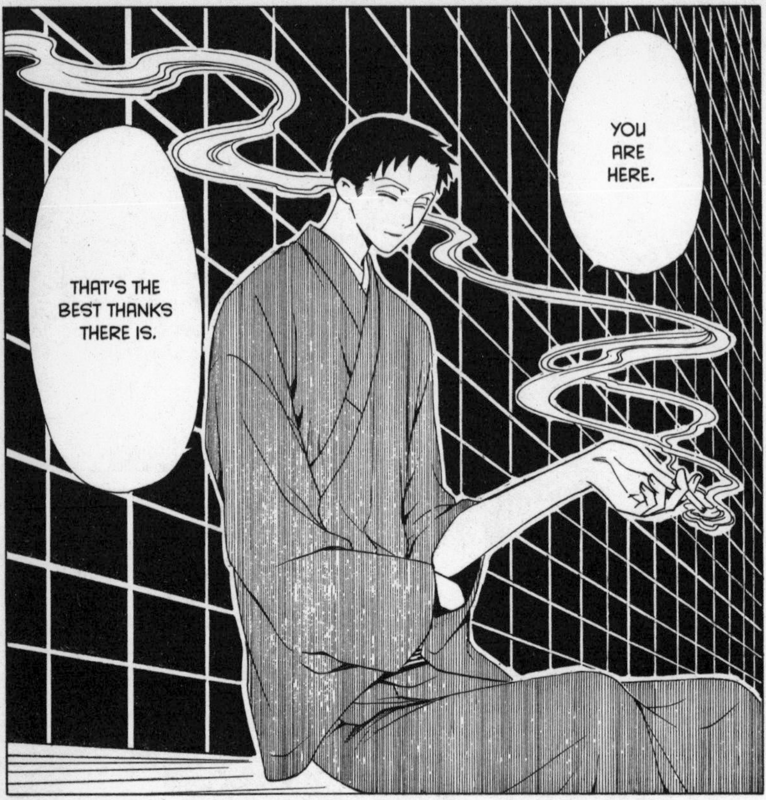
YOU ARE HERE.
THAT'S THE BEST THANKS THERE IS.

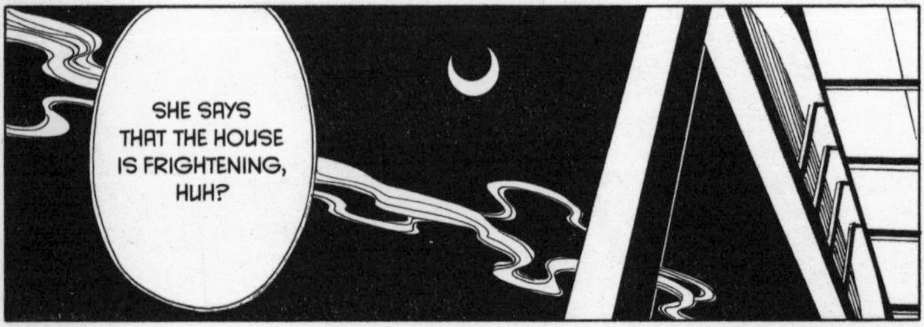
SHE SAYS THAT THE HOUSE IS FRIGHTENING, HUH?

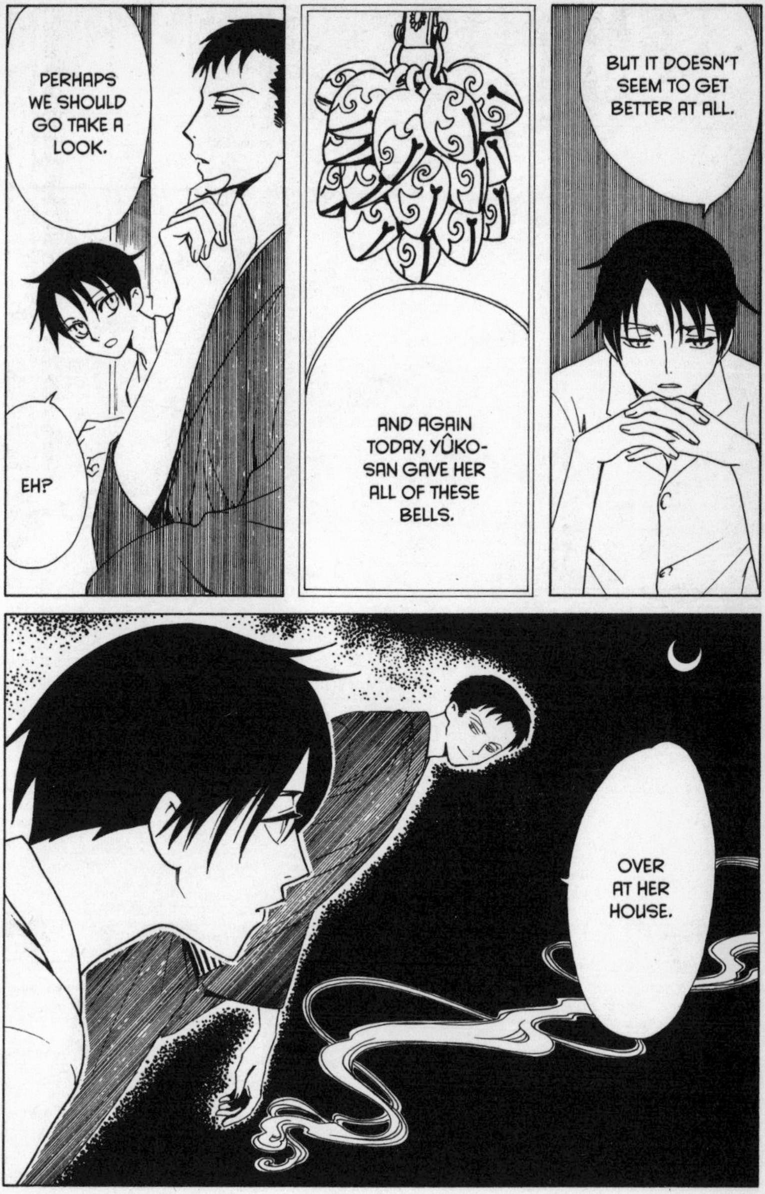
BUT IT DOESN'T SEEM TO GET BETTER AT ALL.
AND AGAIN TODAY, YÛKO-SAN GAVE HER ALL OF THESE BELLS.
PERHAPS WE SHOULD GO TAKE A LOOK.
EH?
OVER AT HER HOUSE.

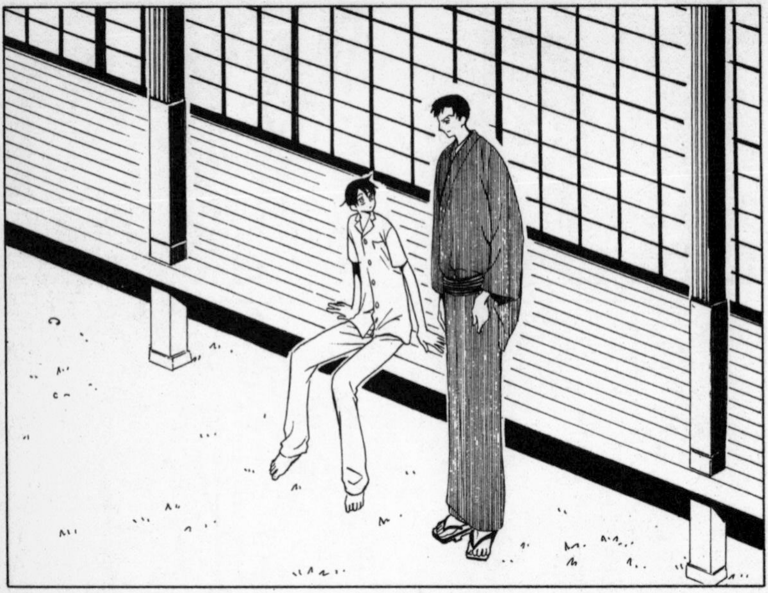
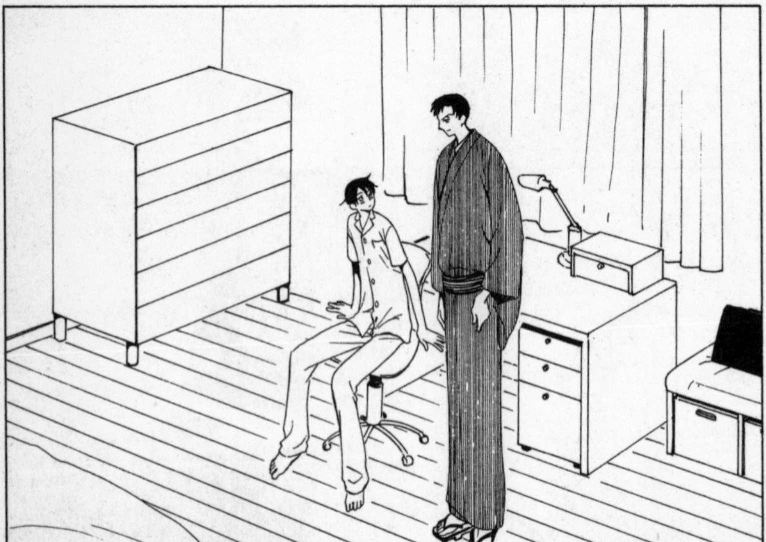

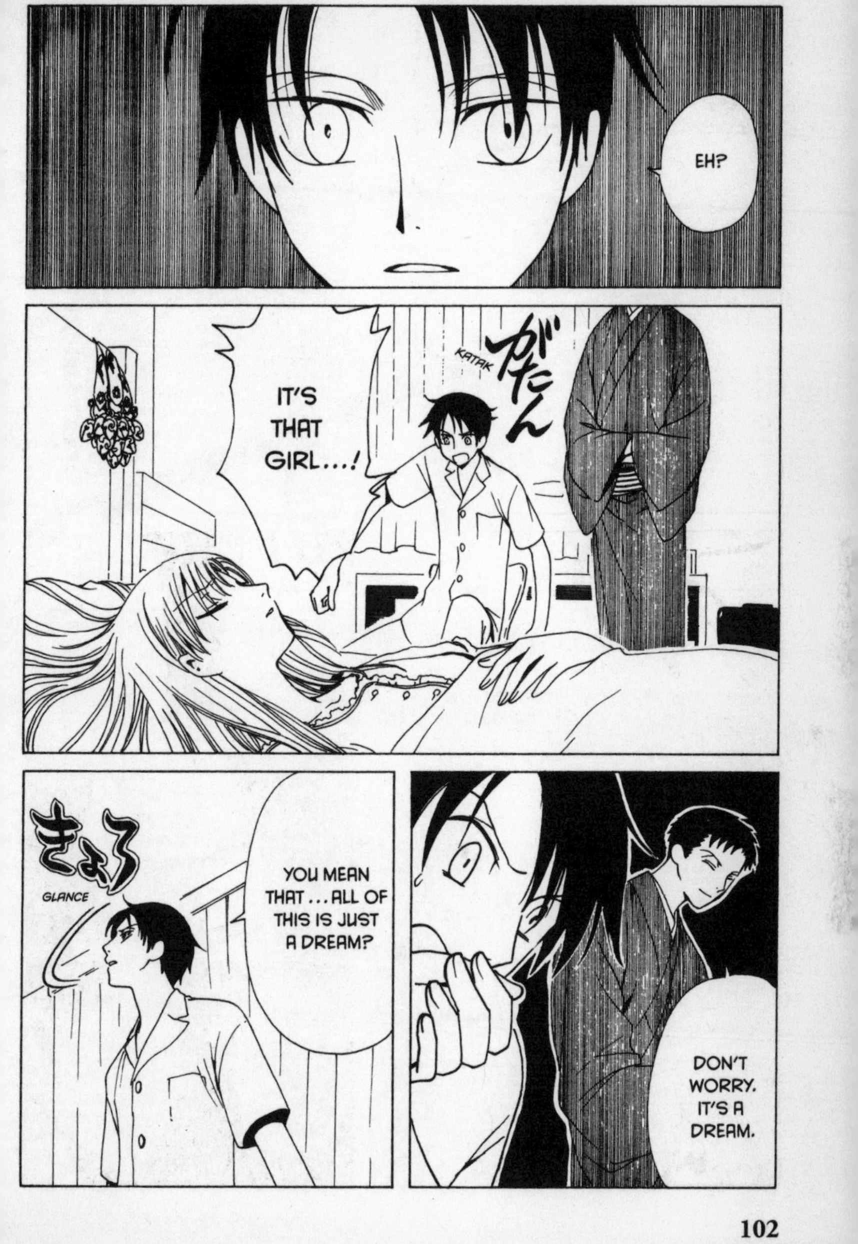
EH?
KATAK
がたん
IT'S THAT GIRL...!
DON'T WORRY. IT'S A DREAM.
きょろ
GLANCE
YOU MEAN THAT...ALL OF THIS IS JUST A DREAM?

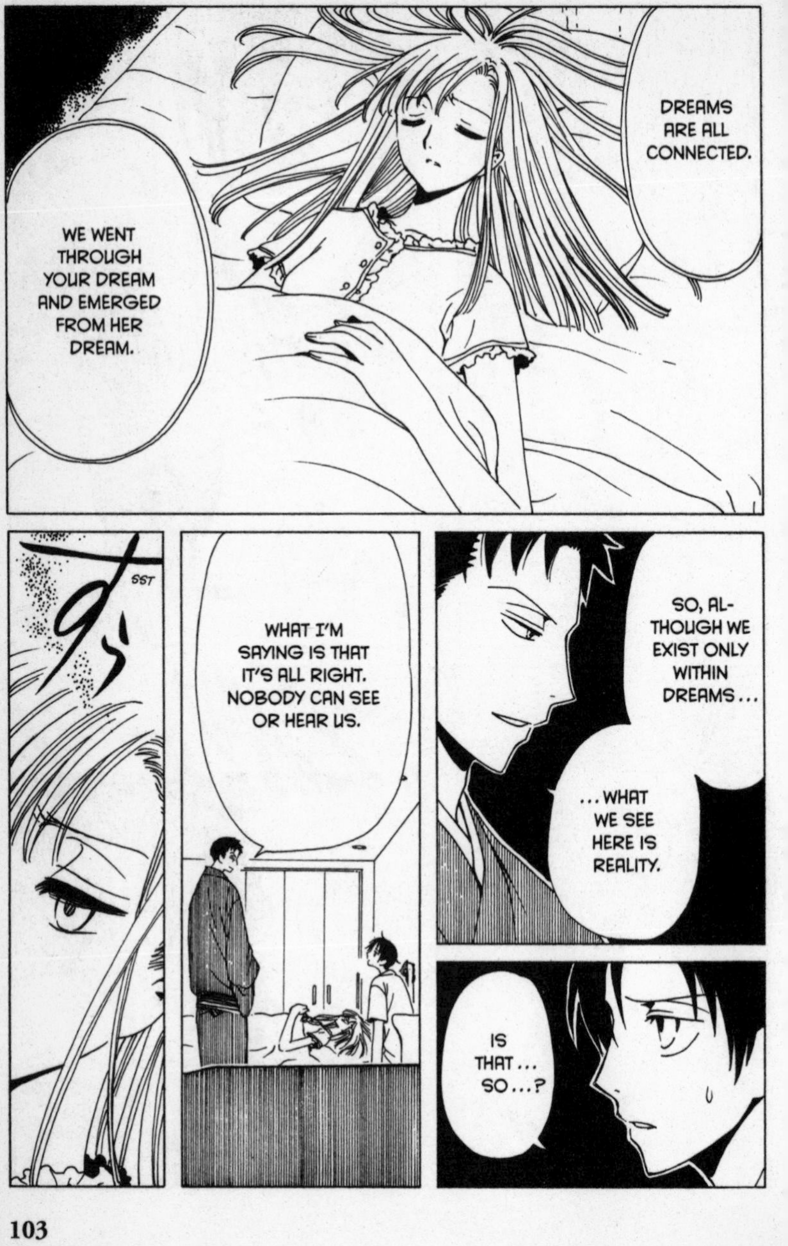
DREAMS ARE ALL CONNECTED.
WE WENT THROUGH YOUR DREAM AND EMERGED FROM HER DREAM.
SO, AL- THOUGH WE EXIST ONLY WITHIN DREAMS...
...WHAT WE SEE HERE IS REALITY.
IS THAT... SO...?
WHAT I'M SAYING IS THAT IT'S ALL RIGHT. NOBODY CAN SEE OR HEAR US.
SST

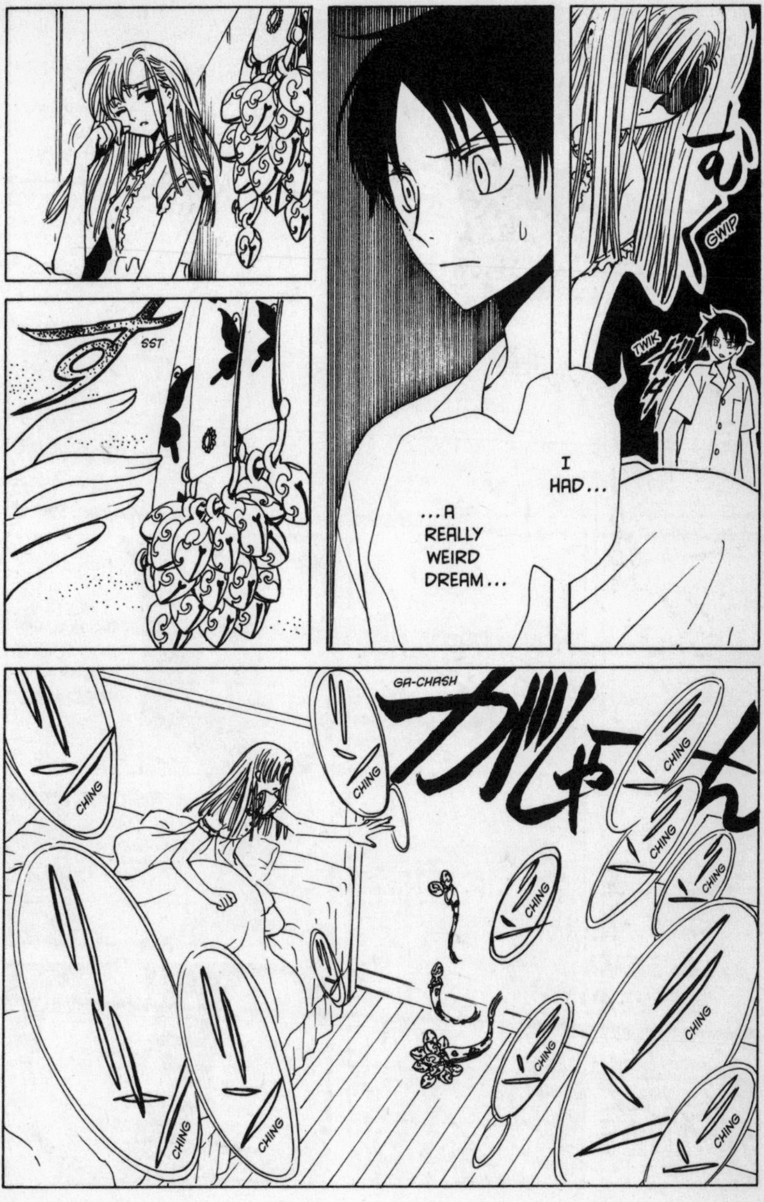
GWIP
TWIK
I HAD...
...A REALLY WEIRD DREAM...
SST
GA-CHASH
CHING
CHING
CHING
CHING
CHING
CHING
CHING
CHING
CHING
CHING
CHING

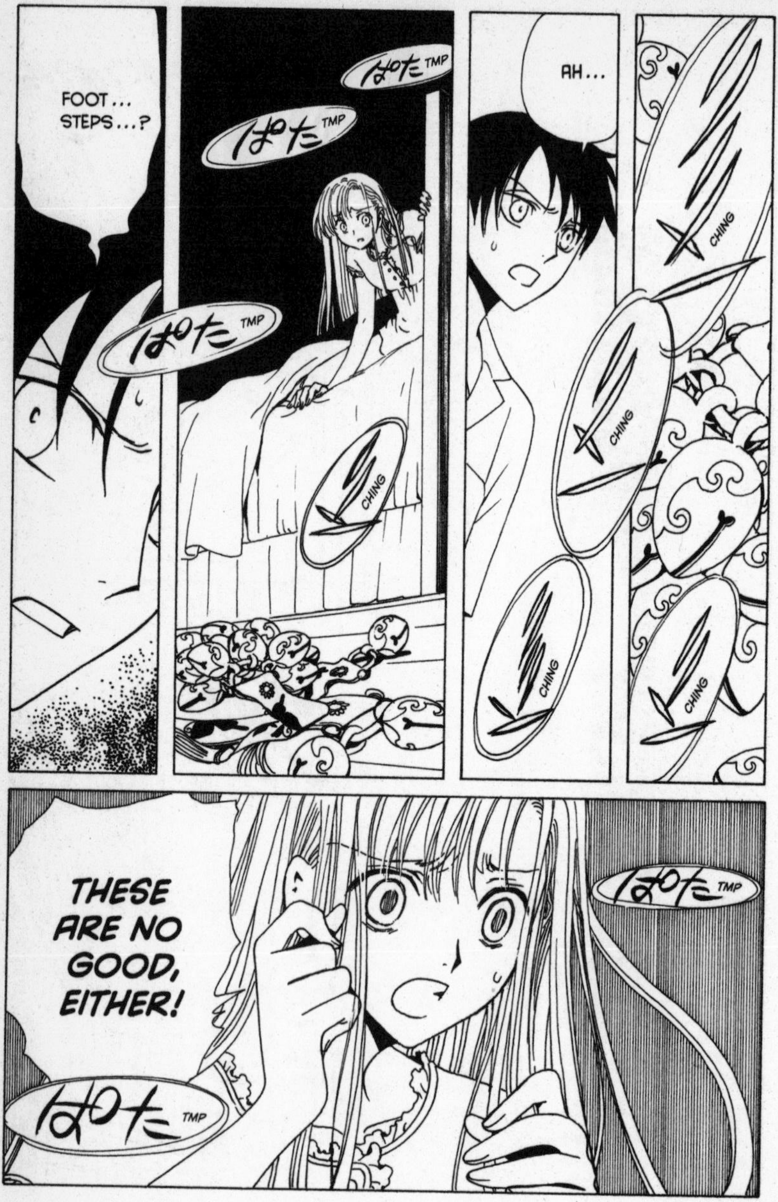
CHING
CHING
AH...
CHING
CHING
ぱた TMP
ぱた TMP
ぱた TMP
CHING
FOOT... STEPS...?
ぱた TMP
THESE ARE NO GOOD, EITHER!
ぱた TMP

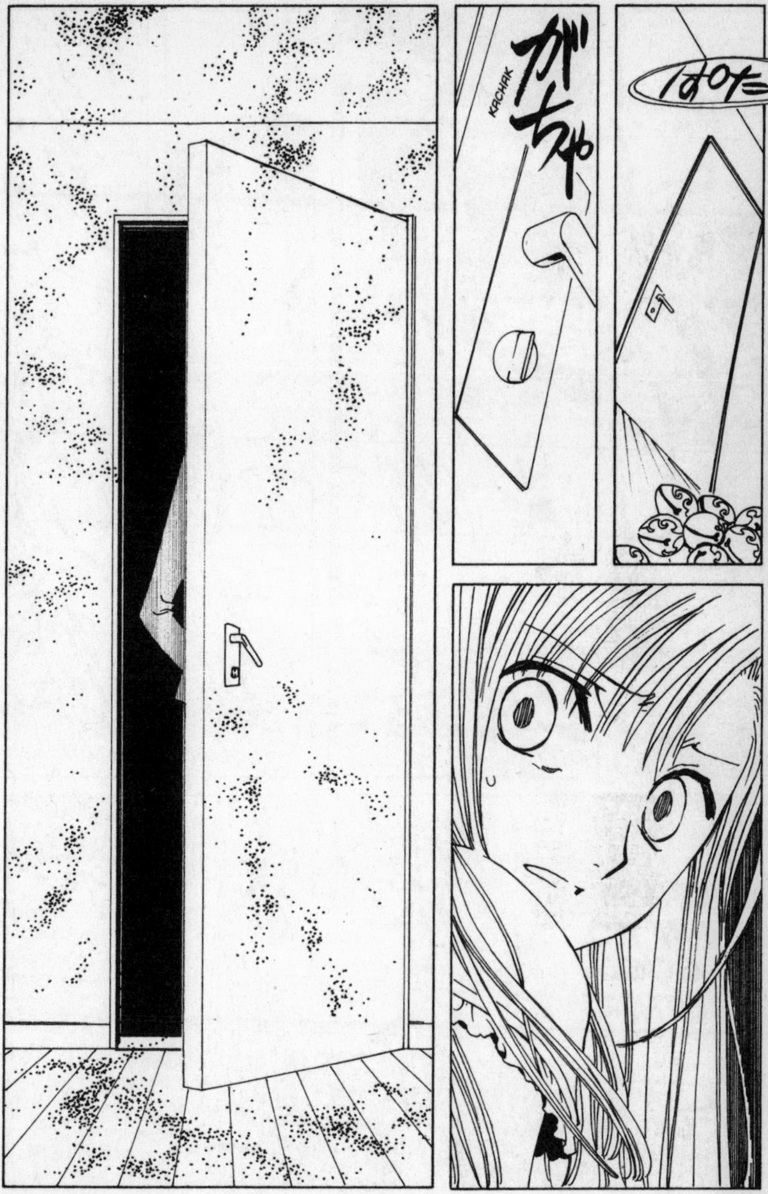
TMP
がちゃ
KACHAK

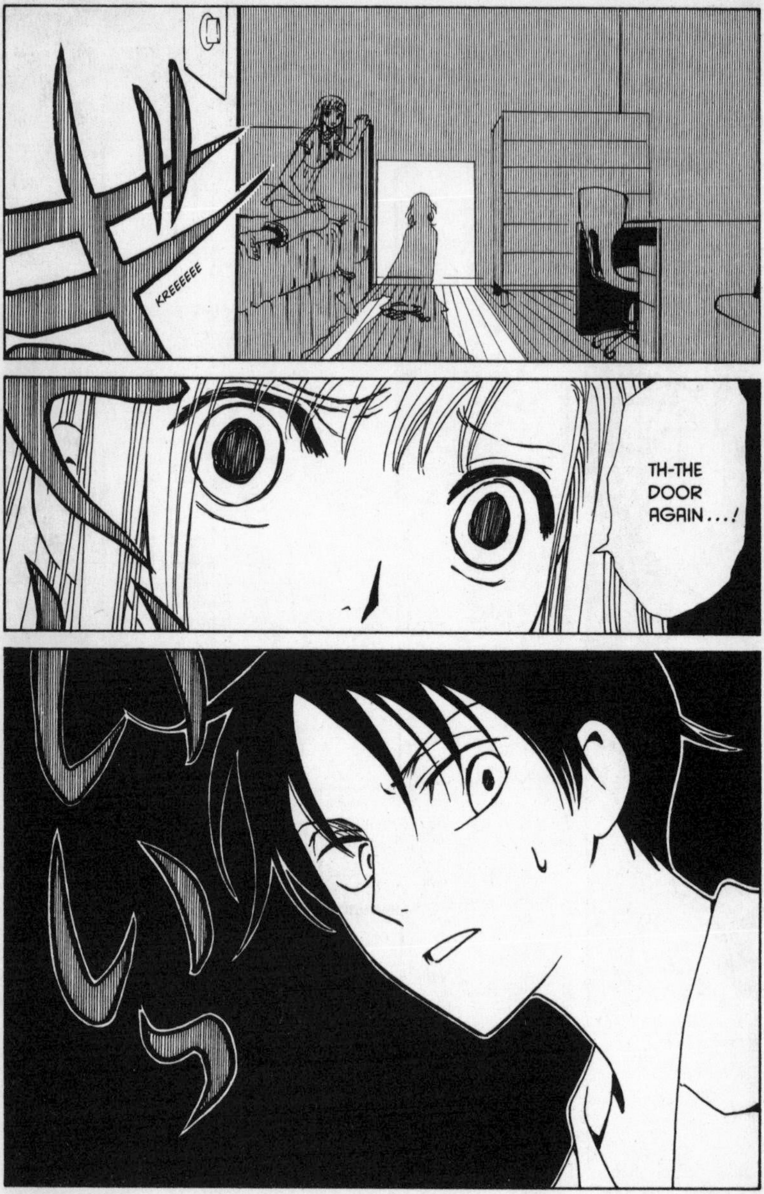
KREEEEEE
TH-THE DOOR AGAIN...!

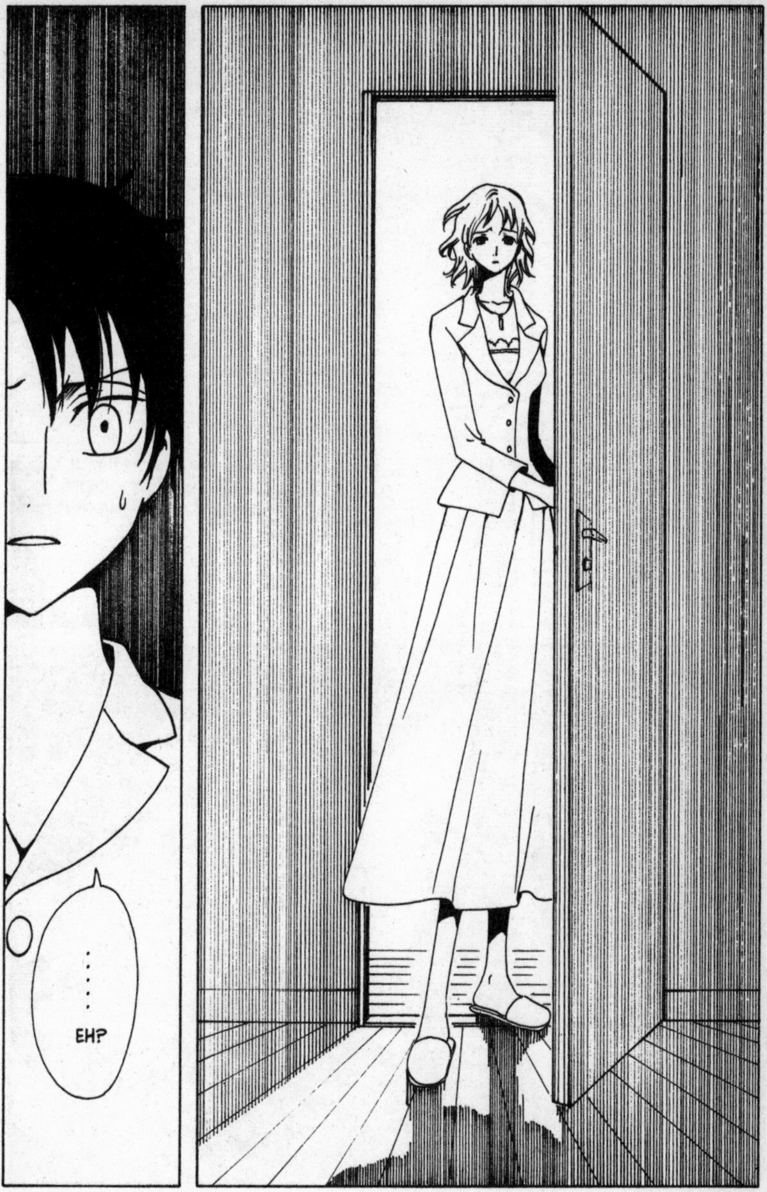

......
EH?

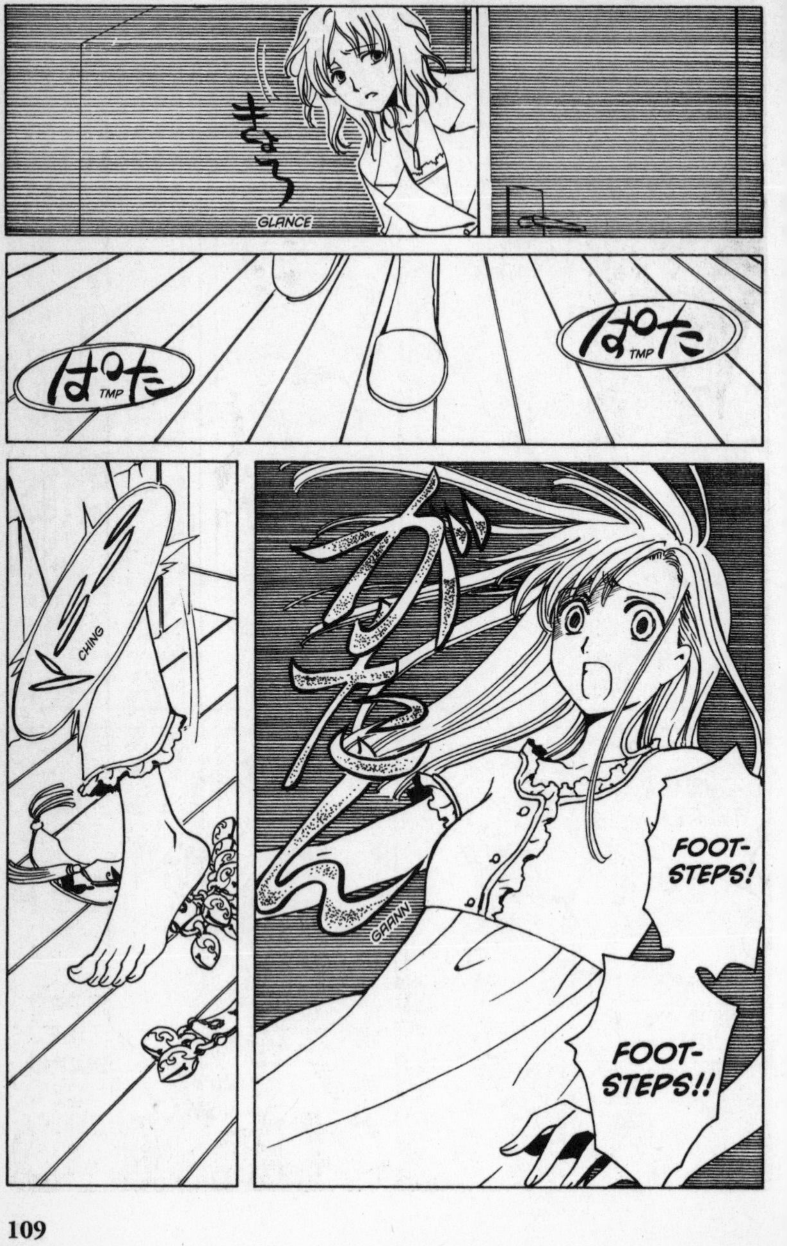
きょろ
GLANCE
ぱた
TMP
ぱた
TMP
GAANN
FOOT-STEPS!
FOOT-STEPS!!
CHING

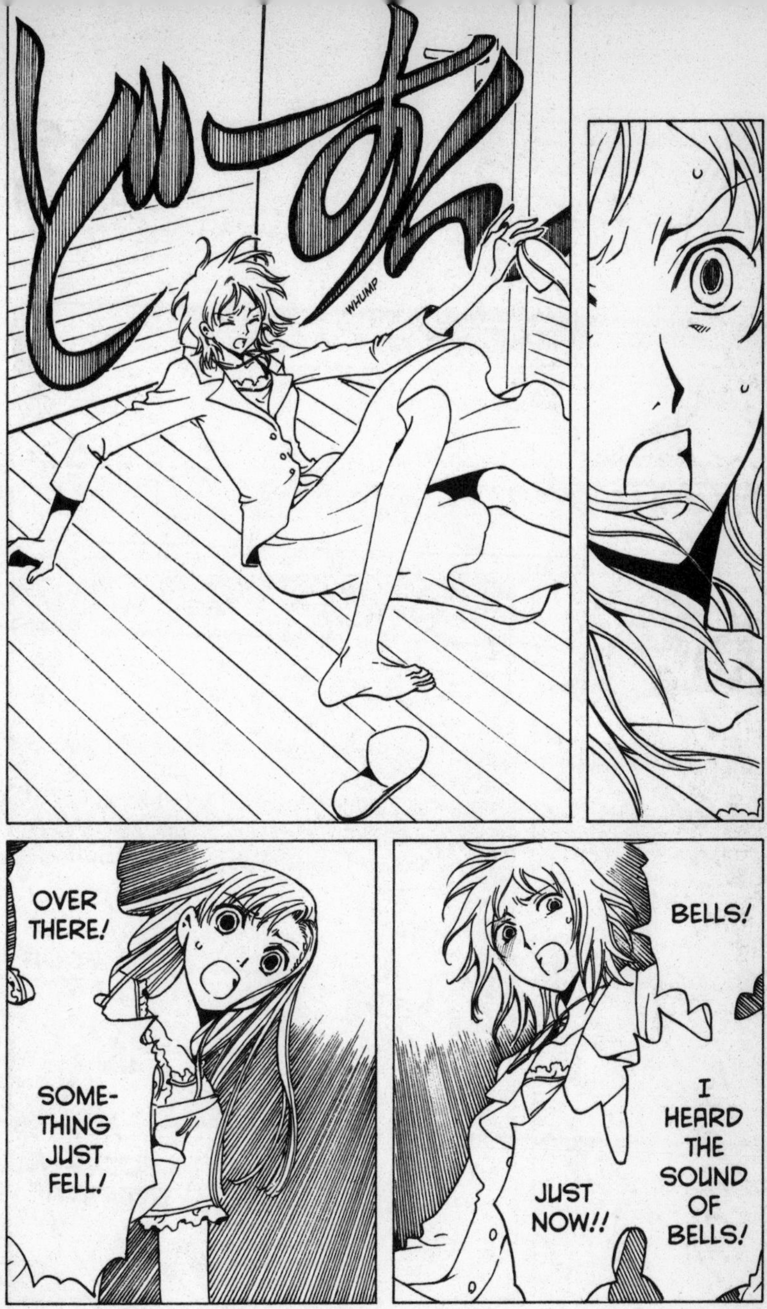

WHUMP
BELLS!
I HEARD THE SOUND OF BELLS!
JUST NOW!!
OVER THERE!
SOME-THING JUST FELL!

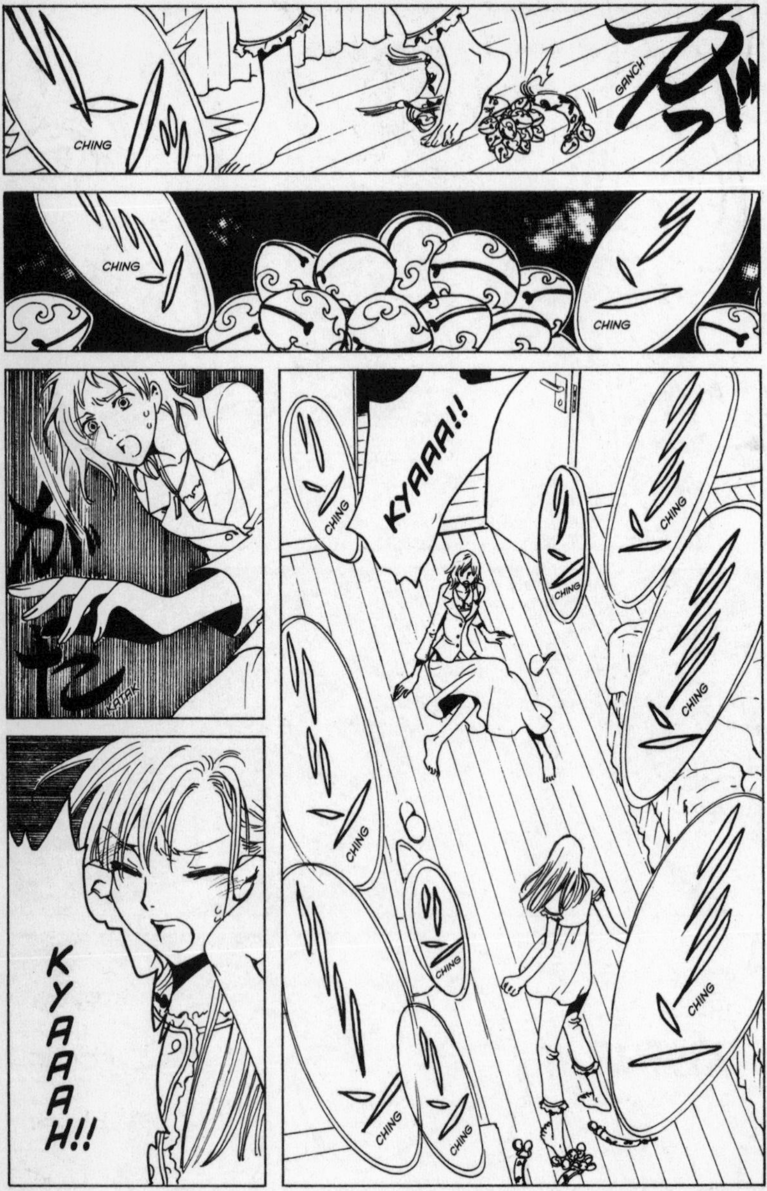

GANCH
CHING
CHING
CHING
CHING
CHING
KYAAA!!
CHING
CHING
CHING
CHING
CHING
CHING
CHING
CHING
KATAK
KYAAAAH!!

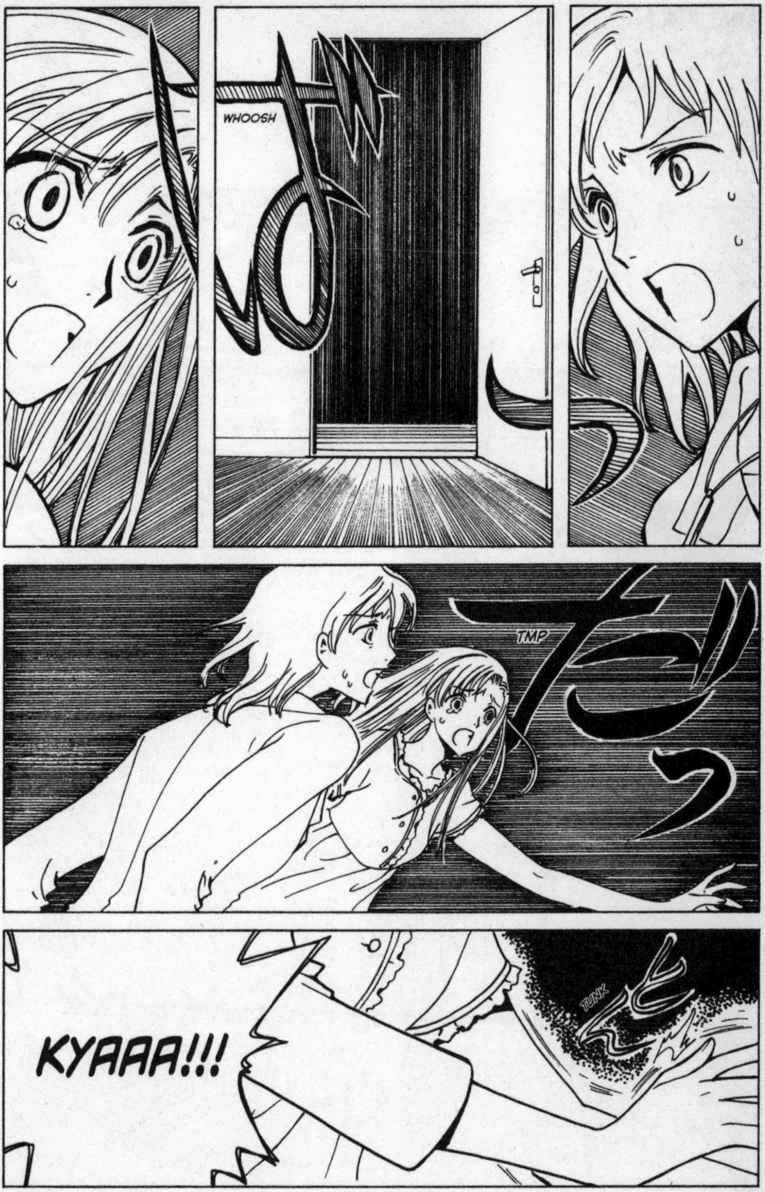
WHOOSH
TMP
TUNK
KYAAA!!!

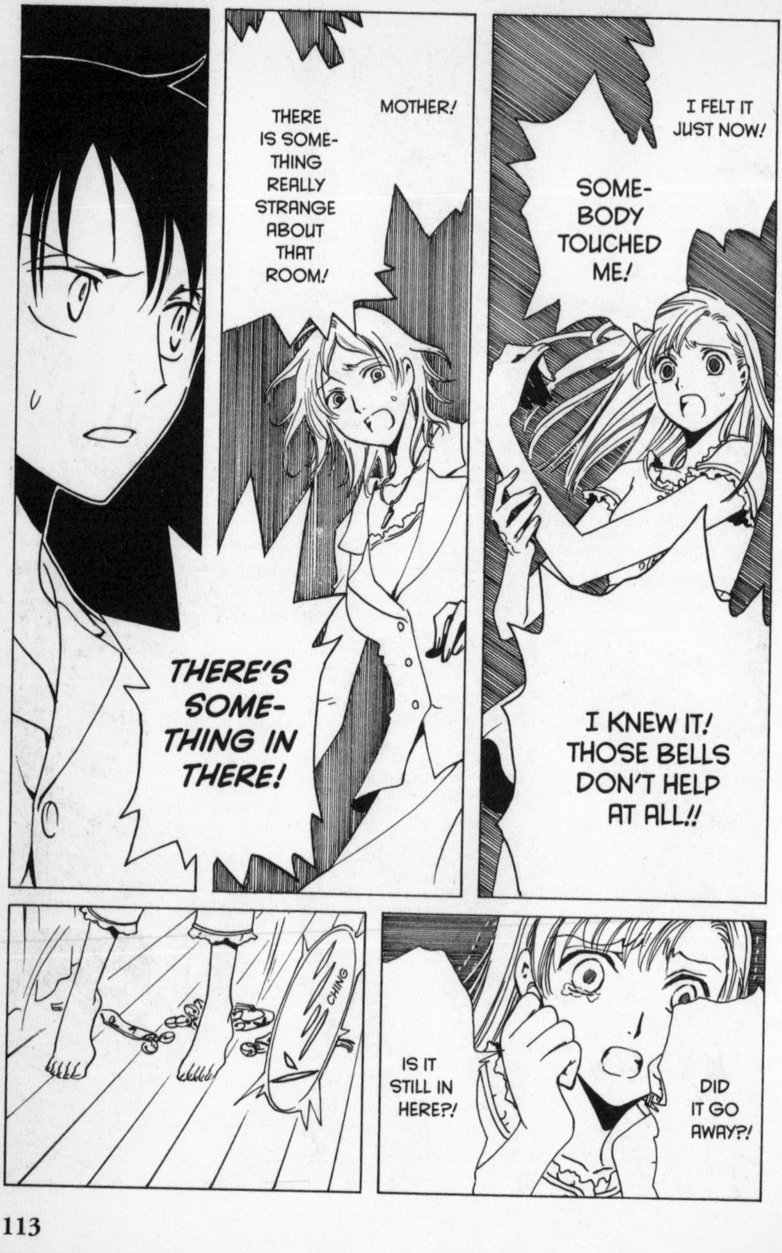
I FELT IT JUST NOW!
SOMEBODY TOUCHED ME!
I KNEW IT! THOSE BELLS DON'T HELP AT ALL!!
MOTHER!
THERE IS SOMETHING REALLY STRANGE ABOUT THAT ROOM!
THERE'S SOMETHING IN THERE!
DID IT GO AWAY?!
IS IT STILL IN HERE?!
CHING

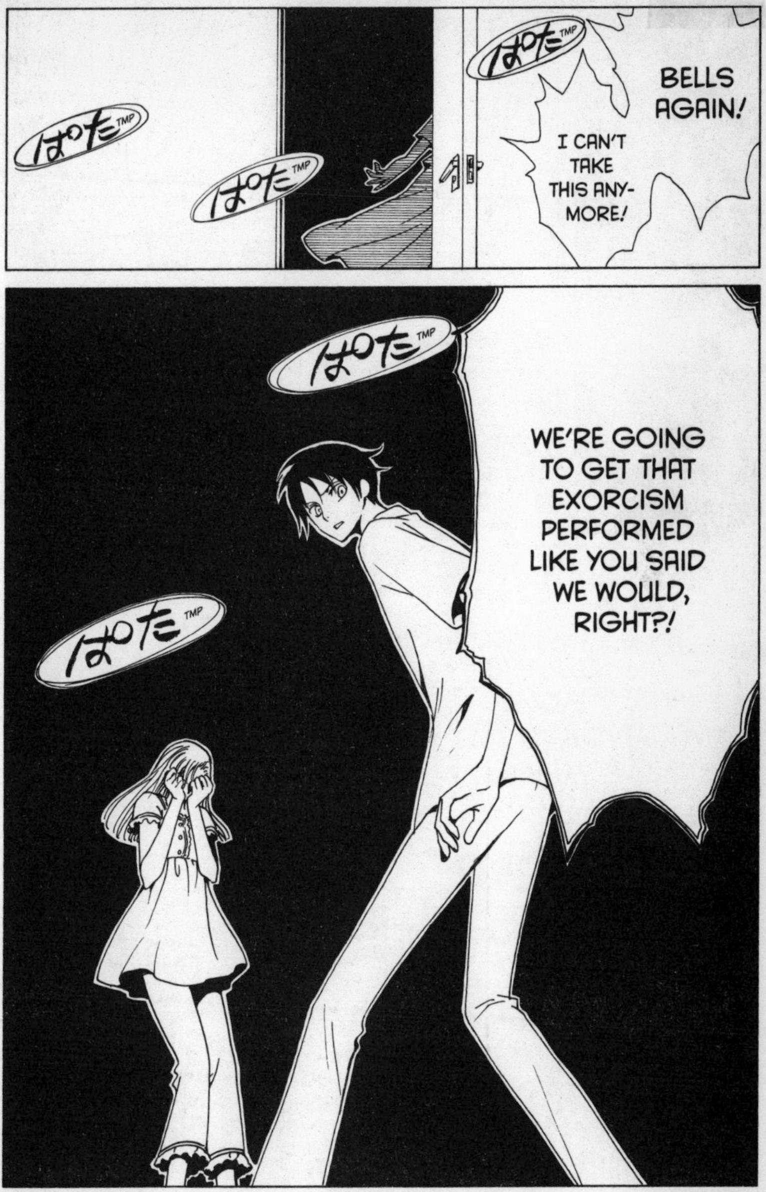
ぱた TMP
BELLS AGAIN!
I CAN'T TAKE THIS ANY-MORE!
ぱた TMP
ぱた TMP
ぱた TMP
WE'RE GOING TO GET THAT EXORCISM PERFORMED LIKE YOU SAID WE WOULD, RIGHT?!
ぱた TMP

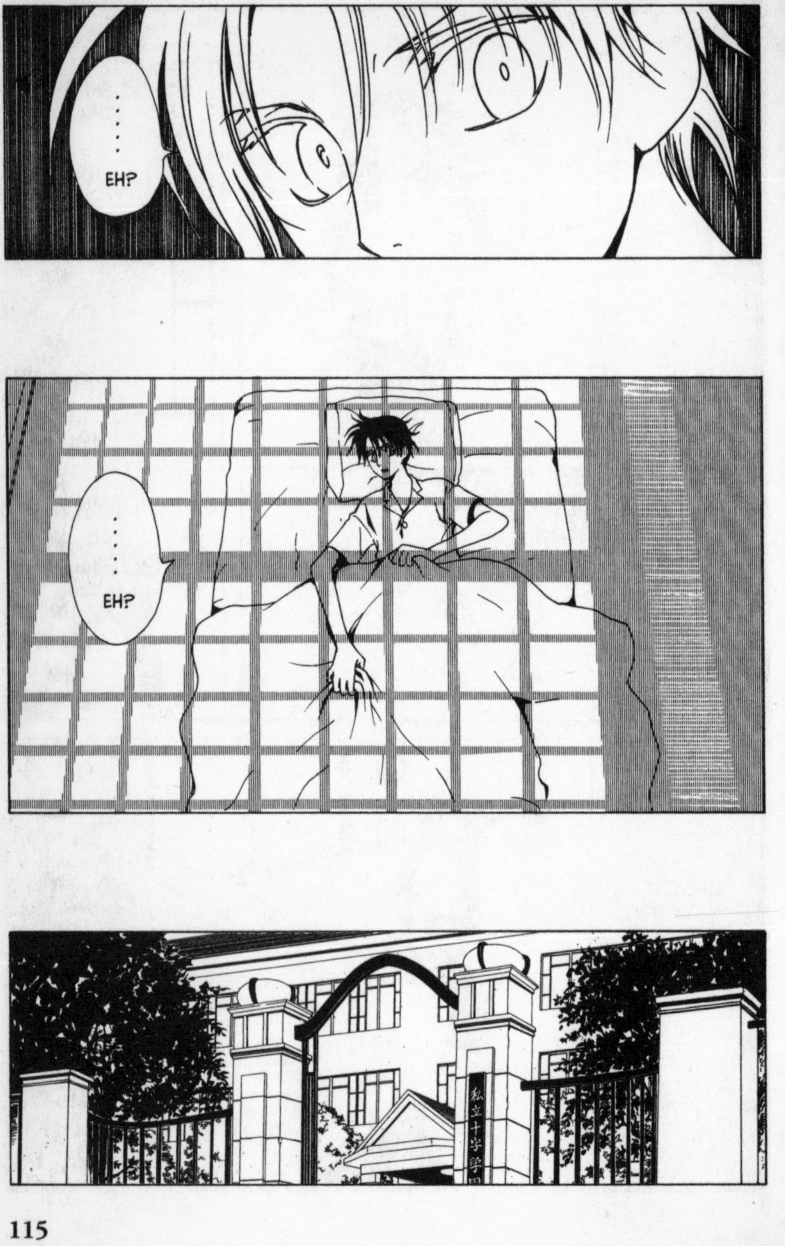

......EH?
......EH?
私立十字学

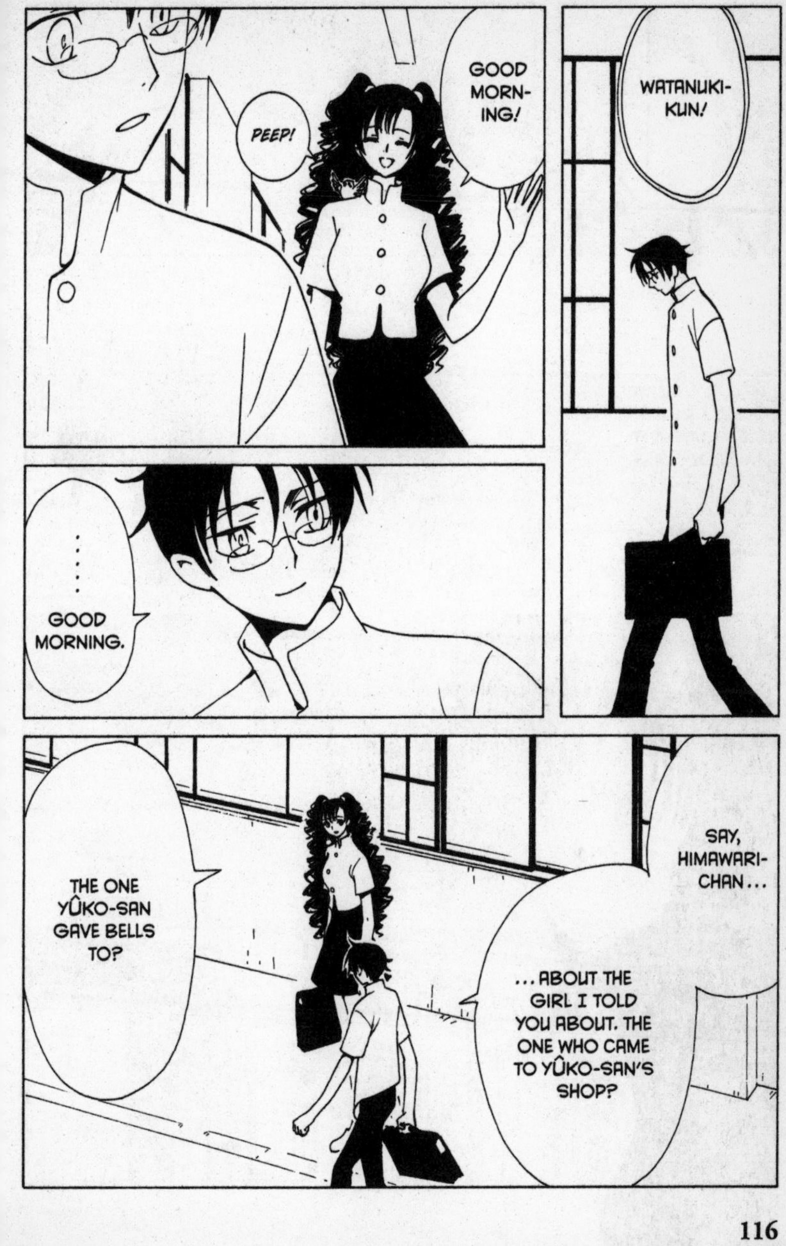
WATANUKI-KUN!
GOOD MORNING!
PEEP!
...... GOOD MORNING.
SAY, HIMAWARI-CHAN...
...ABOUT THE GIRL I TOLD YOU ABOUT. THE ONE WHO CAME TO YÛKO-SAN'S SHOP?
THE ONE YÛKO-SAN GAVE BELLS TO?

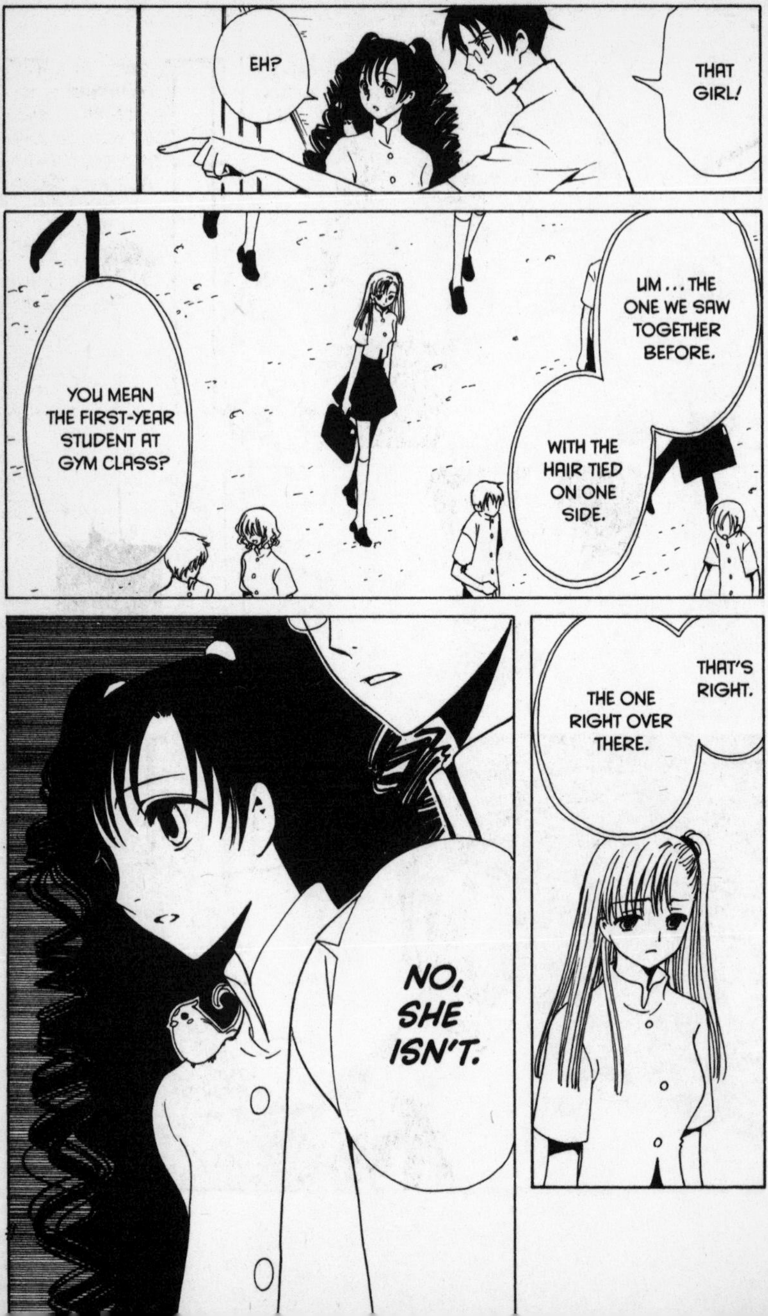
THAT GIRL!
EH?
UM... THE ONE WE SAW TOGETHER BEFORE.
WITH THE HAIR TIED ON ONE SIDE.
YOU MEAN THE FIRST-YEAR STUDENT AT GYM CLASS?
THAT'S RIGHT.
THE ONE RIGHT OVER THERE.
NO, SHE ISN'T.

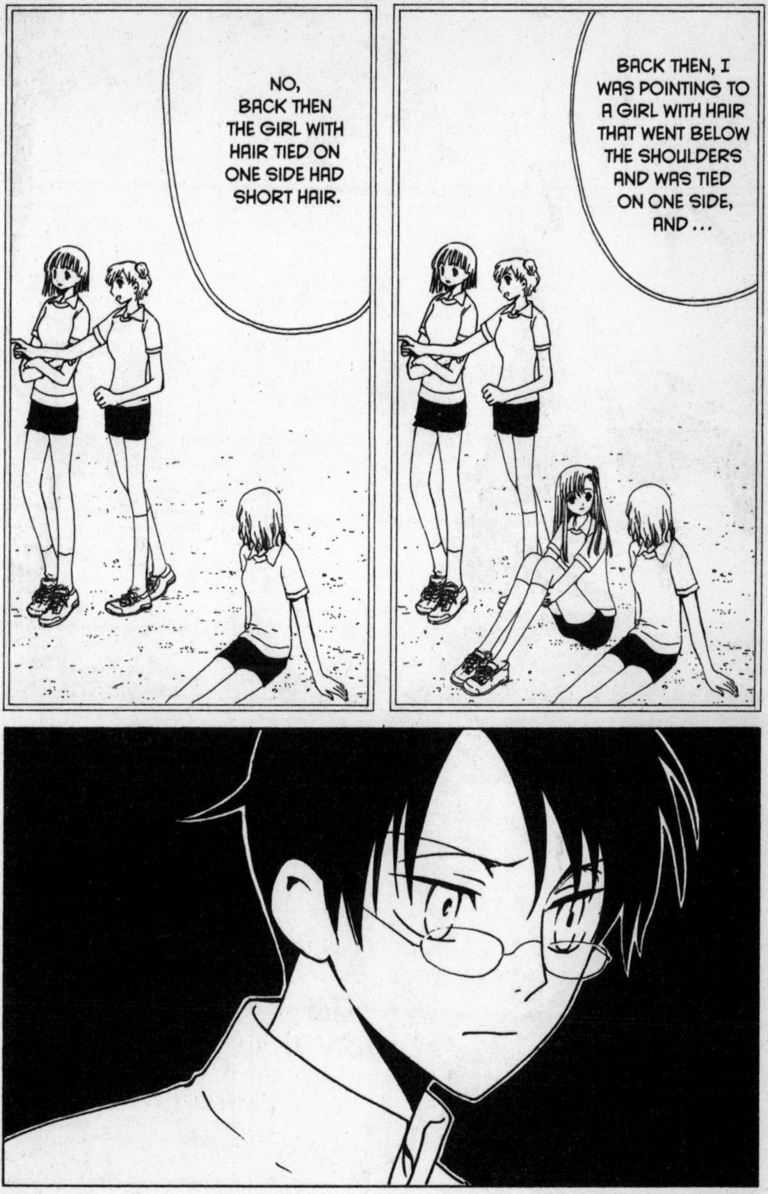
BACK THEN, I WAS POINTING TO A GIRL WITH HAIR THAT WENT BELOW THE SHOULDERS AND WAS TIED ON ONE SIDE, AND ...
NO, BACK THEN THE GIRL WITH HAIR TIED ON ONE SIDE HAD SHORT HAIR.

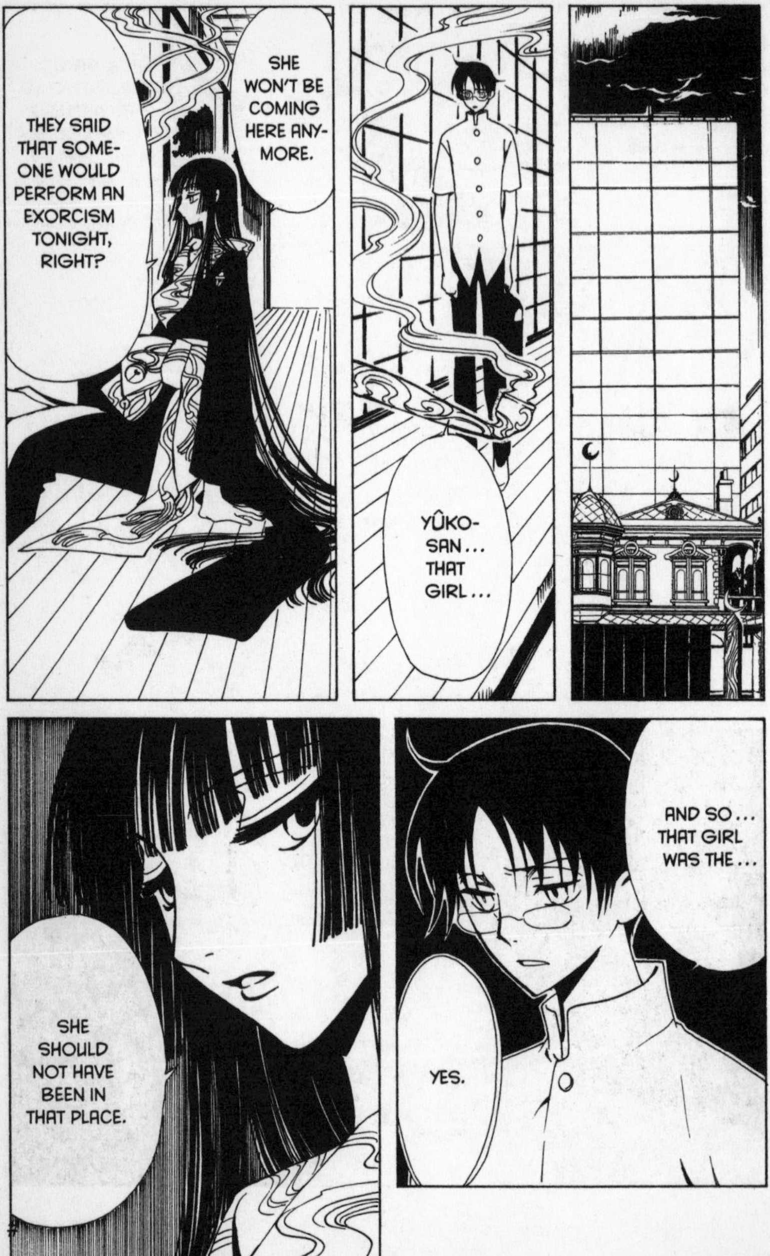
YÛKO-SAN... THAT GIRL...
SHE WON'T BE COMING HERE ANYMORE.
THEY SAID THAT SOMEONE WOULD PERFORM AN EXORCISM TONIGHT, RIGHT?
AND SO... THAT GIRL WAS THE...
YES.
SHE SHOULD NOT HAVE BEEN IN THAT PLACE.

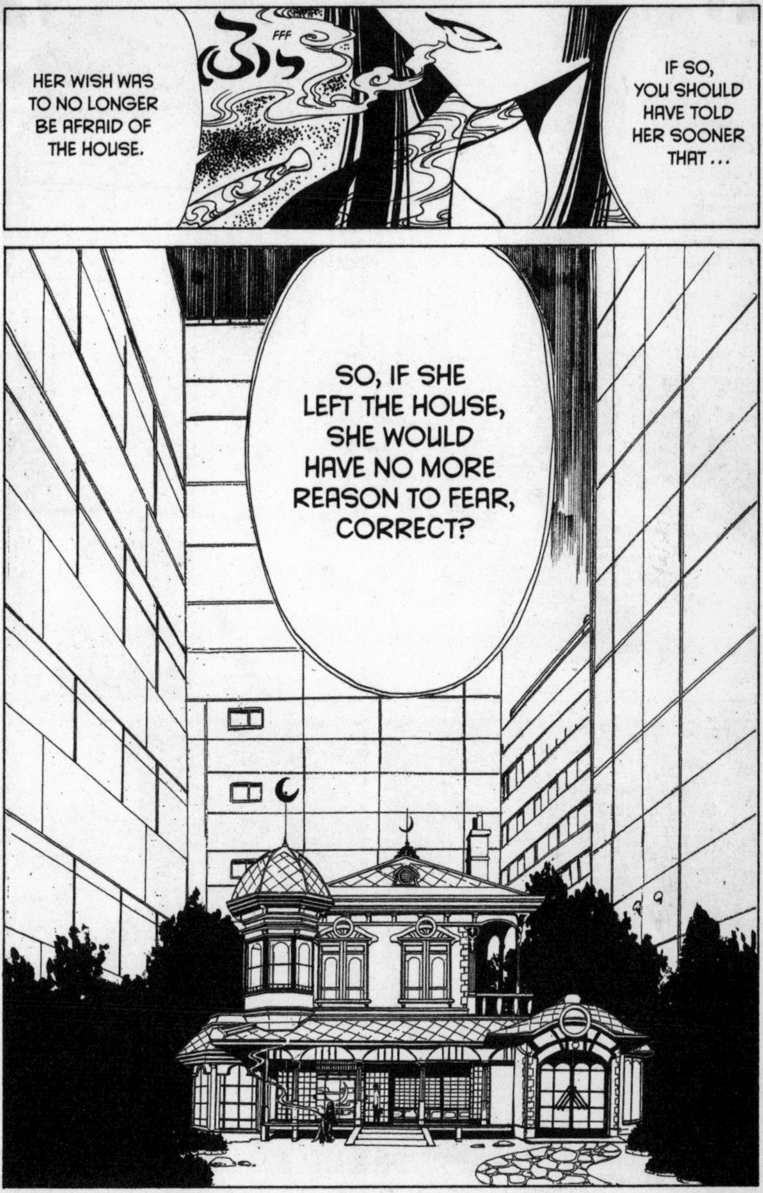
HER WISH WAS TO NO LONGER BE AFRAID OF THE HOUSE.
FFF
IF SO, YOU SHOULD HAVE TOLD HER SOONER THAT ...
SO, IF SHE LEFT THE HOUSE, SHE WOULD HAVE NO MORE REASON TO FEAR, CORRECT?

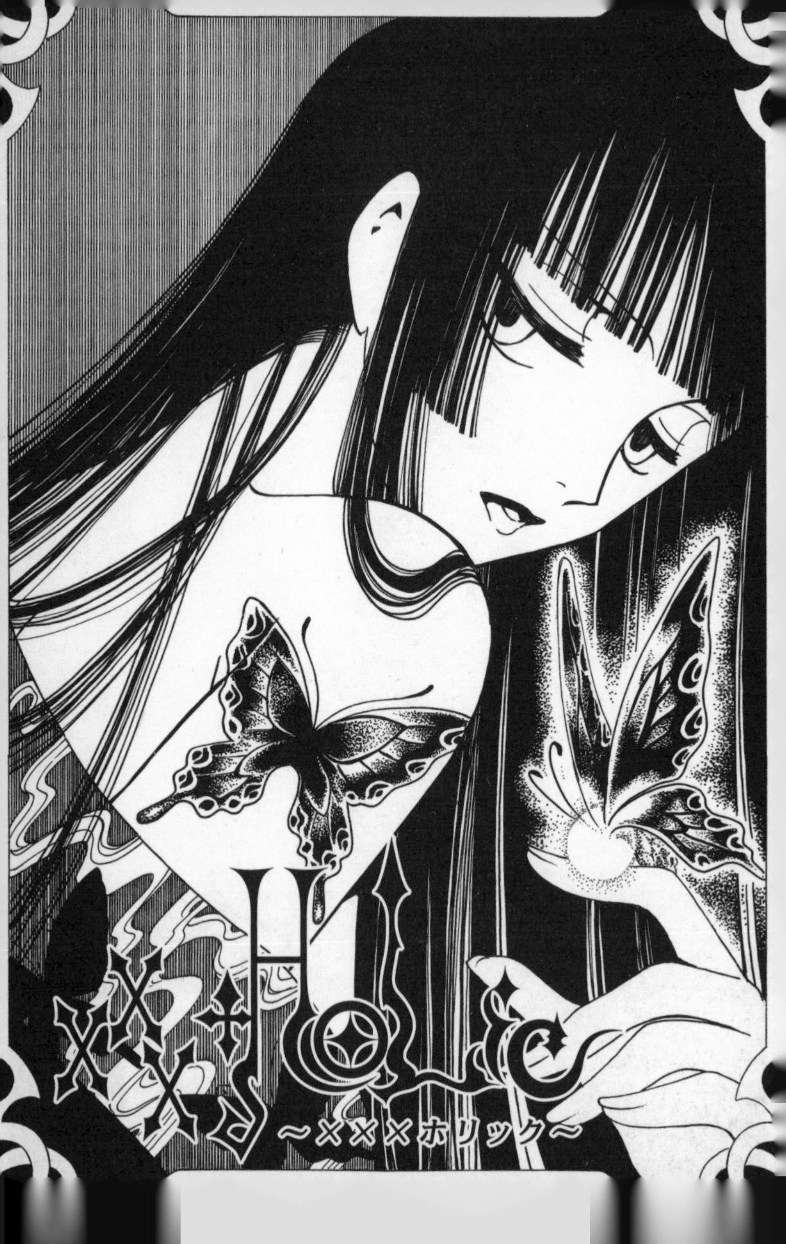
xxxHOLiC
〜×××ホリック〜

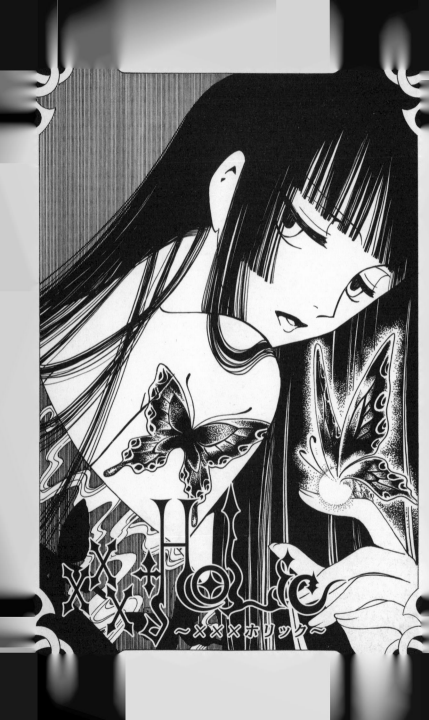

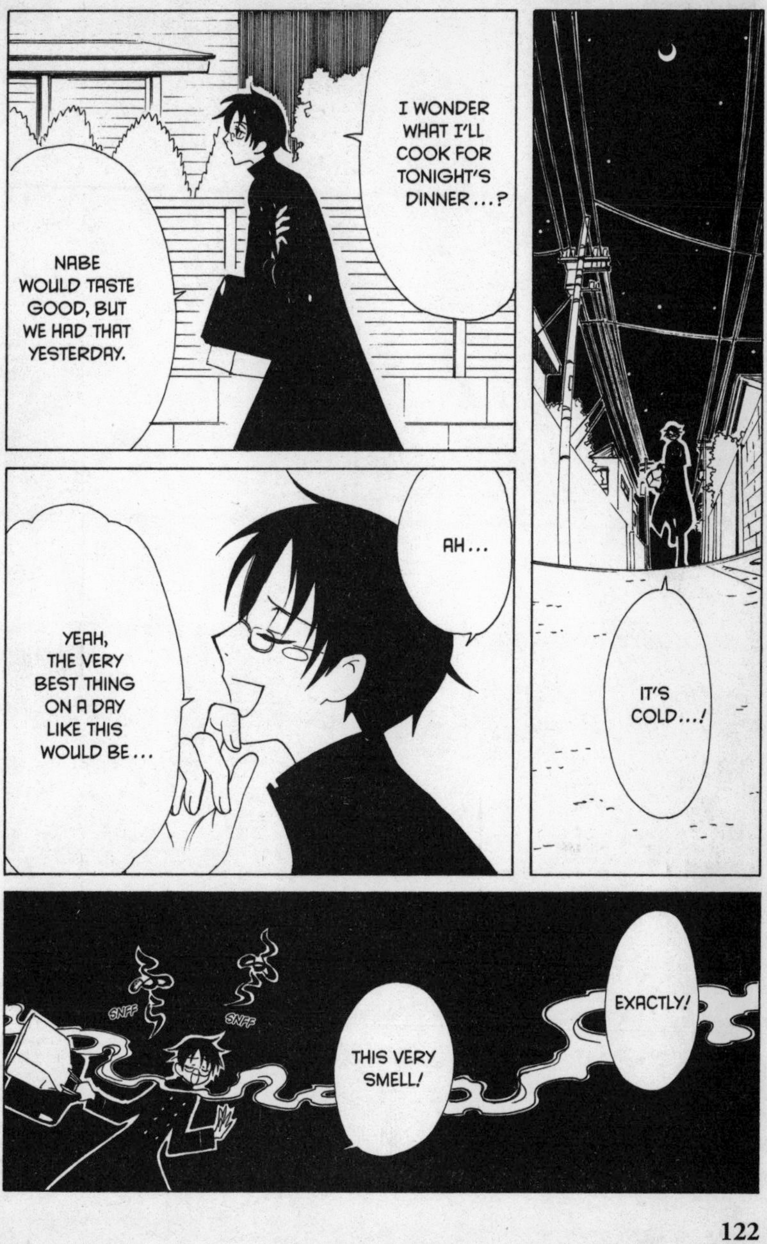
IT'S COLD...!
I WONDER WHAT I'LL COOK FOR TONIGHT'S DINNER...?
NABE WOULD TASTE GOOD, BUT WE HAD THAT YESTERDAY.
AH...
YEAH, THE VERY BEST THING ON A DAY LIKE THIS WOULD BE...
EXACTLY!
THIS VERY SMELL!
SNFF
SNFF

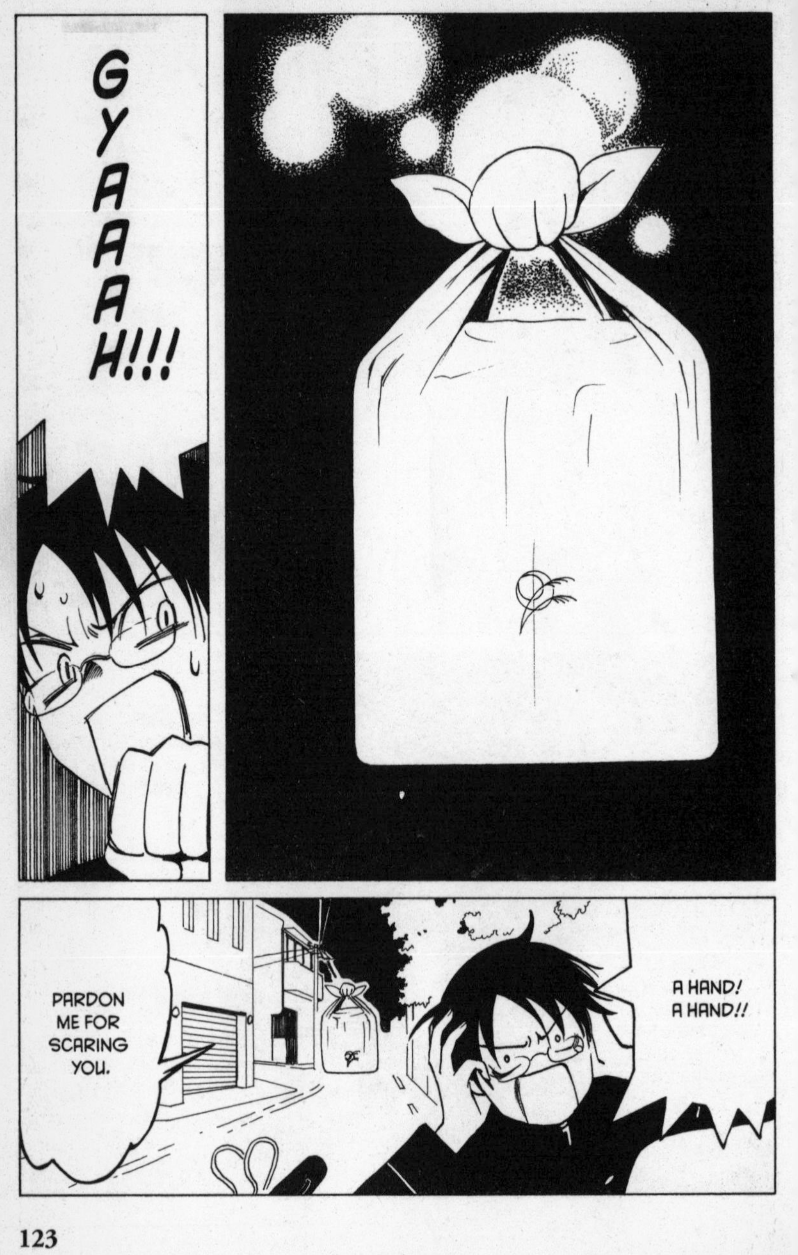
GYAAAAH!!!
A HAND! A HAND!!
PARDON ME FOR SCARING YOU.

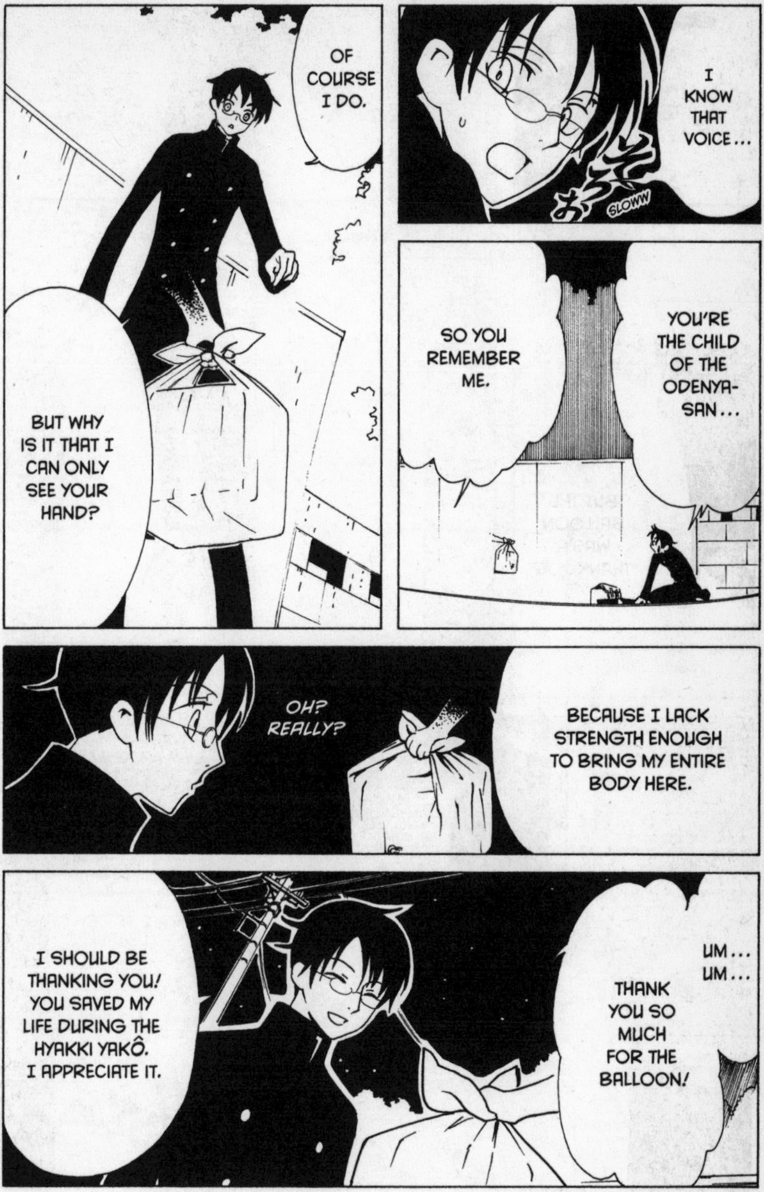
I KNOW THAT VOICE...
SLOWW
YOU'RE THE CHILD OF THE ODENYA-SAN...
SO YOU REMEMBER ME.
OF COURSE I DO.
BUT WHY IS IT THAT I CAN ONLY SEE YOUR HAND?
BECAUSE I LACK STRENGTH ENOUGH TO BRING MY ENTIRE BODY HERE.
OH? REALLY?
UM... UM...
THANK YOU SO MUCH FOR THE BALLOON!
I SHOULD BE THANKING YOU! YOU SAVED MY LIFE DURING THE HYAKKI YAKÔ. I APPRECIATE IT.

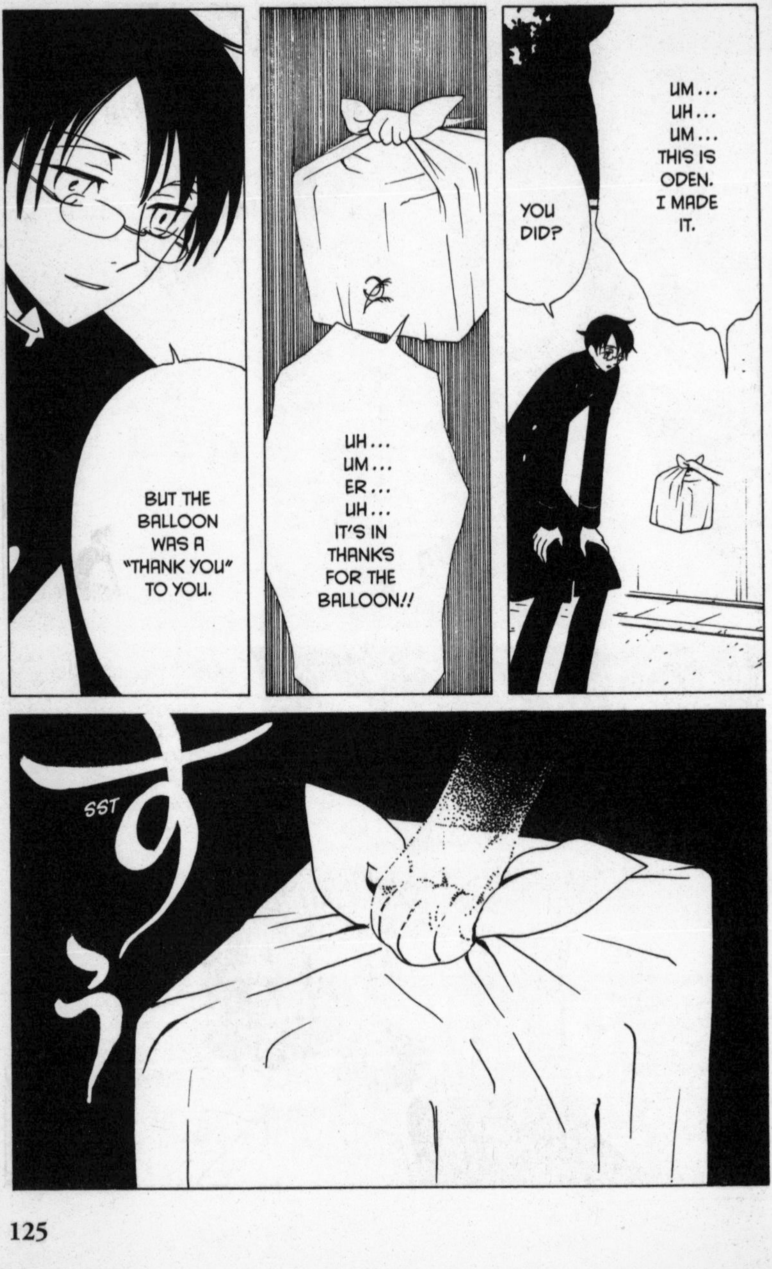
UM... UH... UM... THIS IS ODEN. I MADE IT.
YOU DID?
UH... UM... ER... UH... IT'S IN THANKS FOR THE BALLOON!!
BUT THE BALLOON WAS A "THANK YOU" TO YOU.
すう
SST

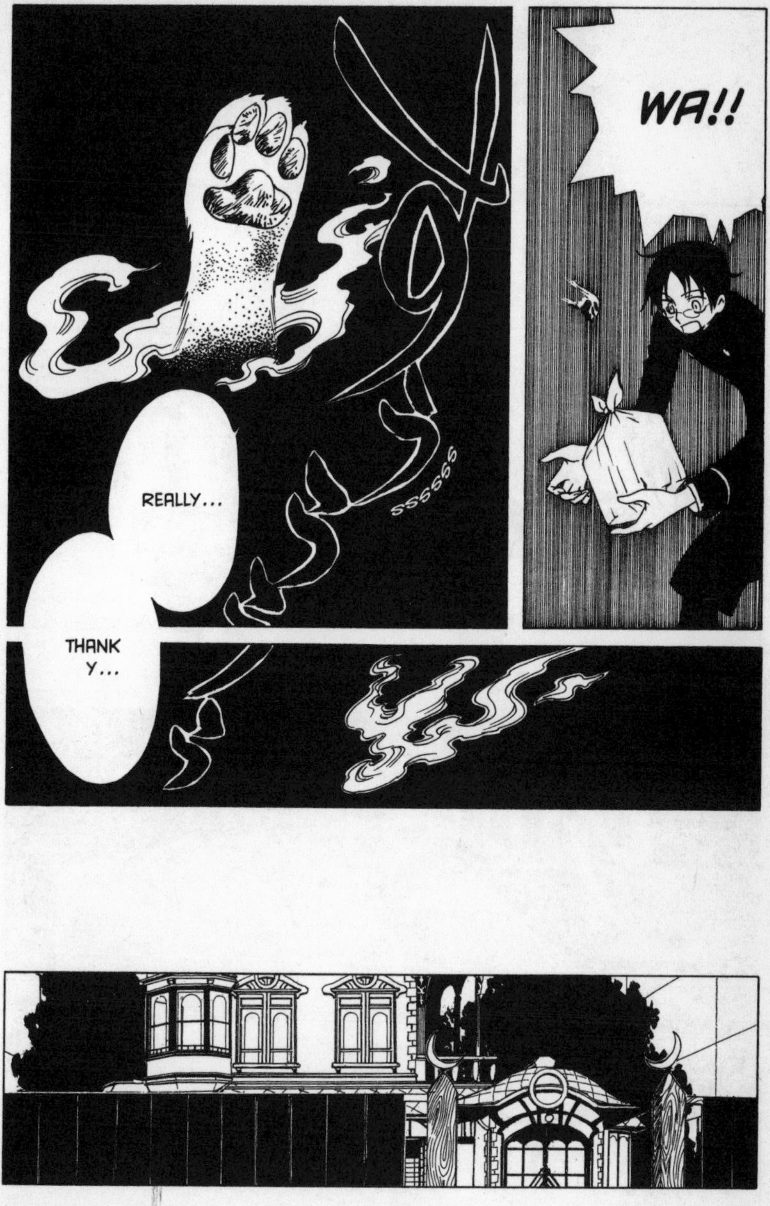
WA!!
REALLY...
SSSSSS
THANK Y...

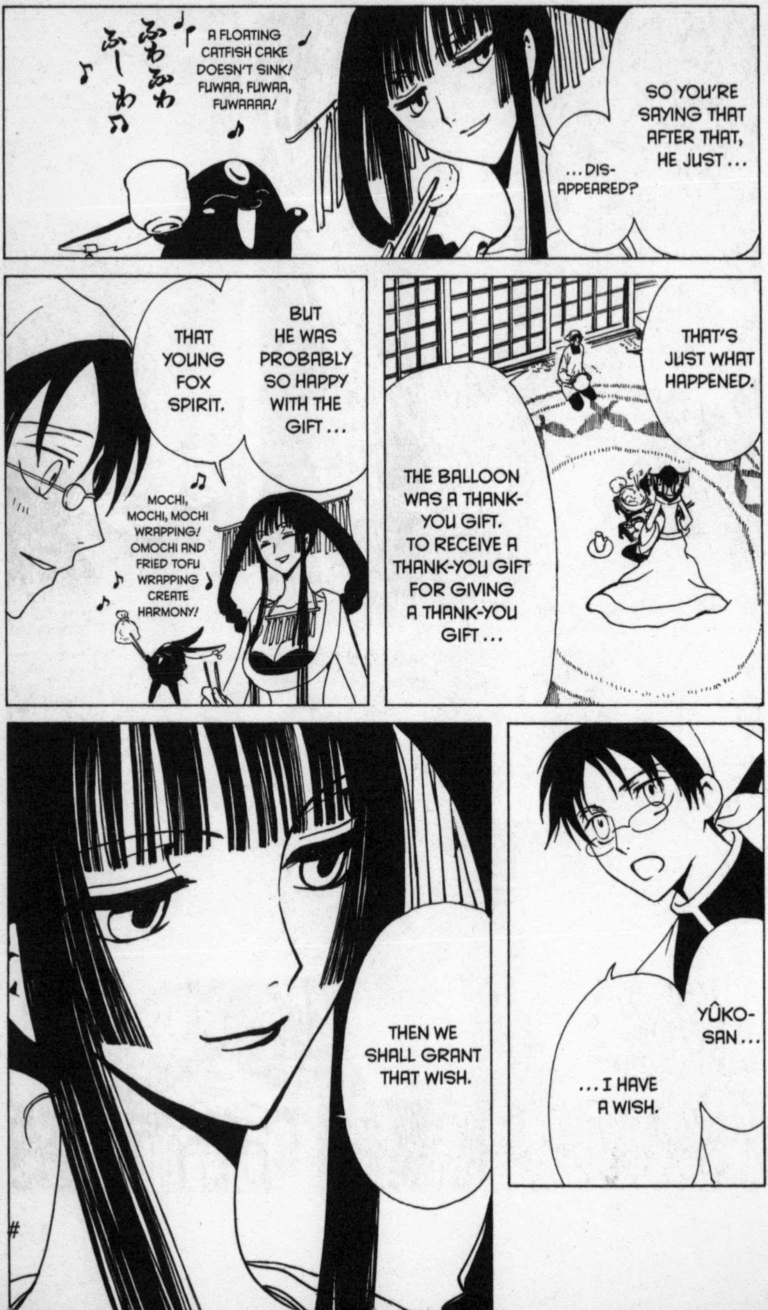
SO YOU'RE SAYING THAT AFTER THAT, HE JUST...
...DIS-APPEARED?
A FLOATING CATFISH CAKE DOESN'T SINK! FUWAA, FUWAA, FUWAAAA!
ふわふわ
ふしわ
THAT'S JUST WHAT HAPPENED.
THE BALLOON WAS A THANK-YOU GIFT. TO RECEIVE A THANK-YOU GIFT FOR GIVING A THANK-YOU GIFT...
BUT HE WAS PROBABLY SO HAPPY WITH THE GIFT...
THAT YOUNG FOX SPIRIT.
MOCHI, MOCHI, MOCHI WRAPPING! OMOCHI AND FRIED TOFU WRAPPING CREATE HARMONY!
YÛKO-SAN...
...I HAVE A WISH.
THEN WE SHALL GRANT THAT WISH.

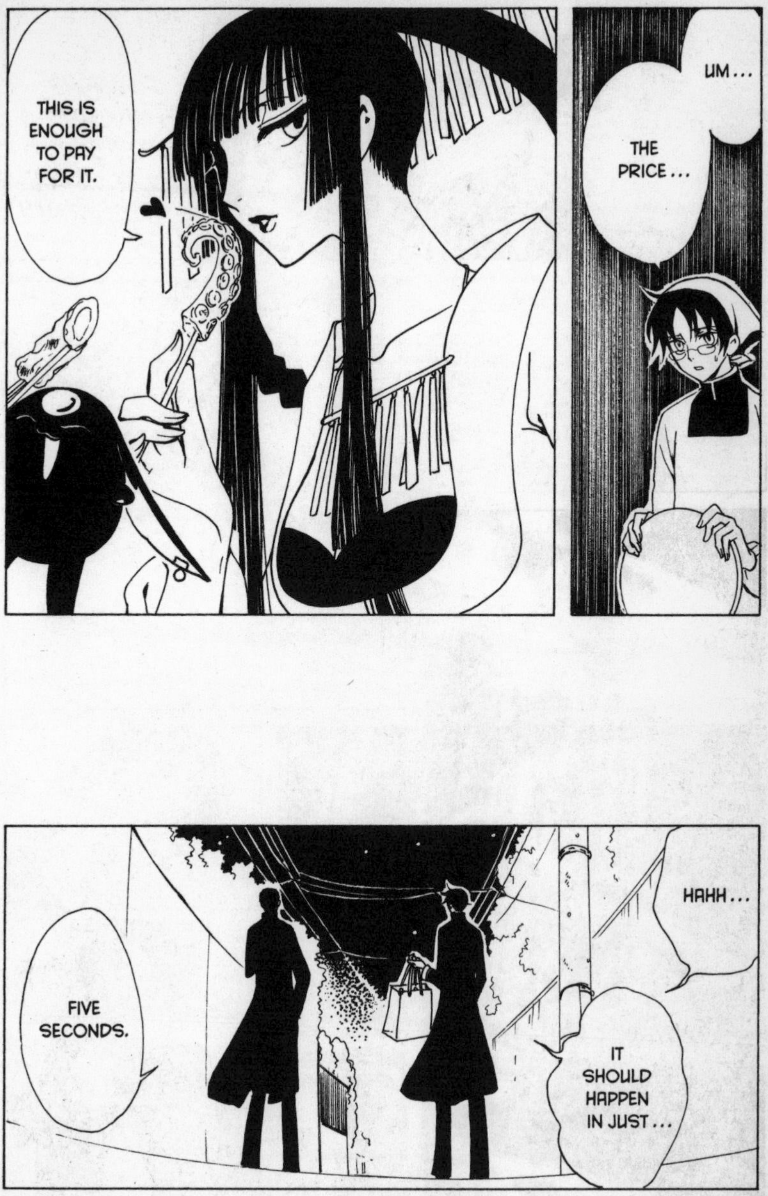
UM…
THE PRICE…
THIS IS ENOUGH TO PAY FOR IT.
HAHH…
IT SHOULD HAPPEN IN JUST…
FIVE SECONDS.

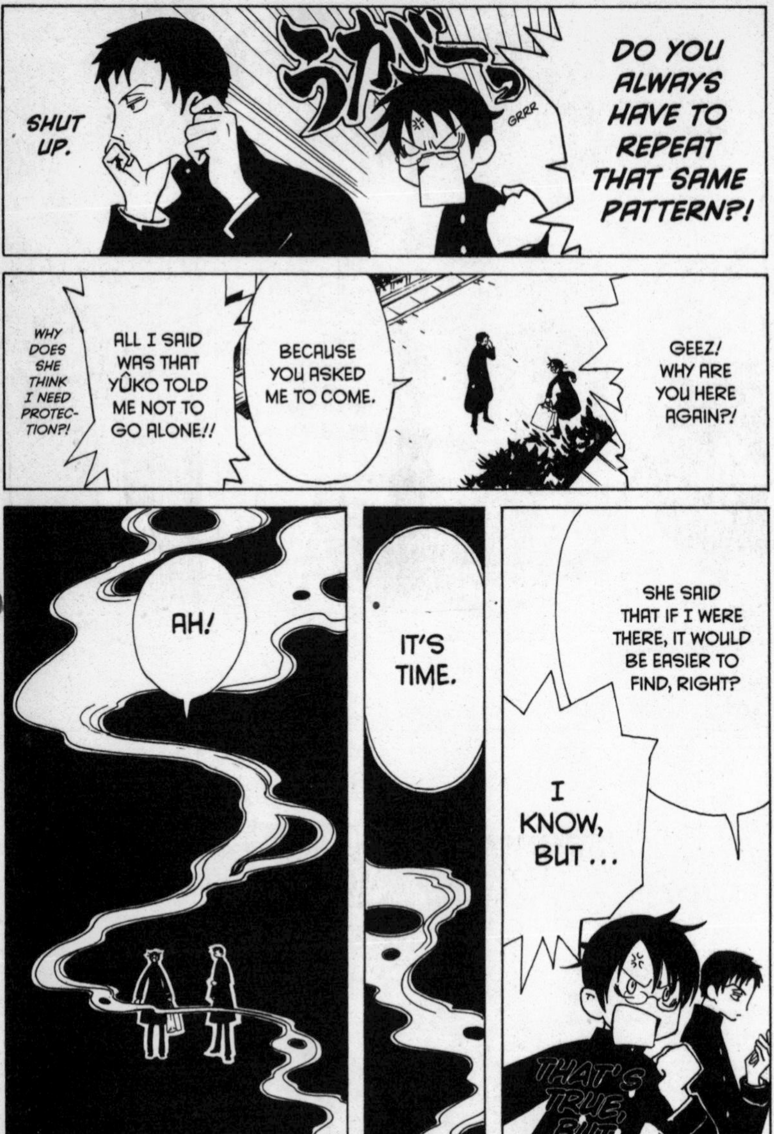
DO YOU ALWAYS HAVE TO REPEAT THAT SAME PATTERN?!
GRRR
SHUT UP.
GEEZ! WHY ARE YOU HERE AGAIN?!
BECAUSE YOU ASKED ME TO COME.
ALL I SAID WAS THAT YÛKO TOLD ME NOT TO GO ALONE!!
WHY DOES SHE THINK I NEED PROTECTION?!
SHE SAID THAT IF I WERE THERE, IT WOULD BE EASIER TO FIND, RIGHT?
I KNOW, BUT . . .
THAT'S TRUE, BUT STILL...
IT'S TIME.
AH!

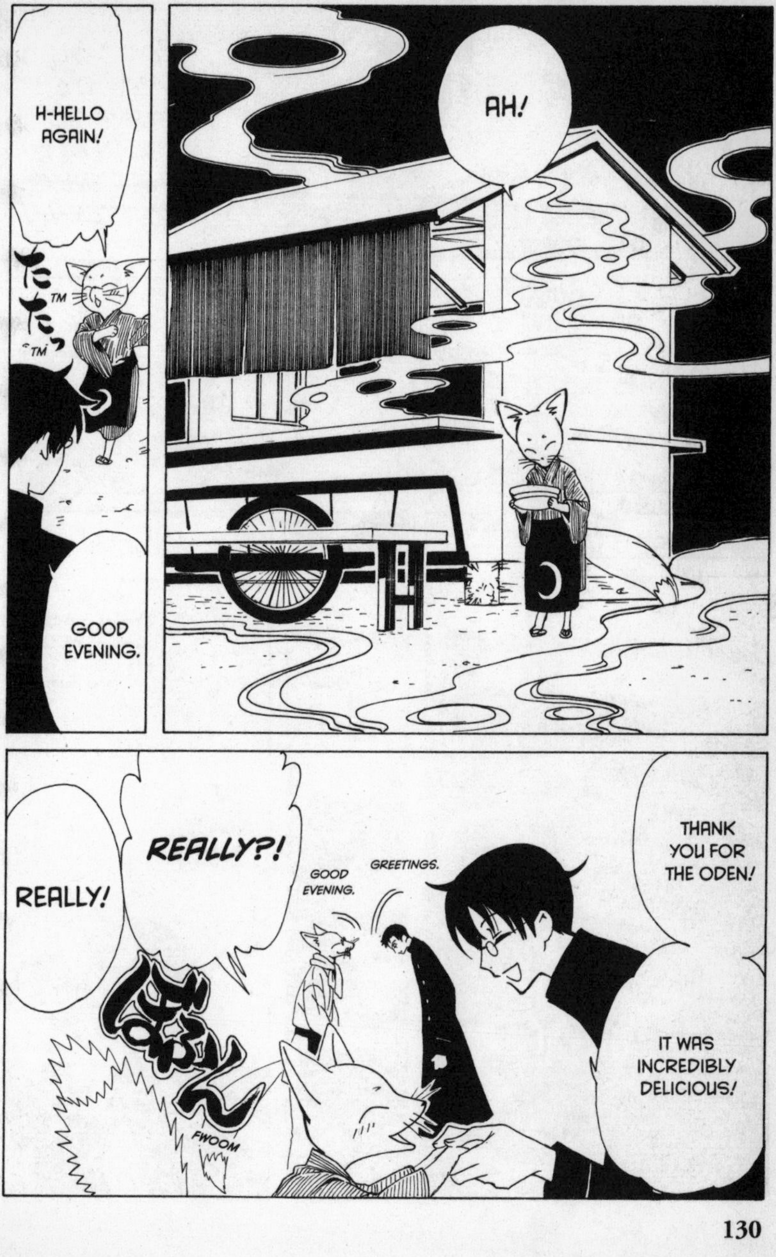
AH!
H-HELLO AGAIN!
たたっ
TM
TM
GOOD EVENING.
THANK YOU FOR THE ODEN!
IT WAS INCREDIBLY DELICIOUS!
GREETINGS.
GOOD EVENING.
REALLY?!
REALLY!
ぽふん
FWOOM

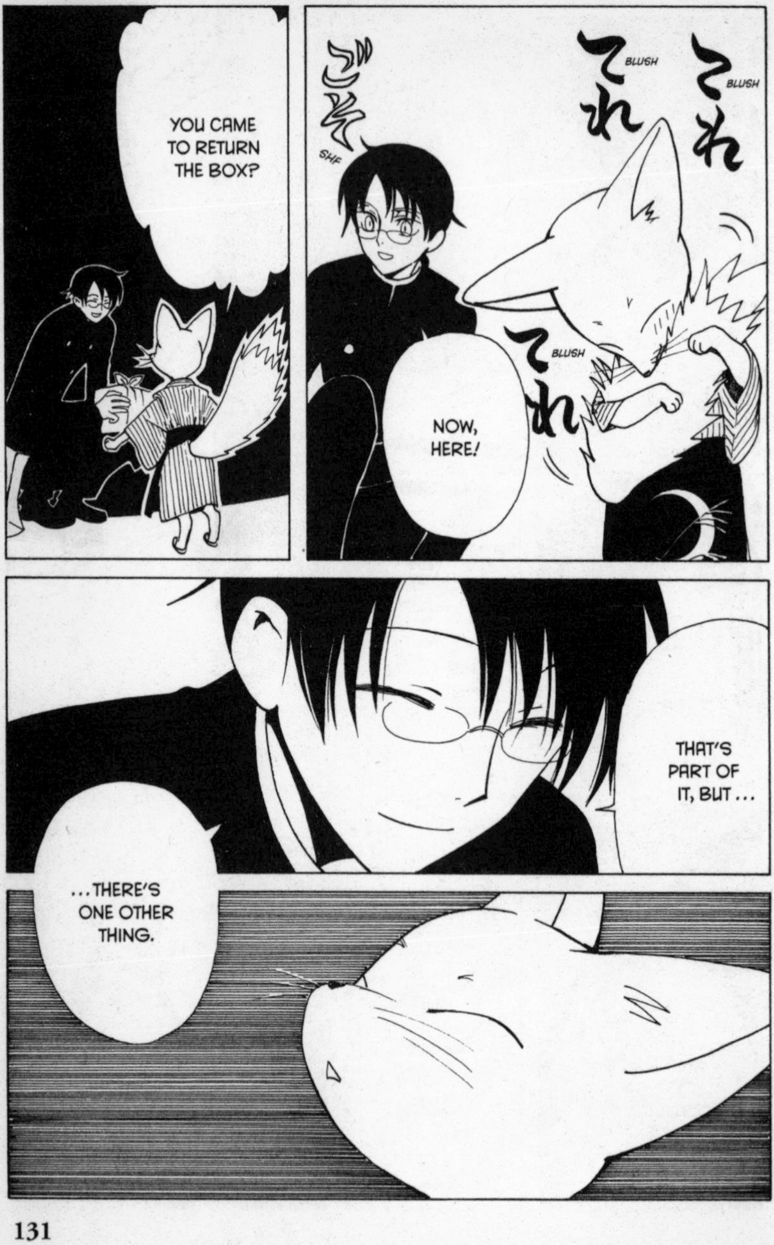
てれ
BLUSH
てれ
BLUSH
ごそ
SHF
てれ
BLUSH
NOW, HERE!
YOU CAME TO RETURN THE BOX?
THAT'S PART OF IT, BUT...
...THERE'S ONE OTHER THING.

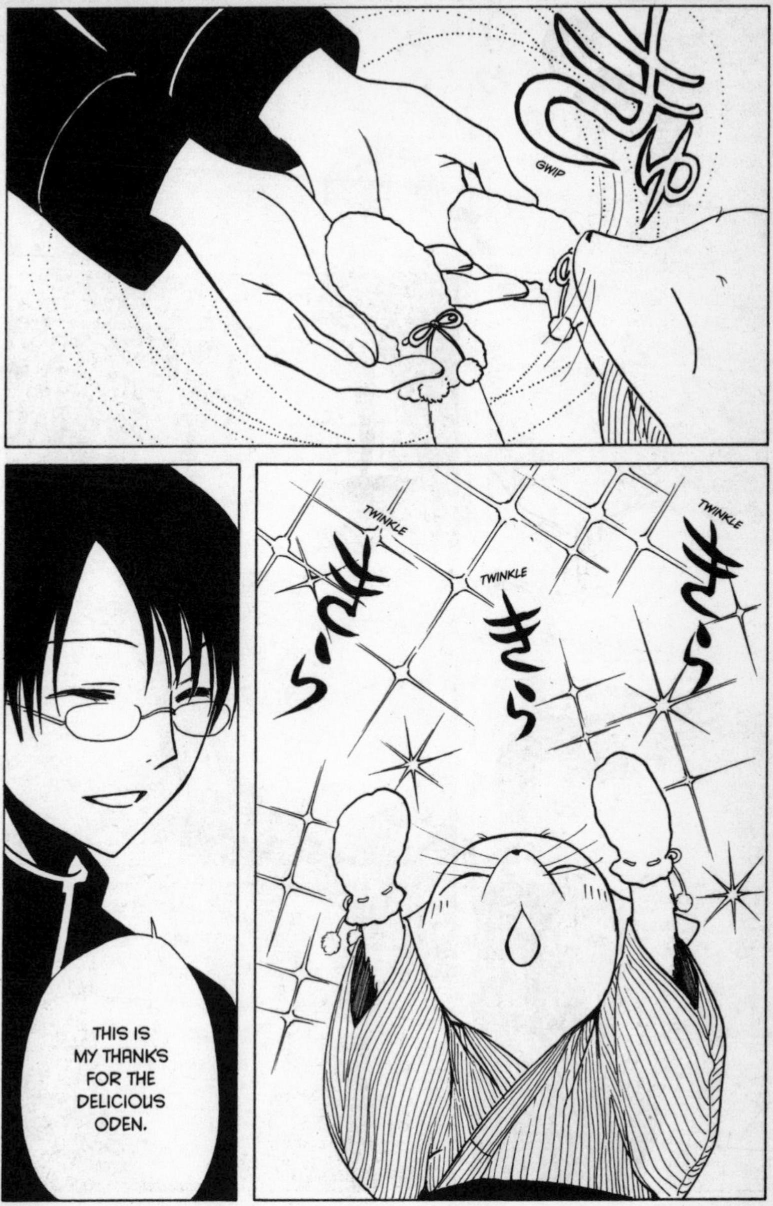
きゅ
GWIP
TWINKLE
きら
TWINKLE
きら
TWINKLE
きら
THIS IS MY THANKS FOR THE DELICIOUS ODEN.

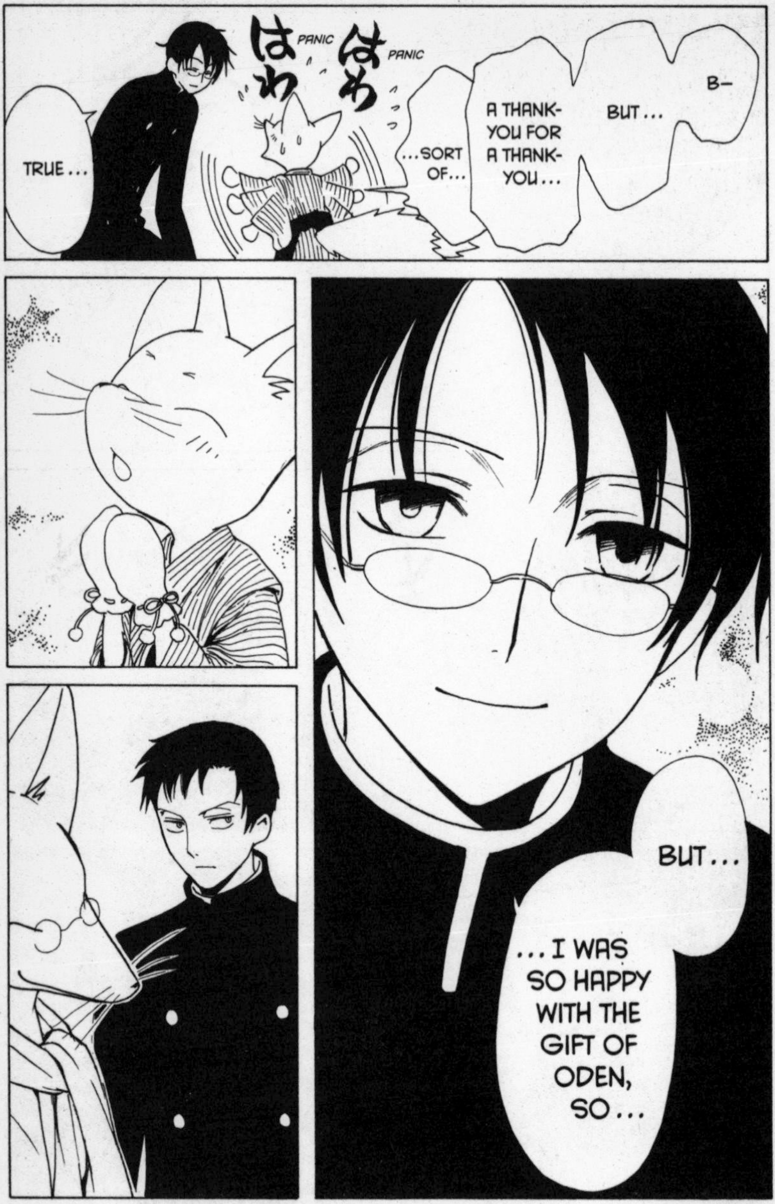
B–
BUT...
A THANK-YOU FOR A THANK-YOU...
...SORT OF...
はわ PANIC
はわ PANIC
TRUE...
BUT...
...I WAS SO HAPPY WITH THE GIFT OF ODEN, SO...

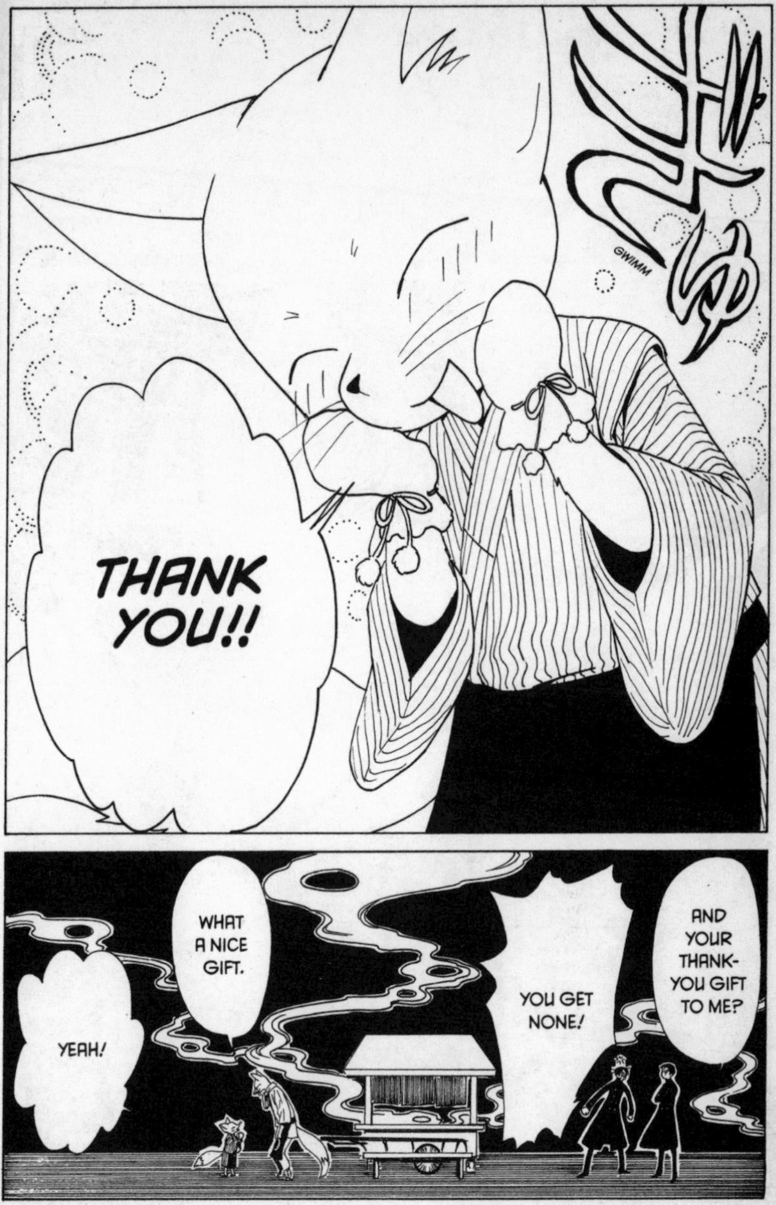
GWIMM
THANK YOU!!
AND YOUR THANK-YOU GIFT TO ME?
YOU GET NONE!
WHAT A NICE GIFT.
YEAH!

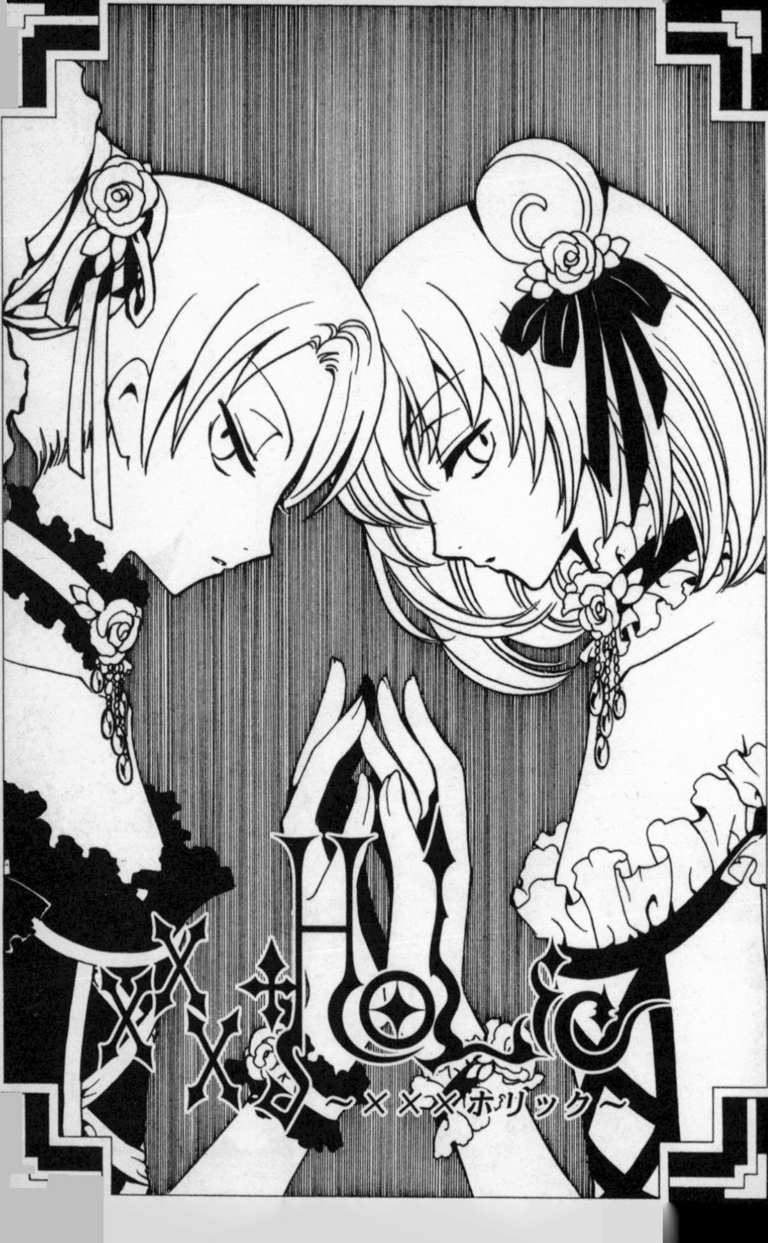
xxxHOLiC
〜×××ホリック〜

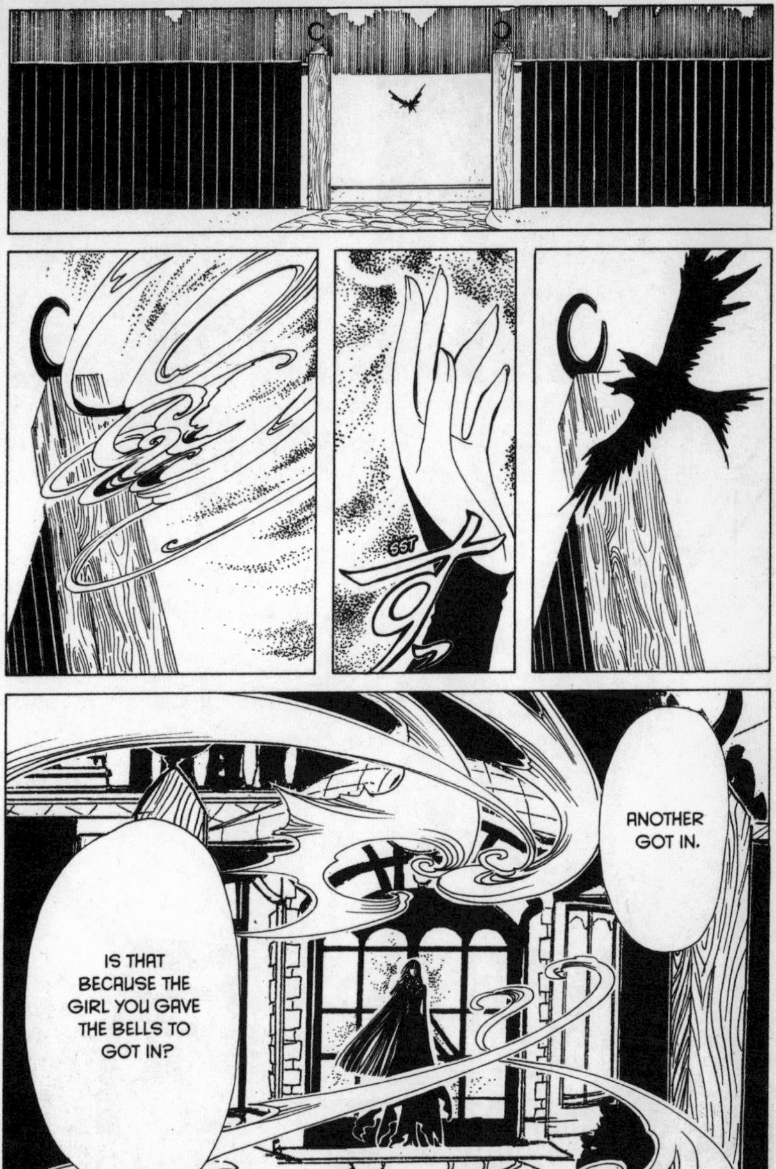
SST
ANOTHER GOT IN.
IS THAT BECAUSE THE GIRL YOU GAVE THE BELLS TO GOT IN?

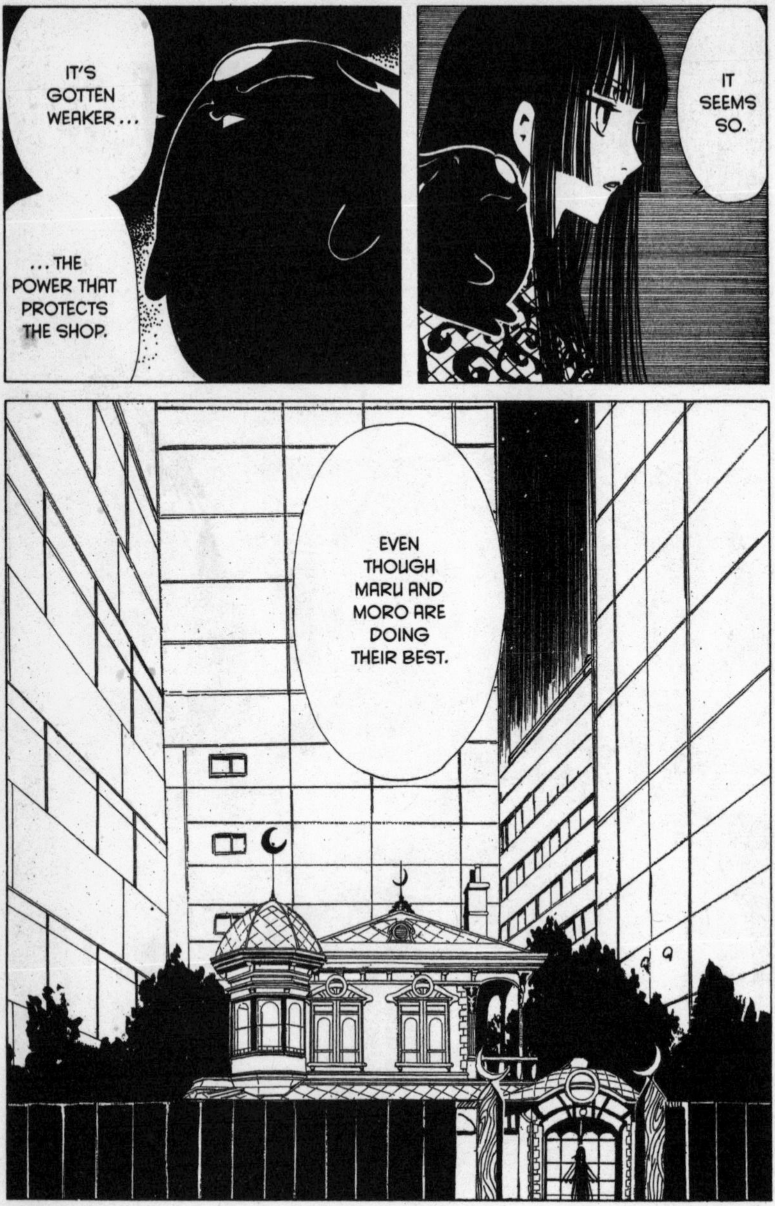
IT SEEMS SO.
IT'S GOTTEN WEAKER...
...THE POWER THAT PROTECTS THE SHOP.
EVEN THOUGH MARU AND MORO ARE DOING THEIR BEST.

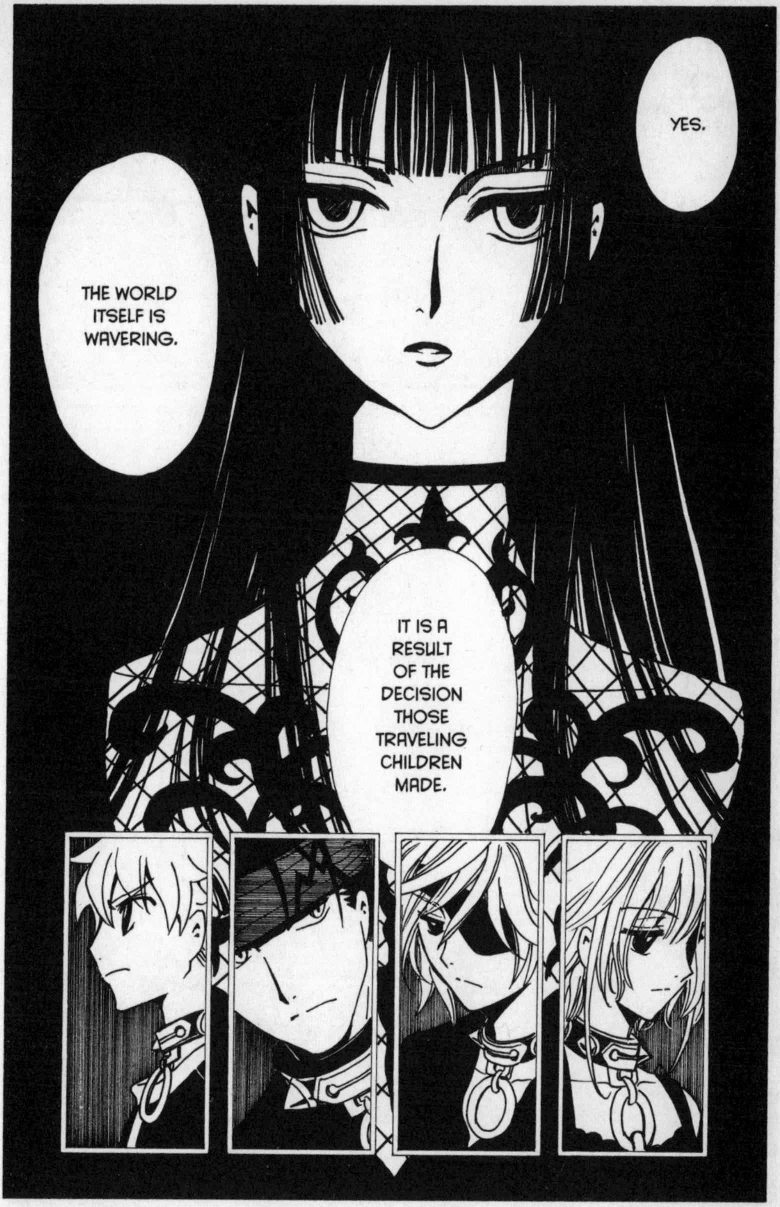
YES.
THE WORLD ITSELF IS WAVERING.
IT IS A RESULT OF THE DECISION THOSE TRAVELING CHILDREN MADE.

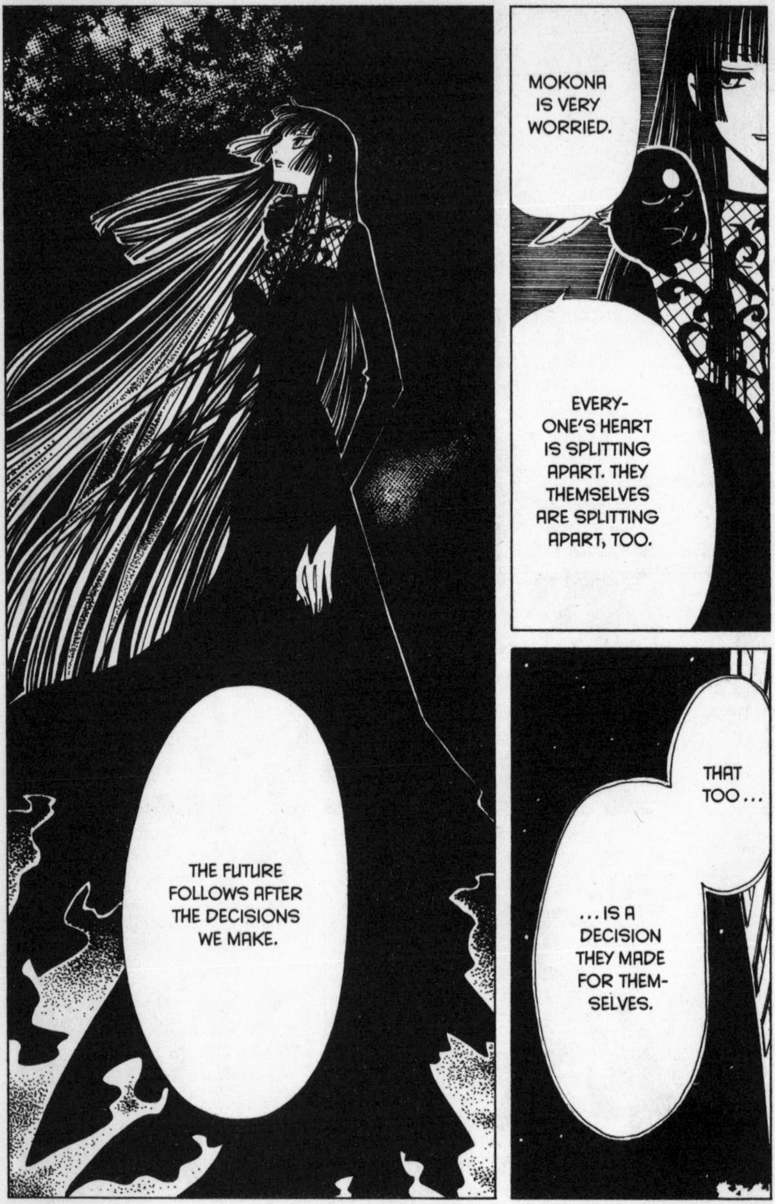
MOKONA IS VERY WORRIED.
EVERY-ONE'S HEART IS SPLITTING APART. THEY THEMSELVES ARE SPLITTING APART, TOO.
THAT TOO...
...IS A DECISION THEY MADE FOR THEM-SELVES.
THE FUTURE FOLLOWS AFTER THE DECISIONS WE MAKE.

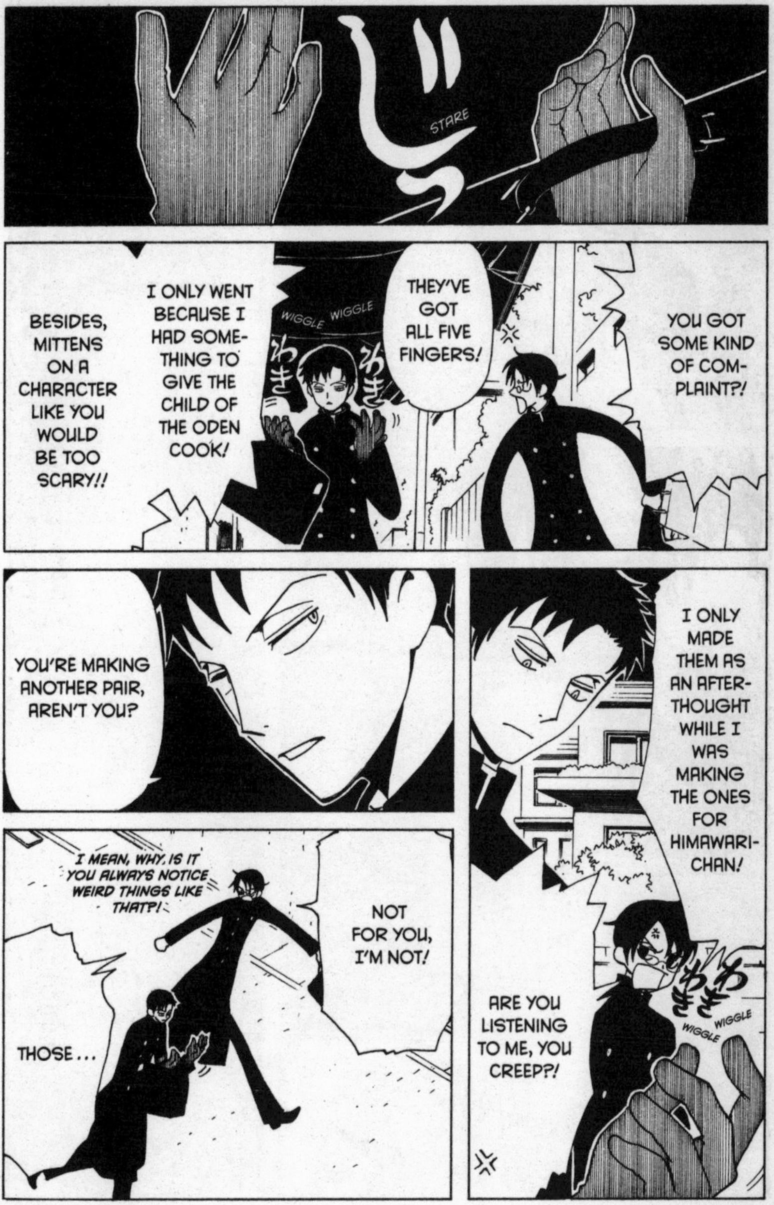
STARE
YOU GOT SOME KIND OF COM-PLAINT?!
THEY'VE GOT ALL FIVE FINGERS!
WIGGLE WIGGLE
I ONLY WENT BECAUSE I HAD SOME-THING TO GIVE THE CHILD OF THE ODEN COOK!
BESIDES, MITTENS ON A CHARACTER LIKE YOU WOULD BE TOO SCARY!!
I ONLY MADE THEM AS AN AFTER-THOUGHT WHILE I WAS MAKING THE ONES FOR HIMAWARI-CHAN!
ARE YOU LISTENING TO ME, YOU CREEP?!
WIGGLE WIGGLE
YOU'RE MAKING ANOTHER PAIR, AREN'T YOU?
NOT FOR YOU, I'M NOT!
I MEAN, WHY IS IT YOU ALWAYS NOTICE WEIRD THINGS LIKE THAT?!
THOSE...

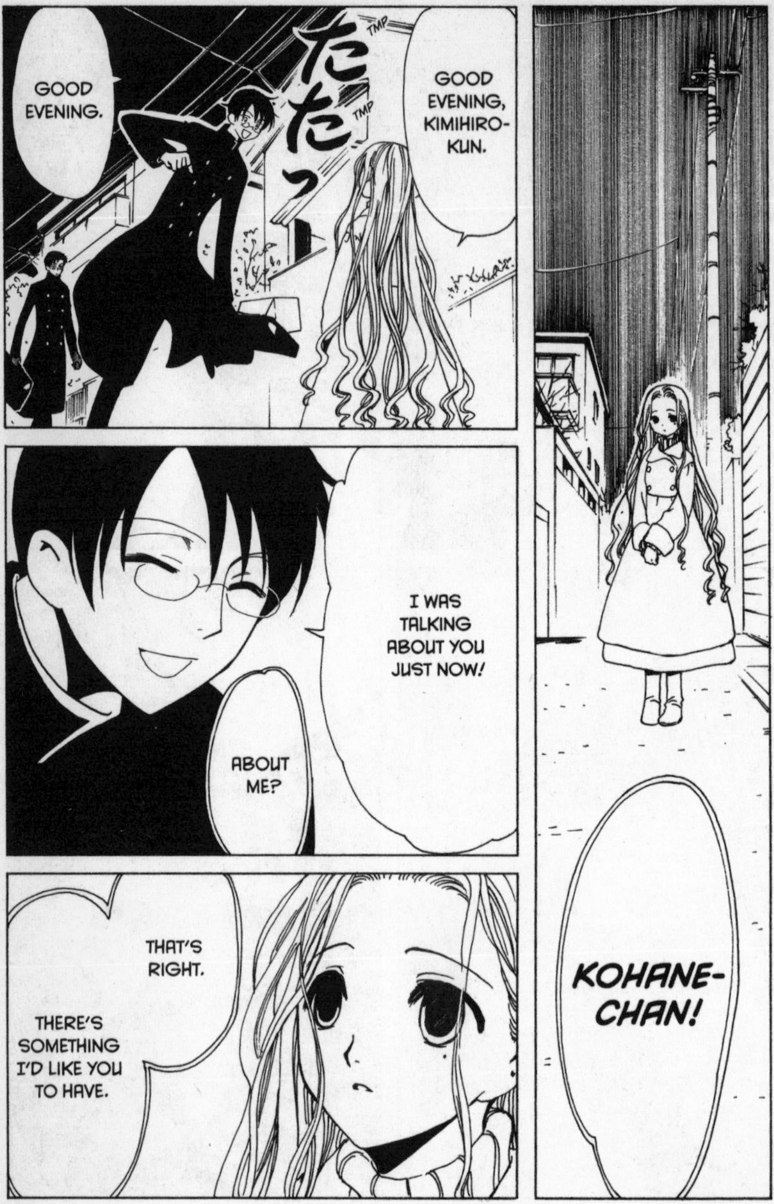
KOHANE-CHAN!
GOOD EVENING, KIMIHIRO-KUN.
たたっ
TMP
TMP
GOOD EVENING.
I WAS TALKING ABOUT YOU JUST NOW!
ABOUT ME?
THAT'S RIGHT.
THERE'S SOMETHING I'D LIKE YOU TO HAVE.

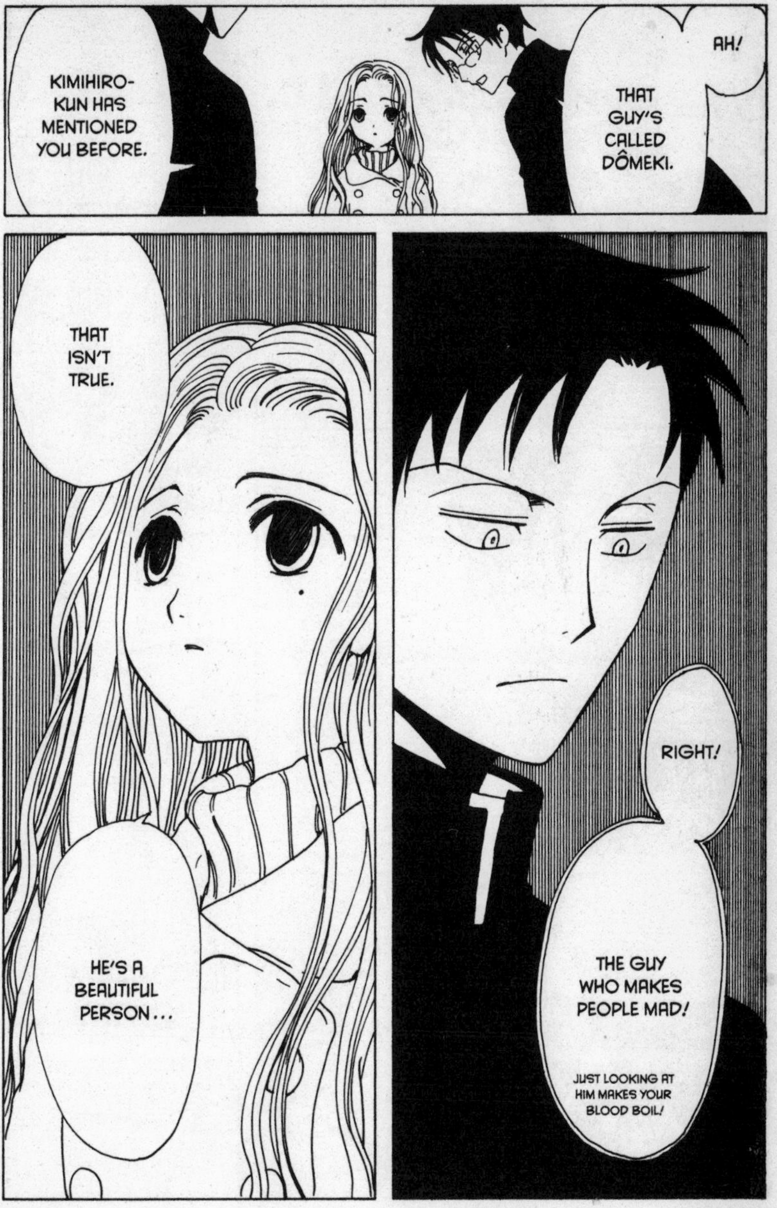
AH!
THAT GUY'S CALLED DÔMEKI.
KIMIHIRO-KUN HAS MENTIONED YOU BEFORE.
RIGHT!
THE GUY WHO MAKES PEOPLE MAD!
JUST LOOKING AT HIM MAKES YOUR BLOOD BOIL!
THAT ISN'T TRUE.
HE'S A BEAUTIFUL PERSON...

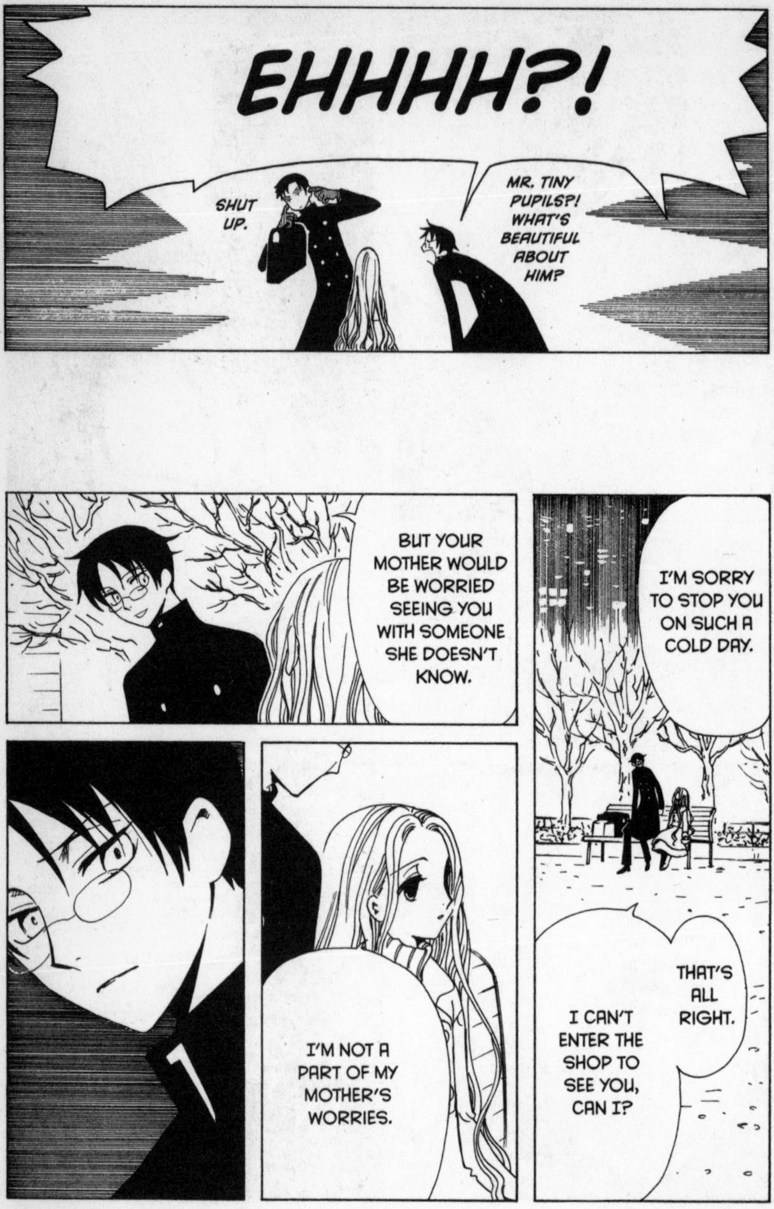
EHHHH?!
MR. TINY PUPILS?! WHAT'S BEAUTIFUL ABOUT HIM?
SHUT UP.
I'M SORRY TO STOP YOU ON SUCH A COLD DAY.
THAT'S ALL RIGHT.
I CAN'T ENTER THE SHOP TO SEE YOU, CAN I?
BUT YOUR MOTHER WOULD BE WORRIED SEEING YOU WITH SOMEONE SHE DOESN'T KNOW.
I'M NOT A PART OF MY MOTHER'S WORRIES.

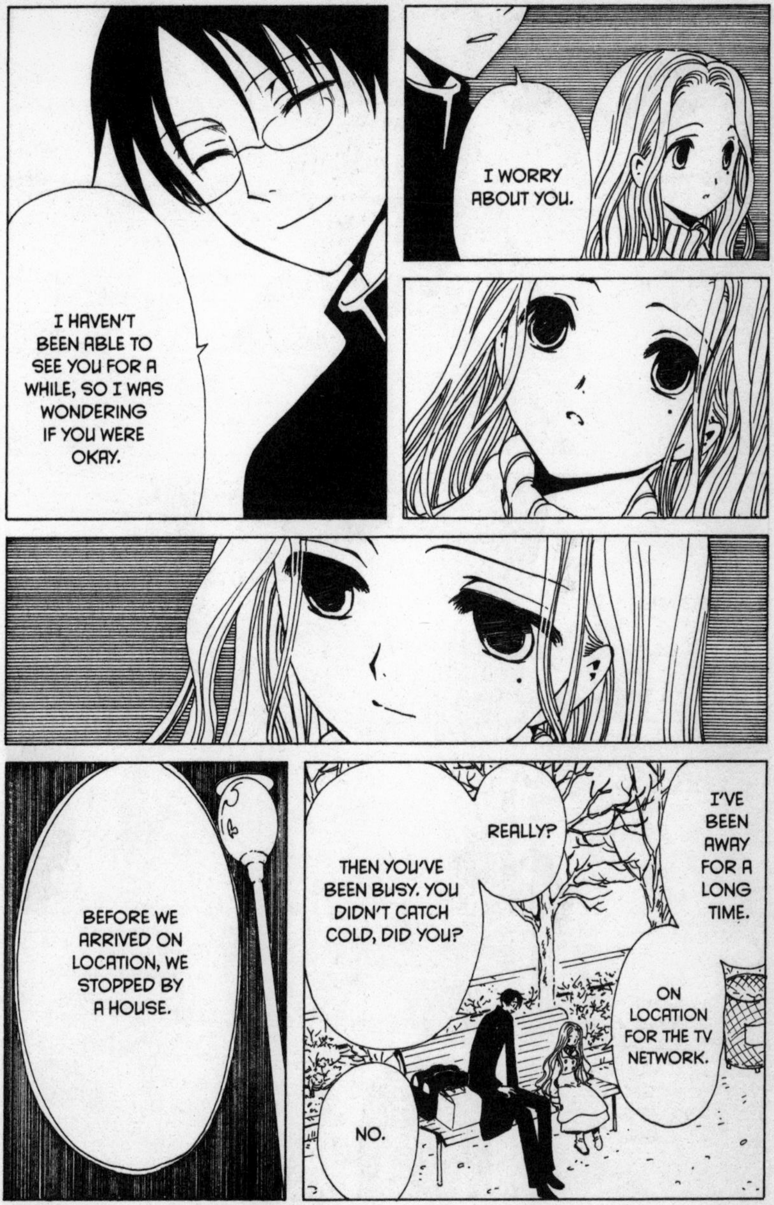
I WORRY ABOUT YOU.
I HAVEN'T BEEN ABLE TO SEE YOU FOR A WHILE, SO I WAS WONDERING IF YOU WERE OKAY.
I'VE BEEN AWAY FOR A LONG TIME.
REALLY?
ON LOCATION FOR THE TV NETWORK.
THEN YOU'VE BEEN BUSY. YOU DIDN'T CATCH COLD, DID YOU?
NO.
BEFORE WE ARRIVED ON LOCATION, WE STOPPED BY A HOUSE.

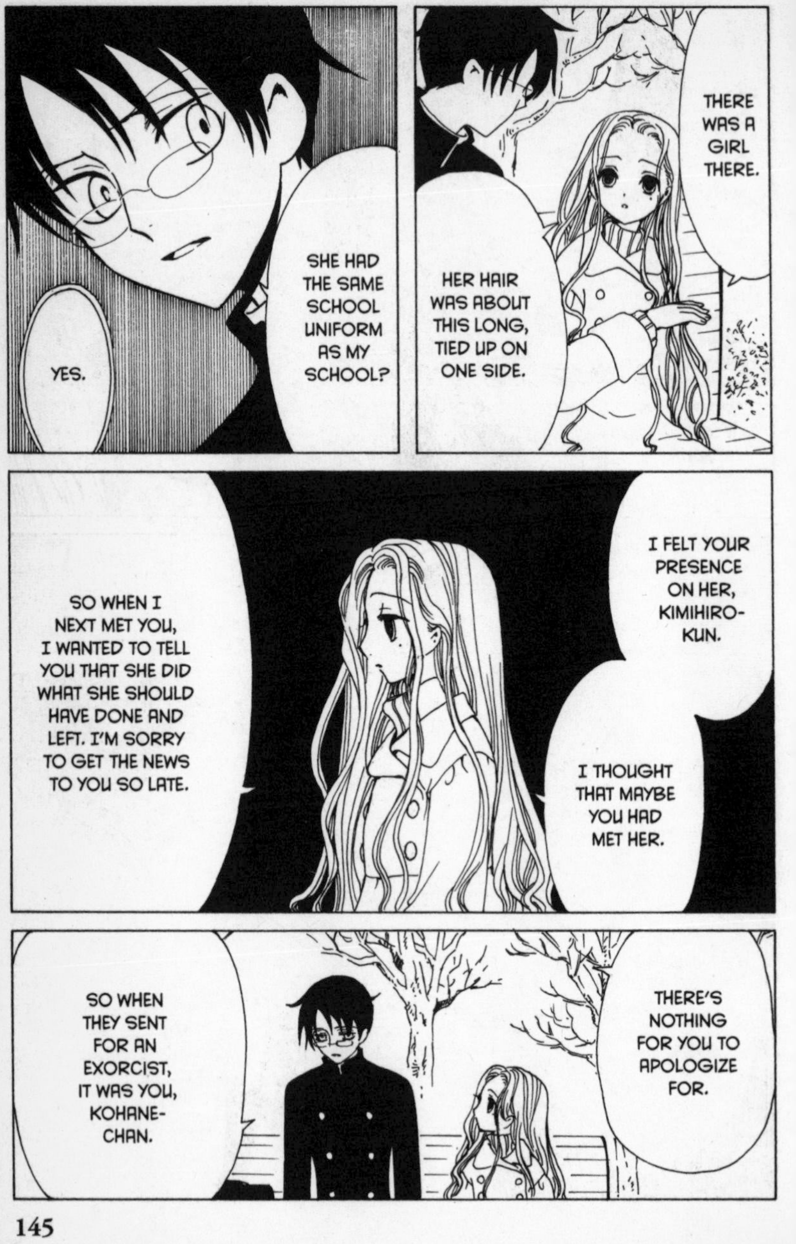
THERE WAS A GIRL THERE.
HER HAIR WAS ABOUT THIS LONG, TIED UP ON ONE SIDE.
SHE HAD THE SAME SCHOOL UNIFORM AS MY SCHOOL?
YES.
I FELT YOUR PRESENCE ON HER, KIMIHIRO-KUN.
I THOUGHT THAT MAYBE YOU HAD MET HER.
SO WHEN I NEXT MET YOU, I WANTED TO TELL YOU THAT SHE DID WHAT SHE SHOULD HAVE DONE AND LEFT. I'M SORRY TO GET THE NEWS TO YOU SO LATE.
THERE'S NOTHING FOR YOU TO APOLOGIZE FOR.
SO WHEN THEY SENT FOR AN EXORCIST, IT WAS YOU, KOHANE-CHAN.

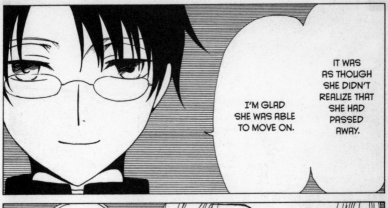

IT WAS AS THOUGH SHE DIDN'T REALIZE THAT SHE HAD PASSED AWAY.

I'M GLAD SHE WAS ABLE TO MOVE ON.

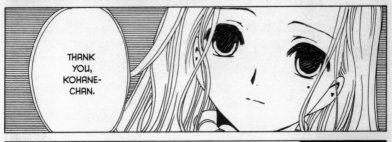

THANK YOU, KOHANE-CHAN.

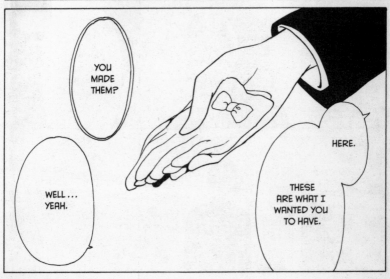

YOU MADE THEM?

WELL... YEAH.

HERE.

THESE ARE WHAT I WANTED YOU TO HAVE.

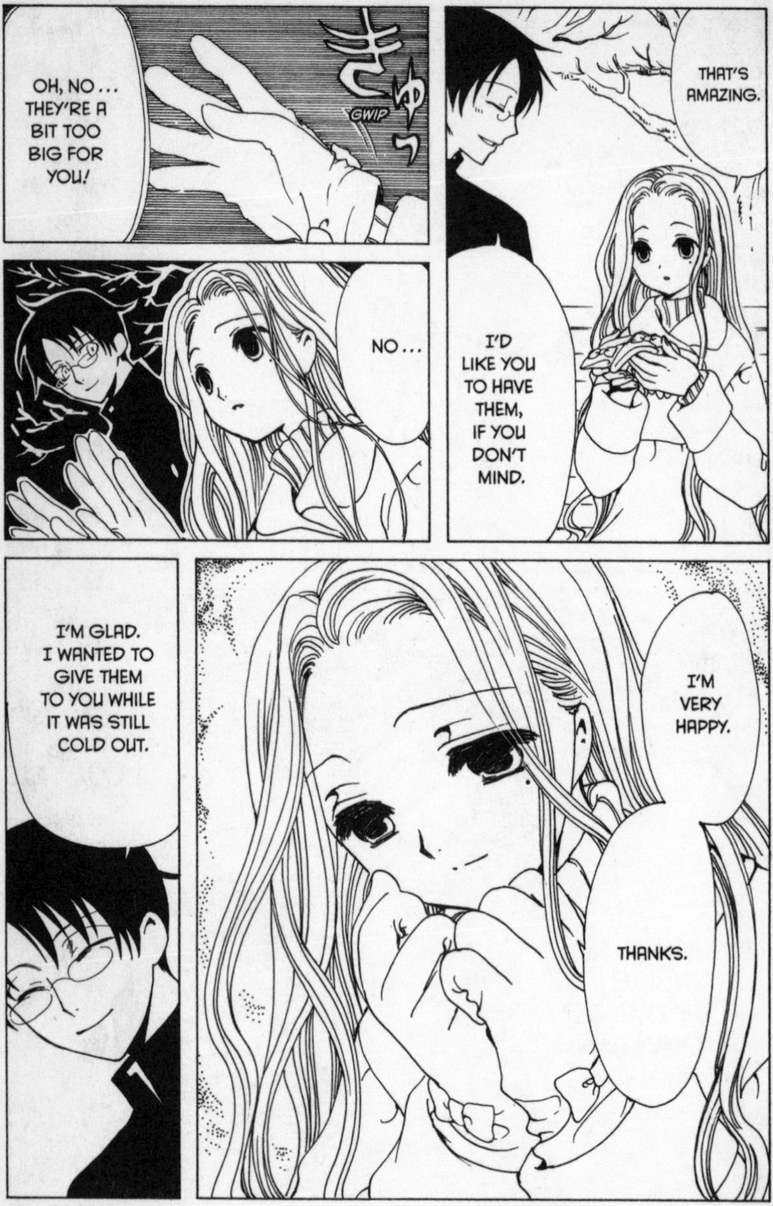
THAT'S AMAZING.
I'D LIKE YOU TO HAVE THEM, IF YOU DON'T MIND.
きゅっ
GWIP
OH, NO... THEY'RE A BIT TOO BIG FOR YOU!
NO...
I'M VERY HAPPY.
THANKS.
I'M GLAD. I WANTED TO GIVE THEM TO YOU WHILE IT WAS STILL COLD OUT.

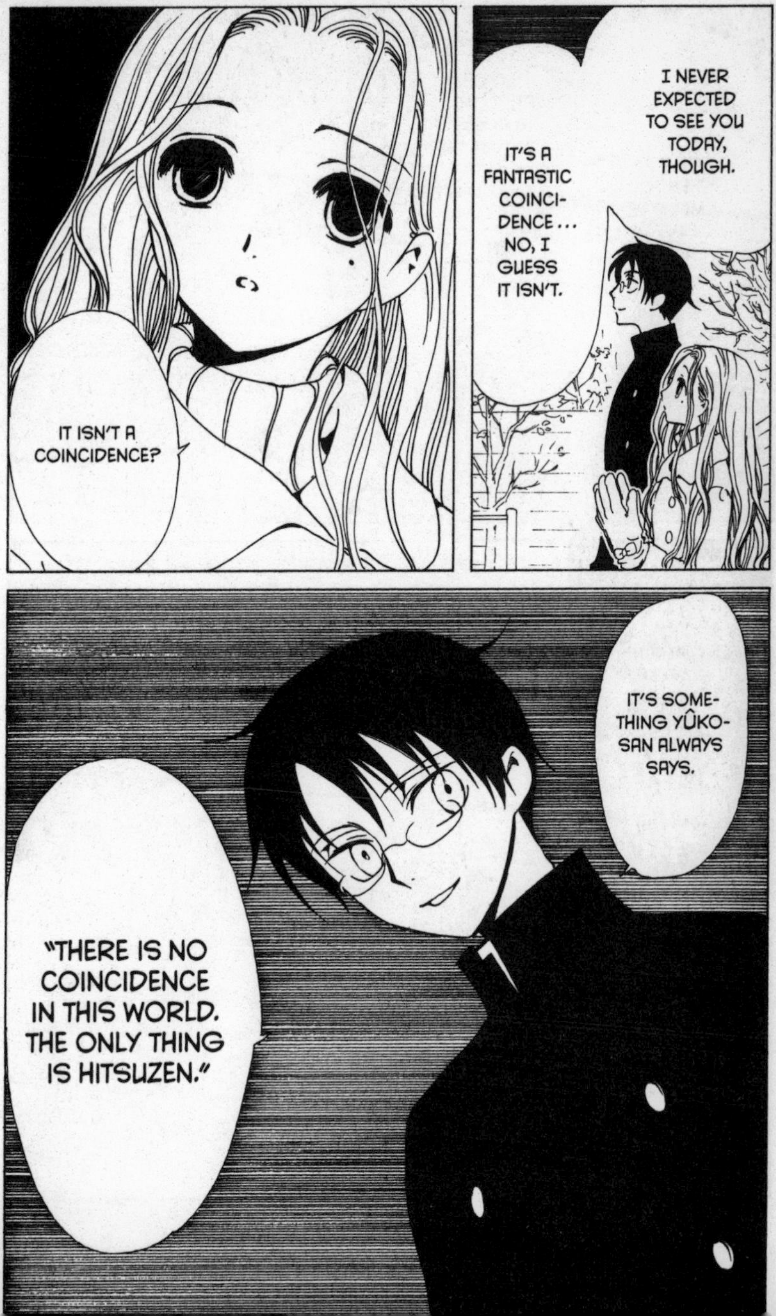
I NEVER EXPECTED TO SEE YOU TODAY, THOUGH.
IT'S A FANTASTIC COINCIDENCE... NO, I GUESS IT ISN'T.
IT ISN'T A COINCIDENCE?
IT'S SOMETHING YÛKO-SAN ALWAYS SAYS.
"THERE IS NO COINCIDENCE IN THIS WORLD. THE ONLY THING IS HITSUZEN."

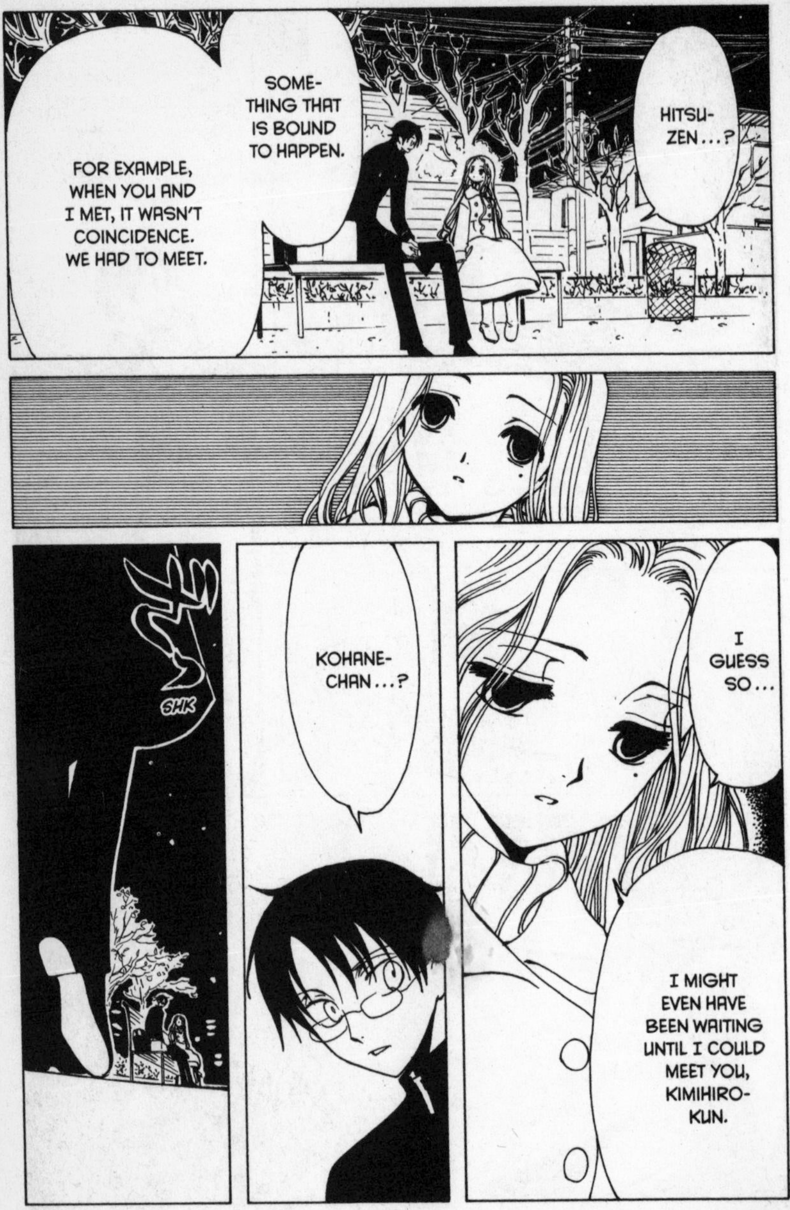
HITSU-ZEN...?
SOME-THING THAT IS BOUND TO HAPPEN.
FOR EXAMPLE, WHEN YOU AND I MET, IT WASN'T COINCIDENCE. WE HAD TO MEET.
I GUESS SO...
I MIGHT EVEN HAVE BEEN WAITING UNTIL I COULD MEET YOU, KIMIHIRO-KUN.
KOHANE-CHAN...?
SHK

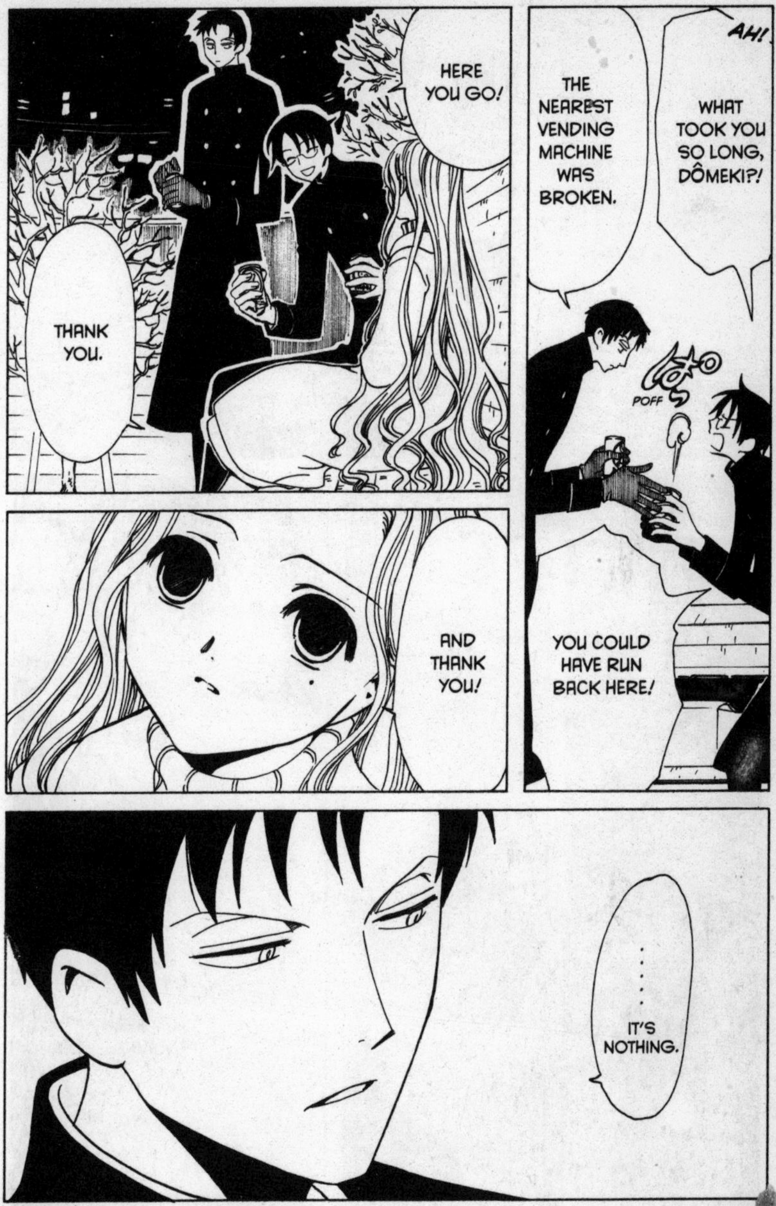
AH!
WHAT TOOK YOU SO LONG, DÔMEKI?!
THE NEAREST VENDING MACHINE WAS BROKEN.
POFF
YOU COULD HAVE RUN BACK HERE!
HERE YOU GO!
THANK YOU.
AND THANK YOU!
.....
IT'S NOTHING.

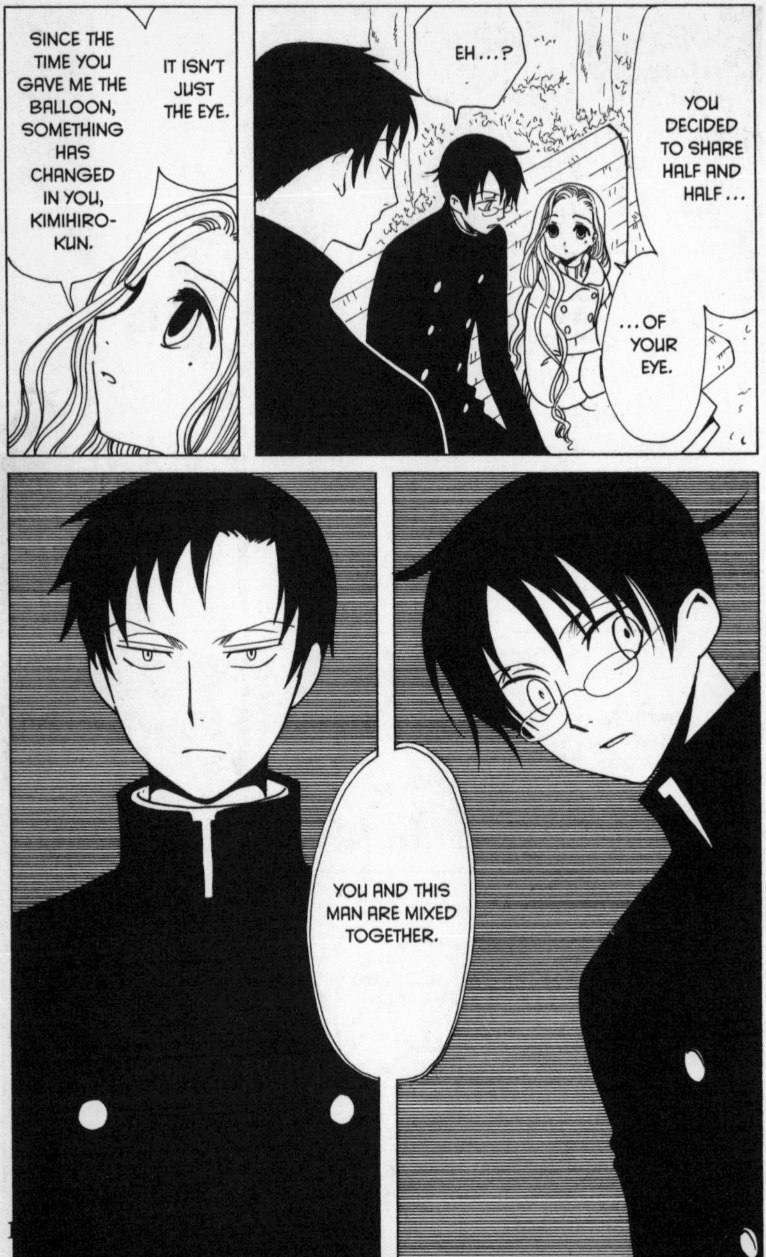
EH...?
YOU DECIDED TO SHARE HALF AND HALF...
...OF YOUR EYE.
IT ISN'T JUST THE EYE.
SINCE THE TIME YOU GAVE ME THE BALLOON, SOMETHING HAS CHANGED IN YOU, KIMIHIRO-KUN.
YOU AND THIS MAN ARE MIXED TOGETHER.

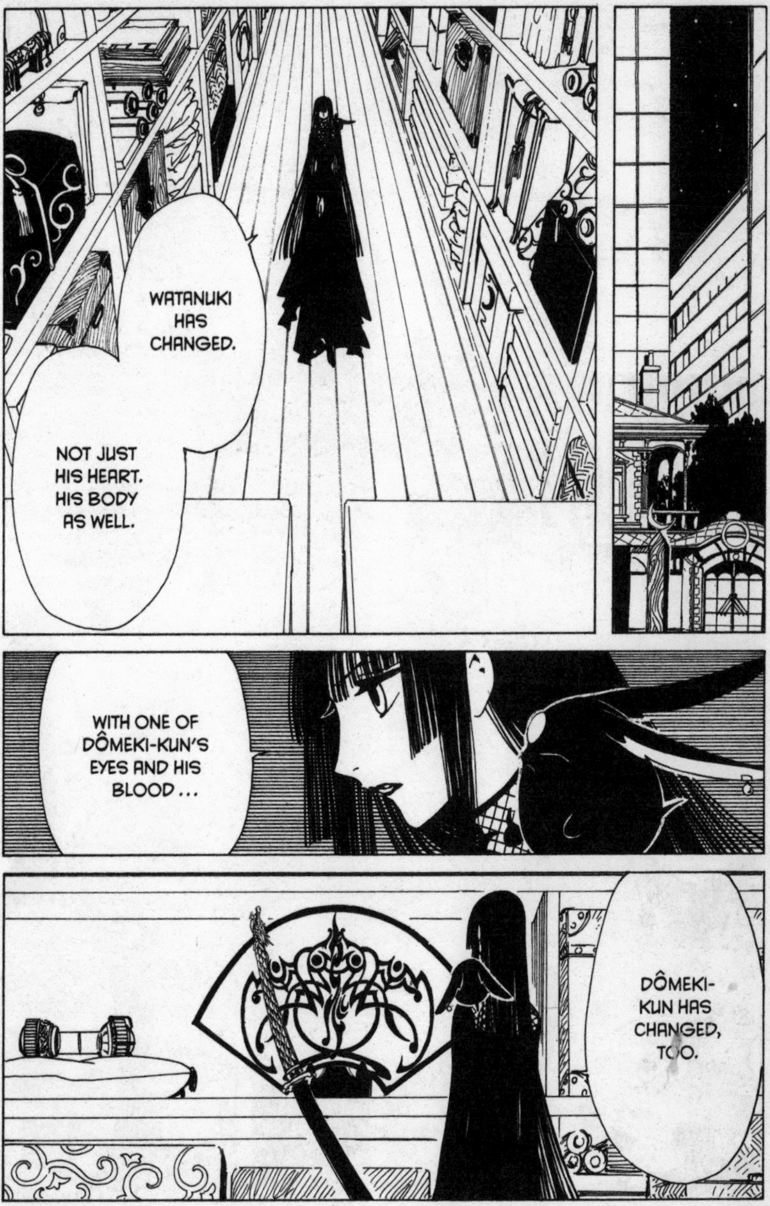
WATANUKI HAS CHANGED.
NOT JUST HIS HEART. HIS BODY AS WELL.
WITH ONE OF DÔMEKI-KUN'S EYES AND HIS BLOOD . . .
DÔMEKI-KUN HAS CHANGED, TOO.

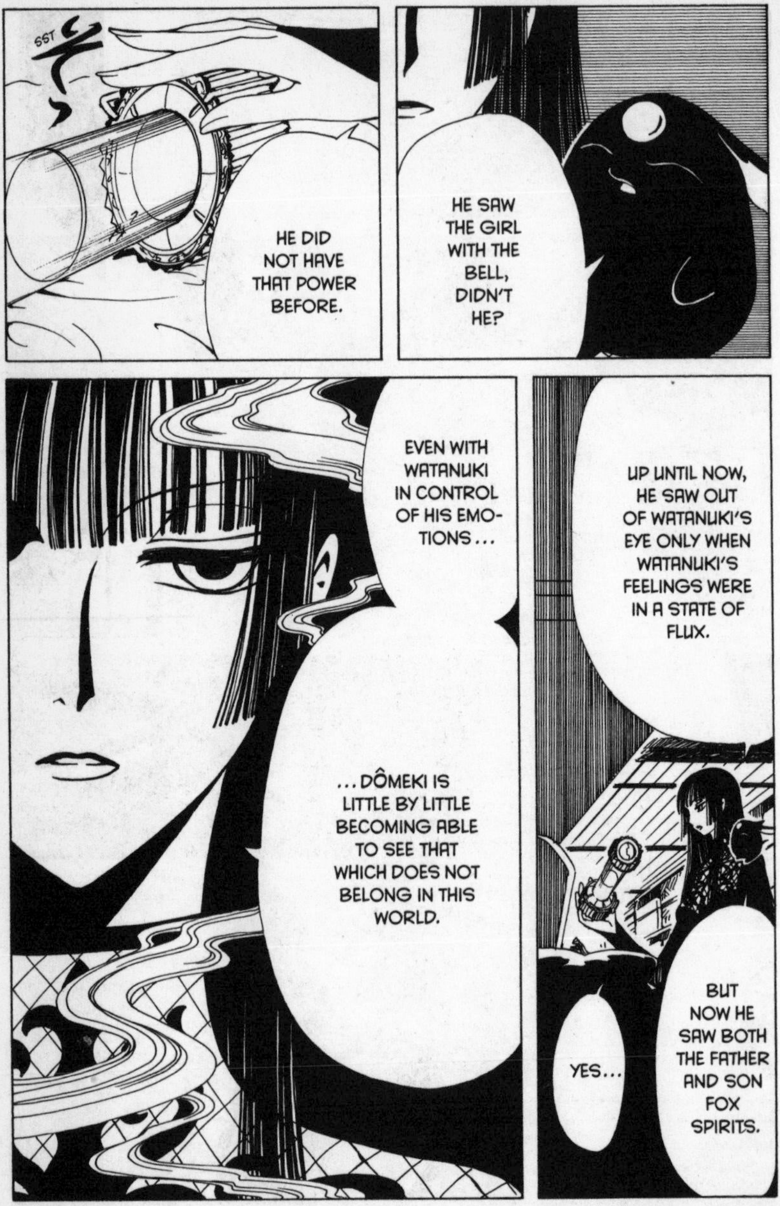
HE SAW THE GIRL WITH THE BELL, DIDN'T HE?
SST
HE DID NOT HAVE THAT POWER BEFORE.
UP UNTIL NOW, HE SAW OUT OF WATANUKI'S EYE ONLY WHEN WATANUKI'S FEELINGS WERE IN A STATE OF FLUX.
BUT NOW HE SAW BOTH THE FATHER AND SON FOX SPIRITS.
YES...
EVEN WITH WATANUKI IN CONTROL OF HIS EMO- TIONS...
...DÔMEKI IS LITTLE BY LITTLE BECOMING ABLE TO SEE THAT WHICH DOES NOT BELONG IN THIS WORLD.

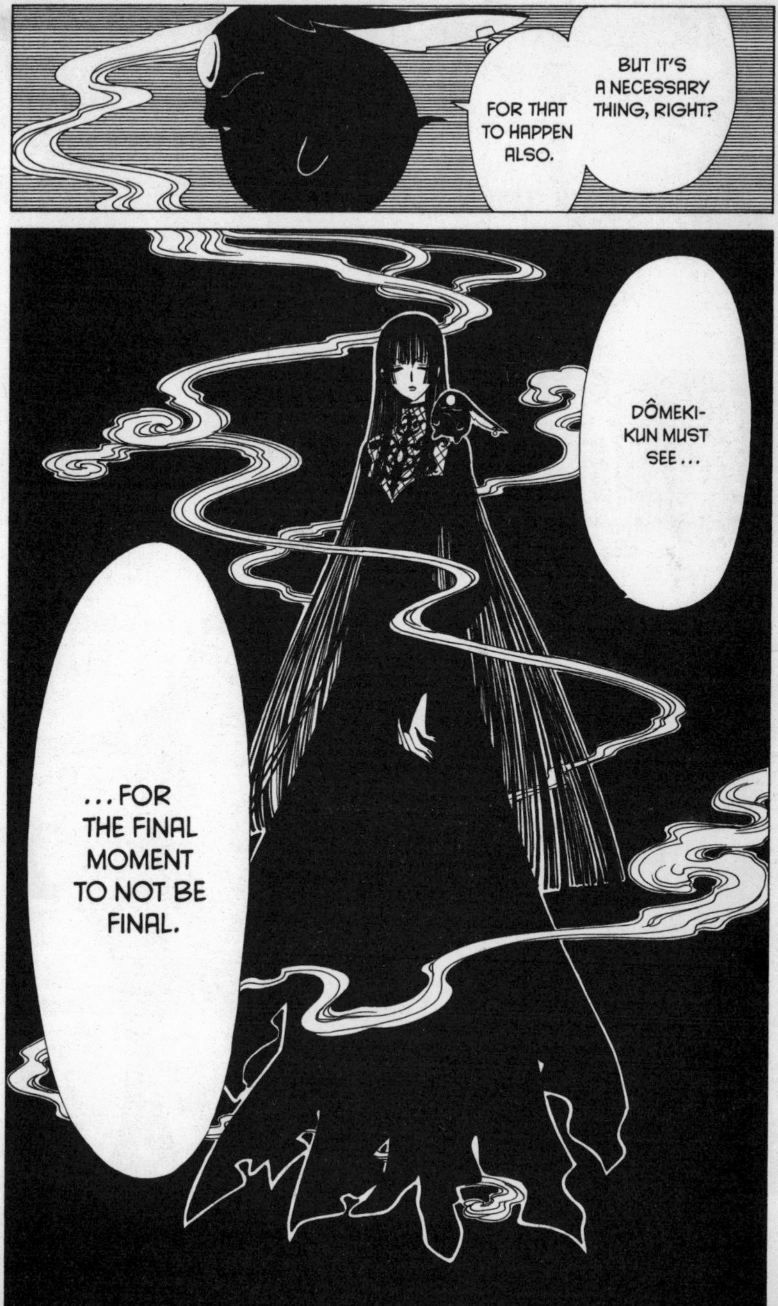
BUT IT'S A NECESSARY THING, RIGHT?
FOR THAT TO HAPPEN ALSO.
DÔMEKI-KUN MUST SEE...
...FOR THE FINAL MOMENT TO NOT BE FINAL.

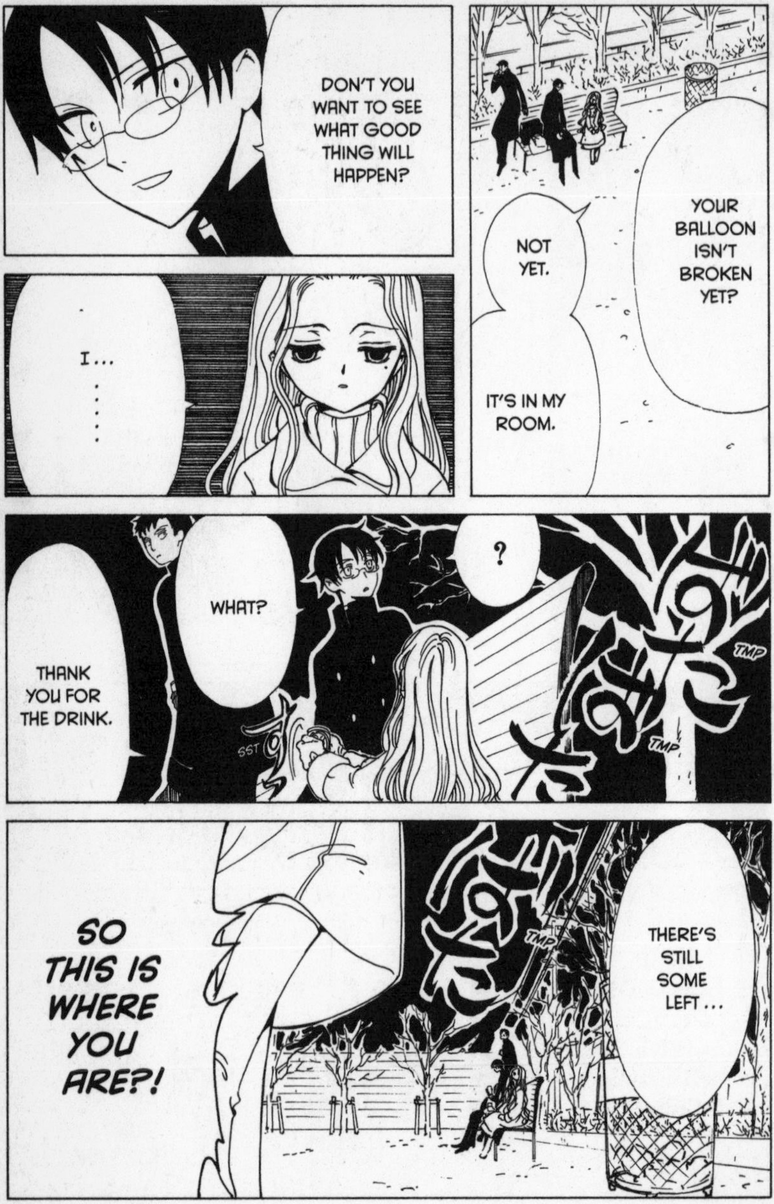
YOUR BALLOON ISN'T BROKEN YET?
NOT YET.
IT'S IN MY ROOM.
DON'T YOU WANT TO SEE WHAT GOOD THING WILL HAPPEN?
I... ......
?
TMP
TMP
WHAT?
THANK YOU FOR THE DRINK.
SST
THERE'S STILL SOME LEFT...
TMP
SO THIS IS WHERE YOU ARE?!

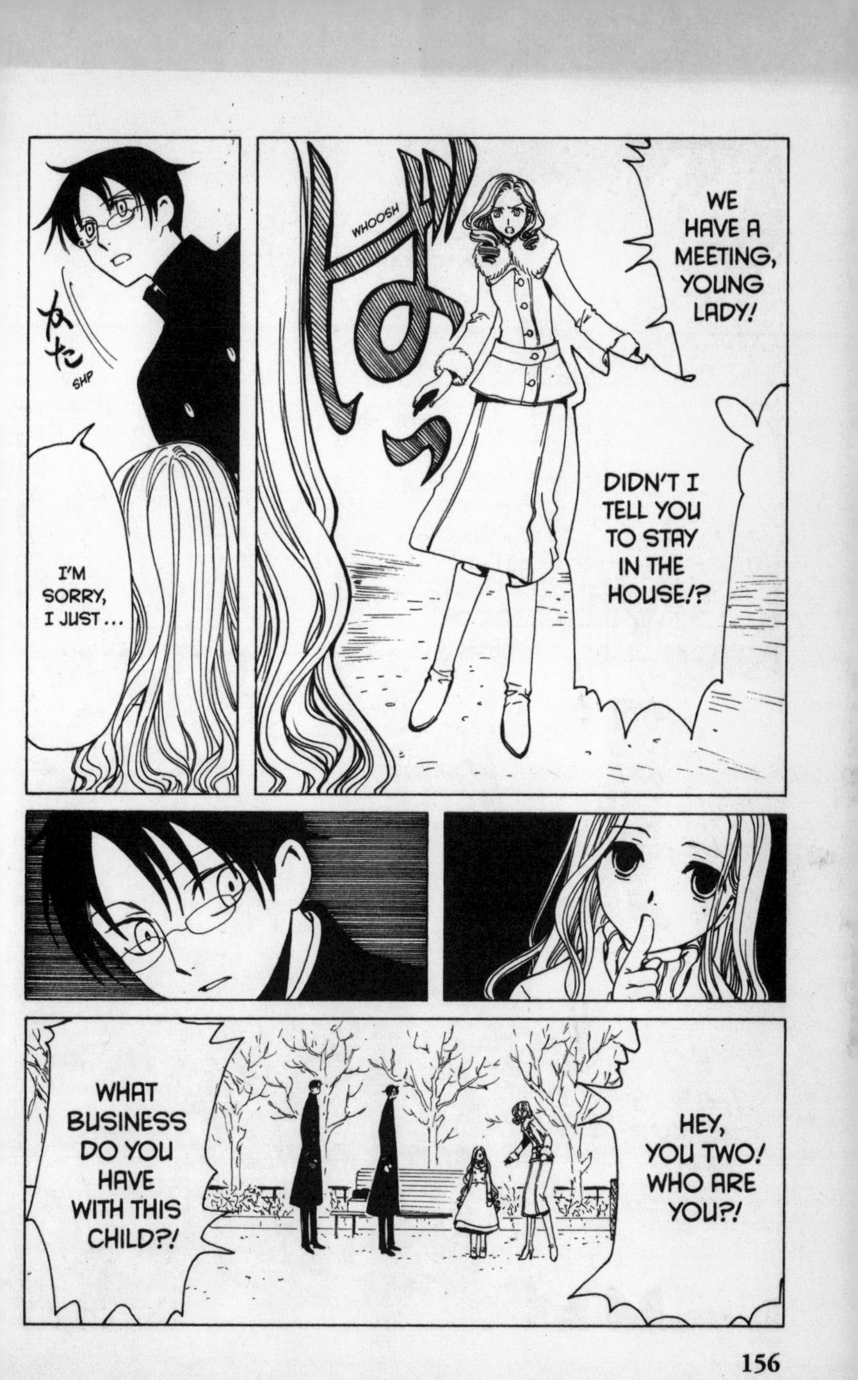
ばっ
WHOOSH
WE HAVE A MEETING, YOUNG LADY!
DIDN'T I TELL YOU TO STAY IN THE HOUSE!?
かた
SHP
I'M SORRY, I JUST...
HEY, YOU TWO! WHO ARE YOU?!
WHAT BUSINESS DO YOU HAVE WITH THIS CHILD?!

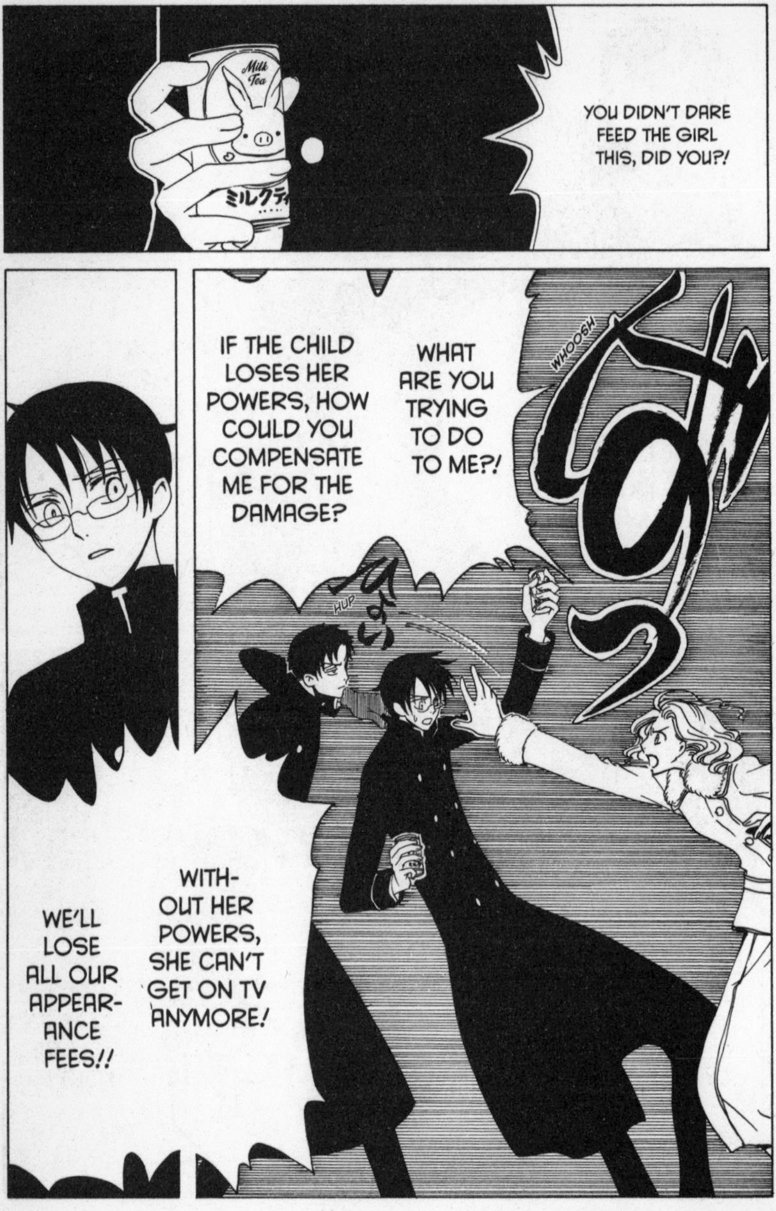
Milk Tea
YOU DIDN'T DARE FEED THE GIRL THIS, DID YOU?!
WHOOSH
WHAT ARE YOU TRYING TO DO TO ME?!
IF THE CHILD LOSES HER POWERS, HOW COULD YOU COMPENSATE ME FOR THE DAMAGE?
HUP
WITH-OUT HER POWERS, SHE CAN'T GET ON TV ANYMORE!
WE'LL LOSE ALL OUR APPEAR-ANCE FEES!!

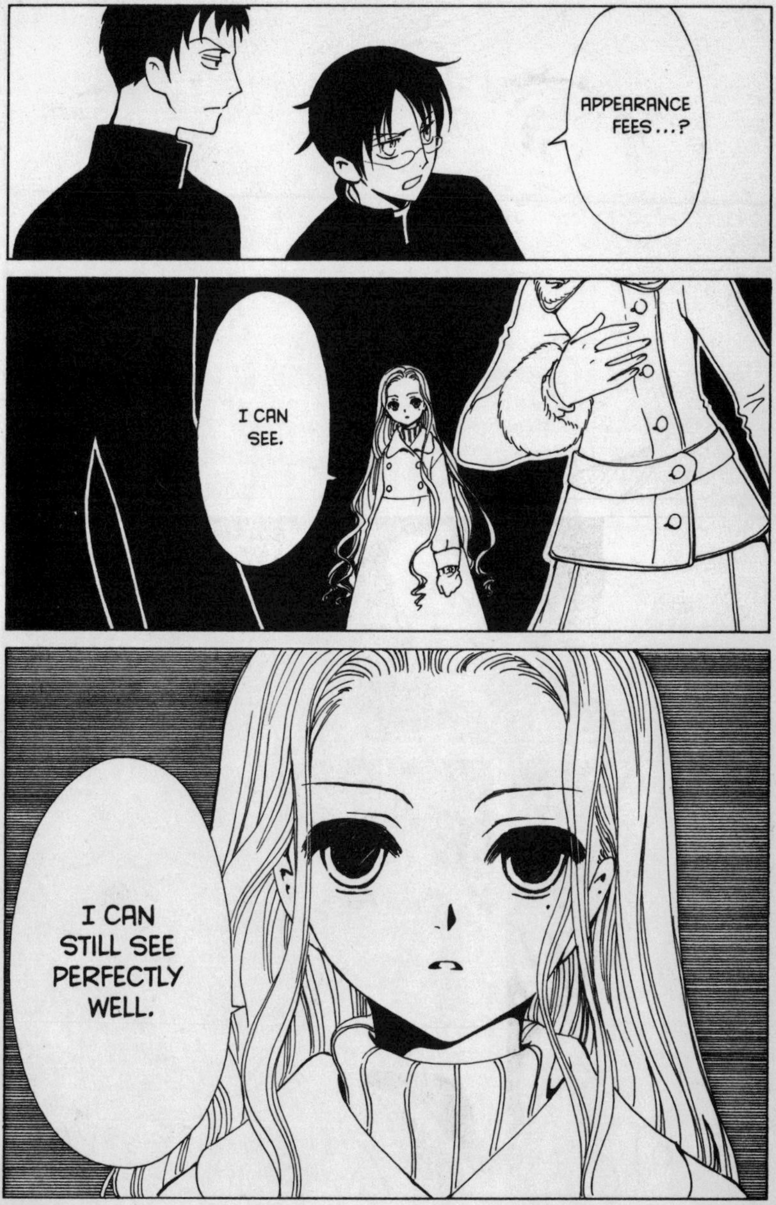
APPEARANCE FEES...?
I CAN SEE.
I CAN STILL SEE PERFECTLY WELL.

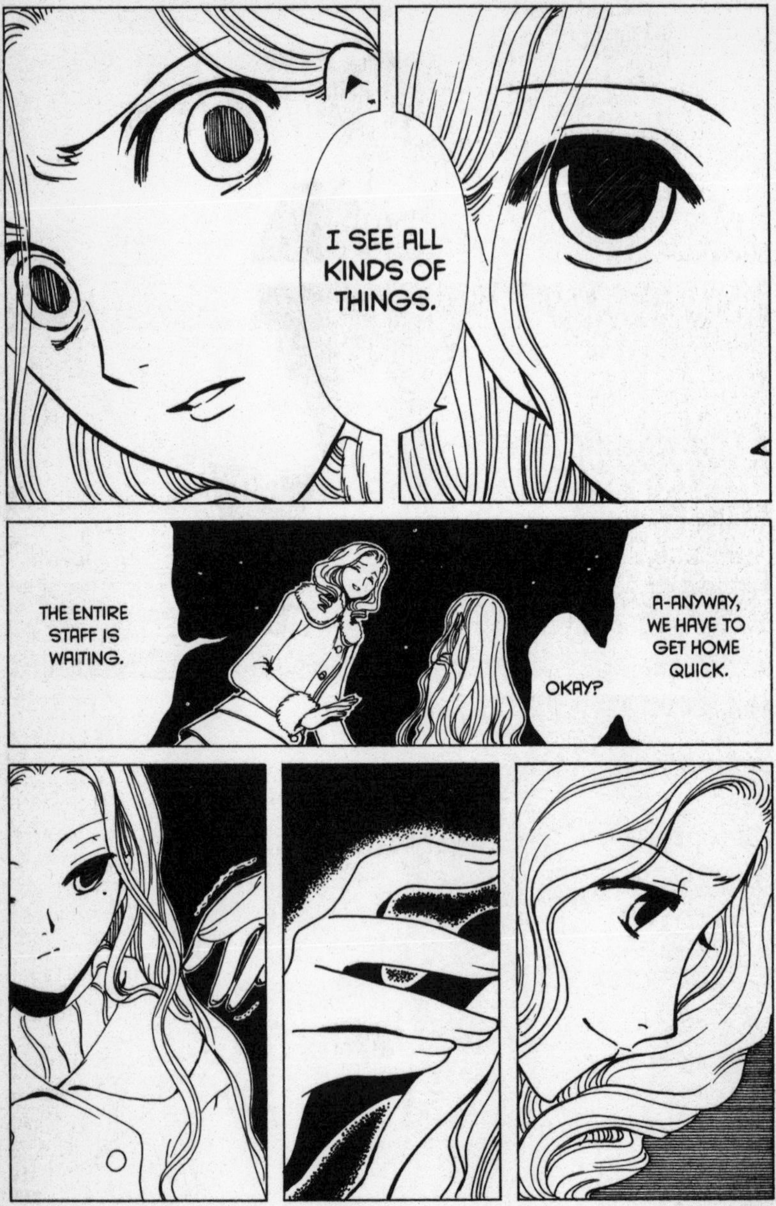
I SEE ALL KINDS OF THINGS.
A-ANYWAY, WE HAVE TO GET HOME QUICK.
OKAY?
THE ENTIRE STAFF IS WAITING.

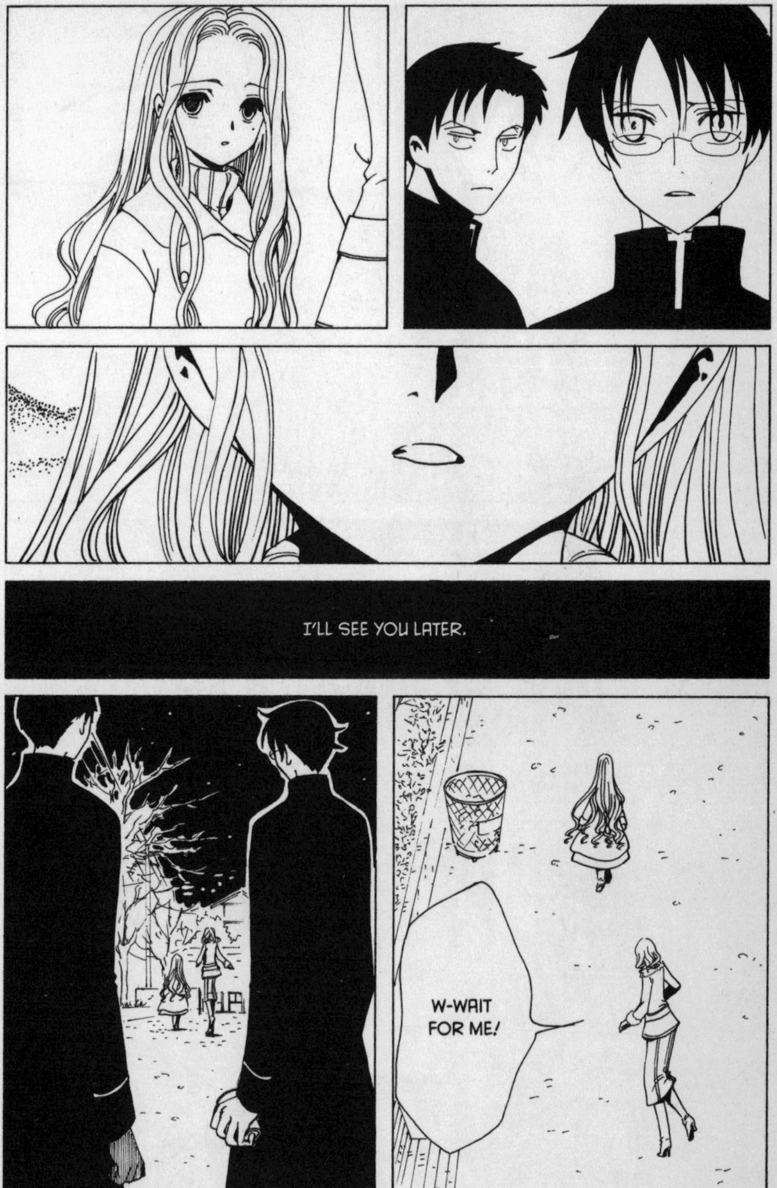
I'LL SEE YOU LATER.
W-WAIT FOR ME!

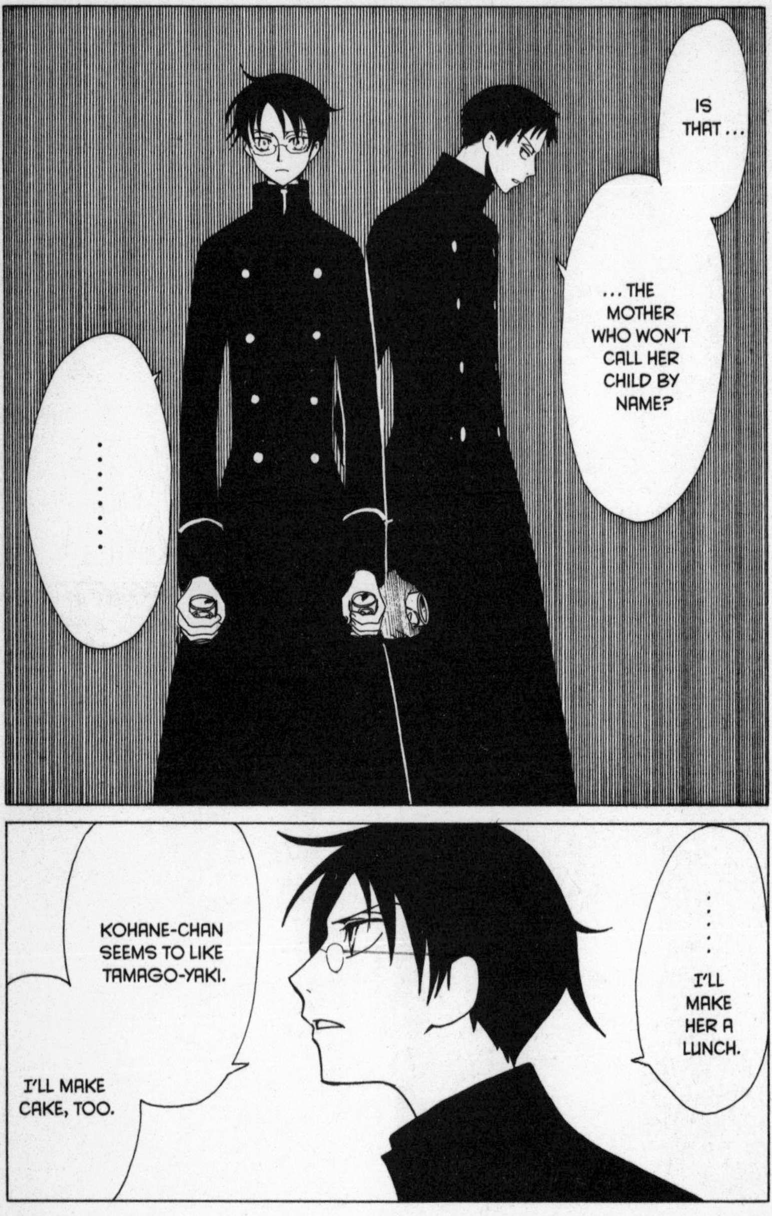
IS THAT . . .
. . . THE MOTHER WHO WON'T CALL HER CHILD BY NAME?
. . . .
. . . . .
I'LL MAKE HER A LUNCH.
KOHANE-CHAN SEEMS TO LIKE TAMAGO-YAKI.
I'LL MAKE CAKE, TOO.

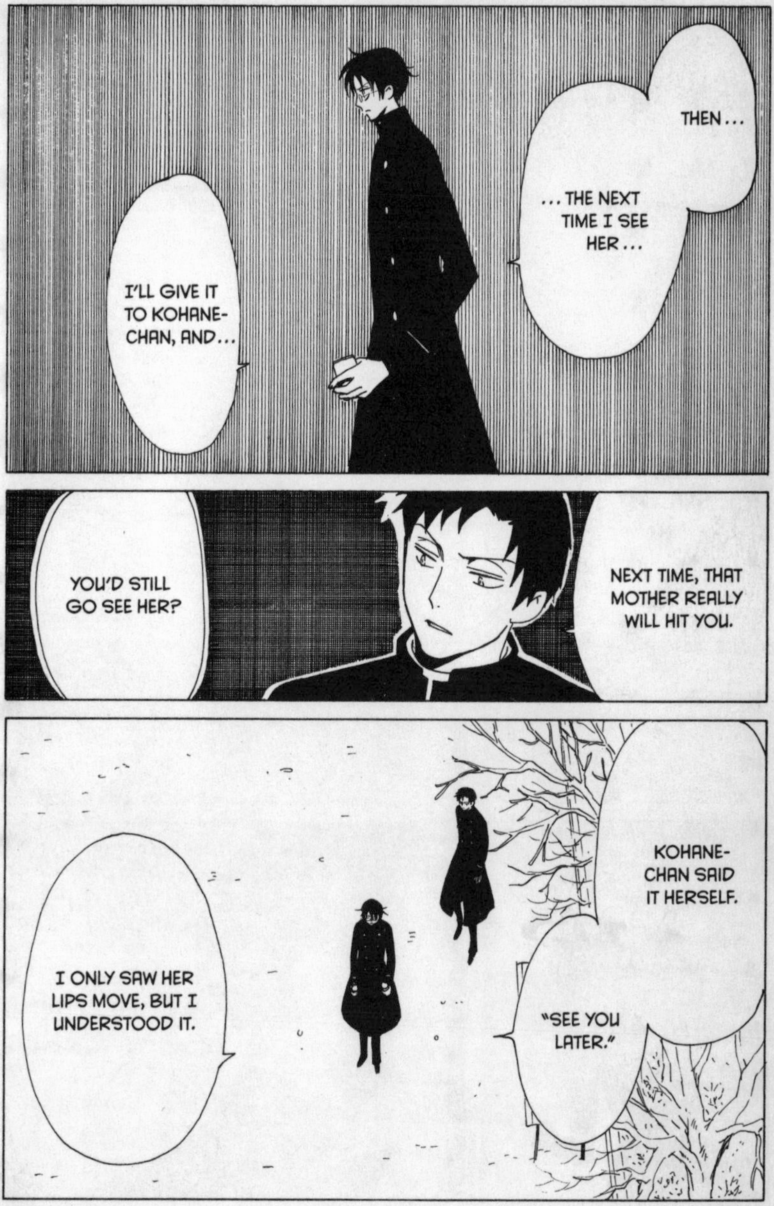
THEN...
...THE NEXT TIME I SEE HER...
I'LL GIVE IT TO KOHANE-CHAN, AND...
NEXT TIME, THAT MOTHER REALLY WILL HIT YOU.
YOU'D STILL GO SEE HER?
KOHANE-CHAN SAID IT HERSELF.
"SEE YOU LATER."
I ONLY SAW HER LIPS MOVE, BUT I UNDERSTOOD IT.

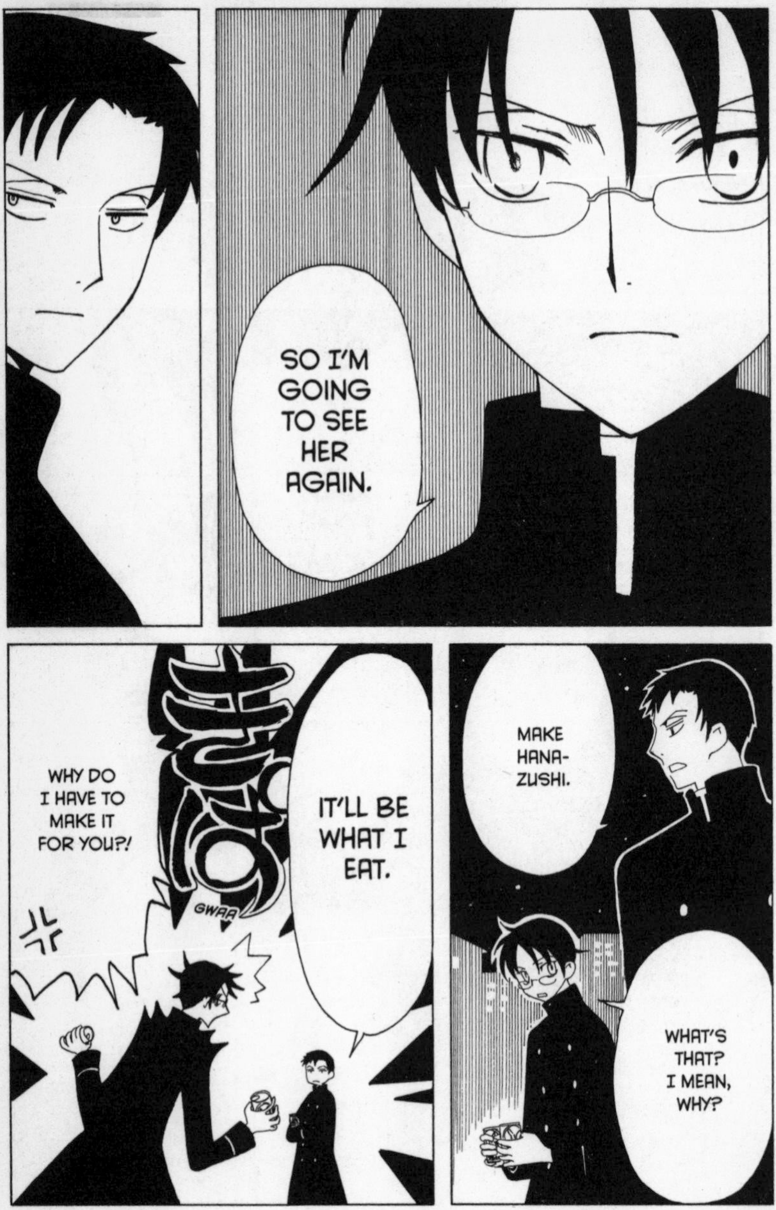
SO I'M GOING TO SEE HER AGAIN.
MAKE HANA-ZUSHI.
WHAT'S THAT? I MEAN, WHY?
IT'LL BE WHAT I EAT.
GWAA
WHY DO I HAVE TO MAKE IT FOR YOU?!

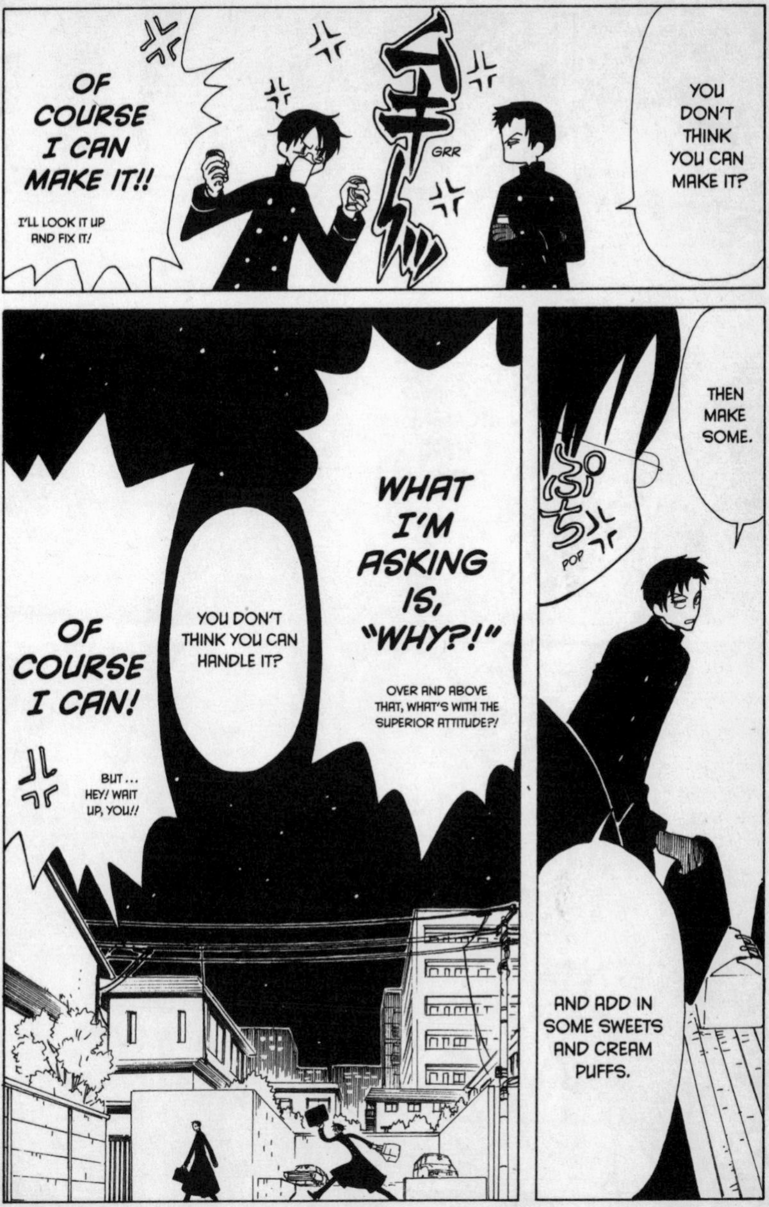
YOU DON'T THINK YOU CAN MAKE IT?
GRR
OF COURSE I CAN MAKE IT!!
I'LL LOOK IT UP AND FIX IT!
THEN MAKE SOME.
POP
AND ADD IN SOME SWEETS AND CREAM PUFFS.
WHAT I'M ASKING IS, "WHY?!"
OVER AND ABOVE THAT, WHAT'S WITH THE SUPERIOR ATTITUDE?!
YOU DON'T THINK YOU CAN HANDLE IT?
OF COURSE I CAN!
BUT... HEY! WAIT UP, YOU!!

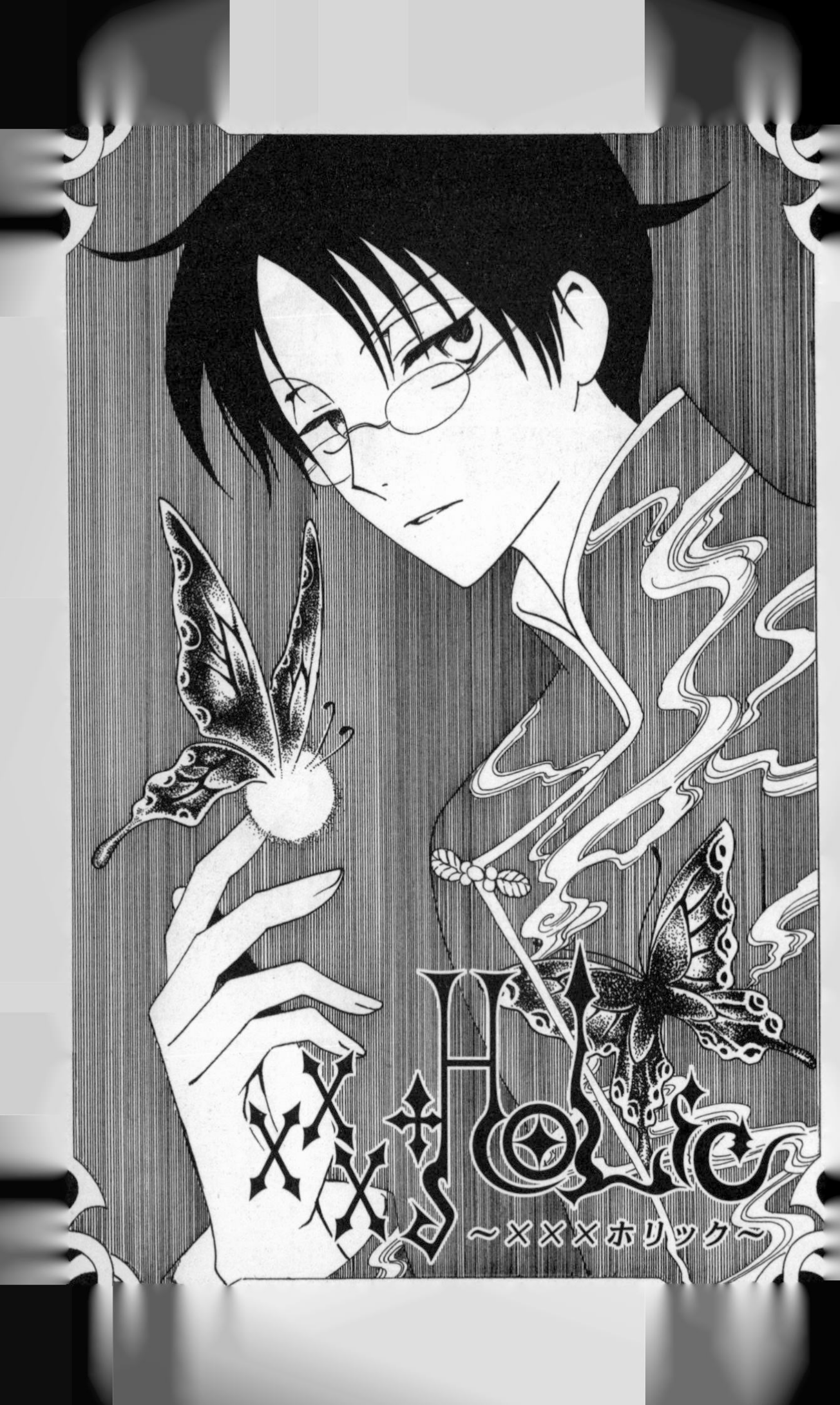
xxxHOLiC
～×××ホリック～

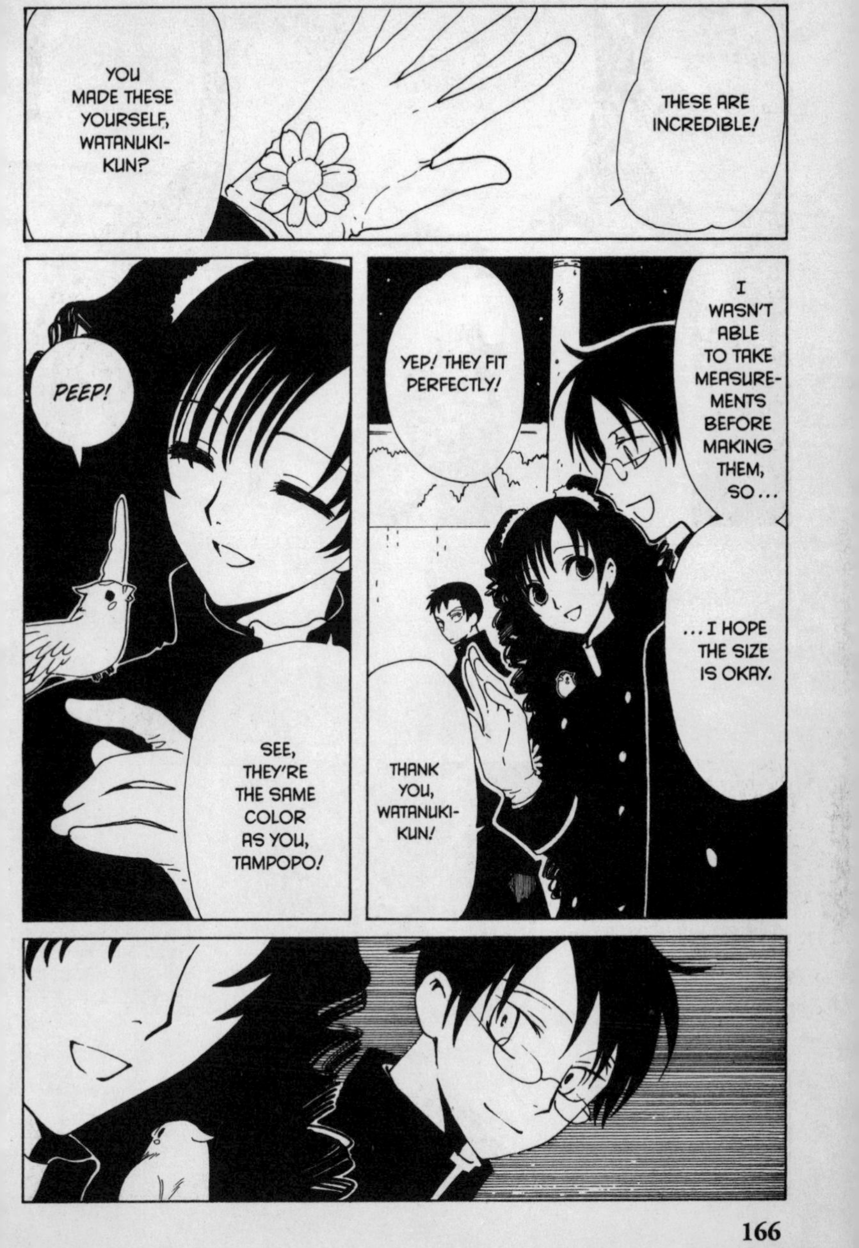

THESE ARE INCREDIBLE!
YOU MADE THESE YOURSELF, WATANUKI-KUN?
I WASN'T ABLE TO TAKE MEASUREMENTS BEFORE MAKING THEM, SO...
...I HOPE THE SIZE IS OKAY.
YEP! THEY FIT PERFECTLY!
THANK YOU, WATANUKI-KUN!
PEEP!
SEE, THEY'RE THE SAME COLOR AS YOU, TAMPOPO!

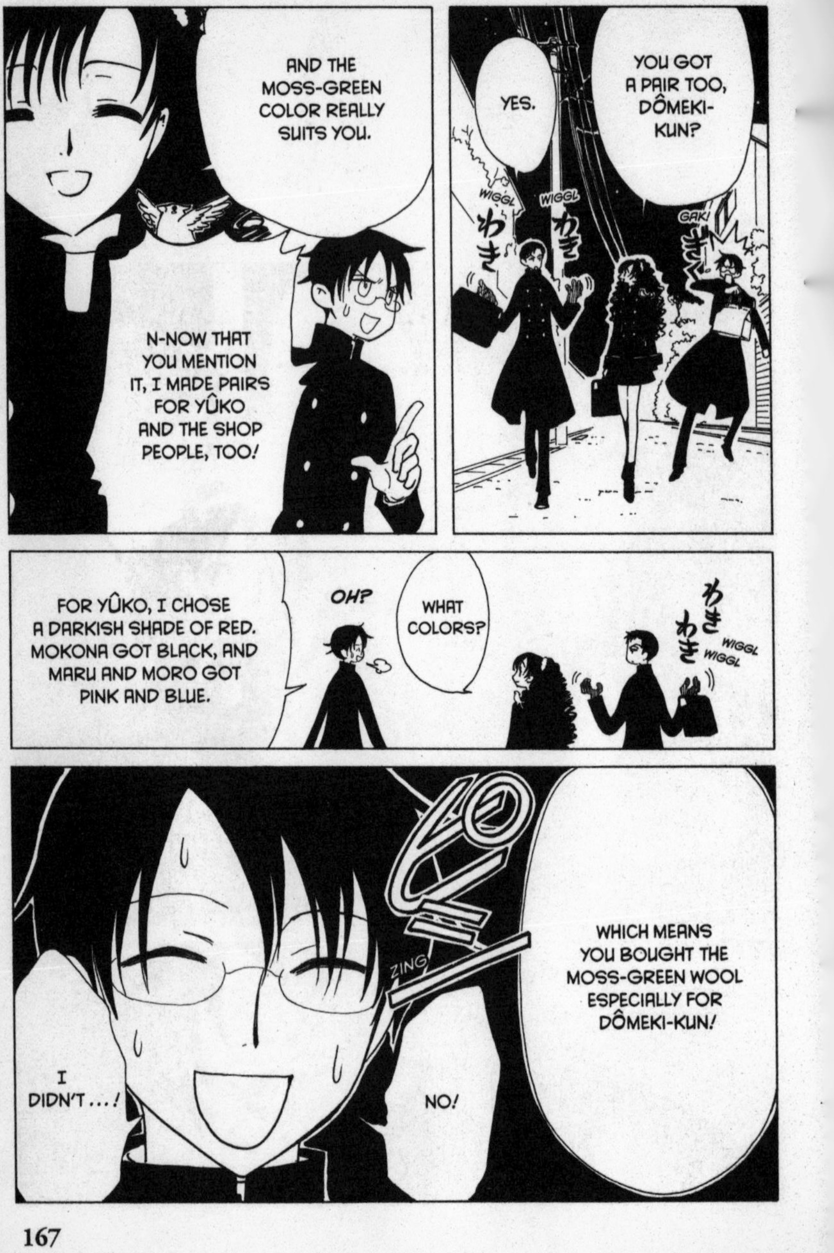
YOU GOT A PAIR TOO, DÔMEKI-KUN?
YES.
GAK!
ぎく
WIGGL
わき
WIGGL
わき
AND THE MOSS-GREEN COLOR REALLY SUITS YOU.
N-NOW THAT YOU MENTION IT, I MADE PAIRS FOR YÛKO AND THE SHOP PEOPLE, TOO!
わき わき
WIGGL WIGGL
WHAT COLORS?
OH?
FOR YÛKO, I CHOSE A DARKISH SHADE OF RED. MOKONA GOT BLACK, AND MARU AND MORO GOT PINK AND BLUE.
WHICH MEANS YOU BOUGHT THE MOSS-GREEN WOOL ESPECIALLY FOR DÔMEKI-KUN!
ZING
NO!
I DIDN'T...!

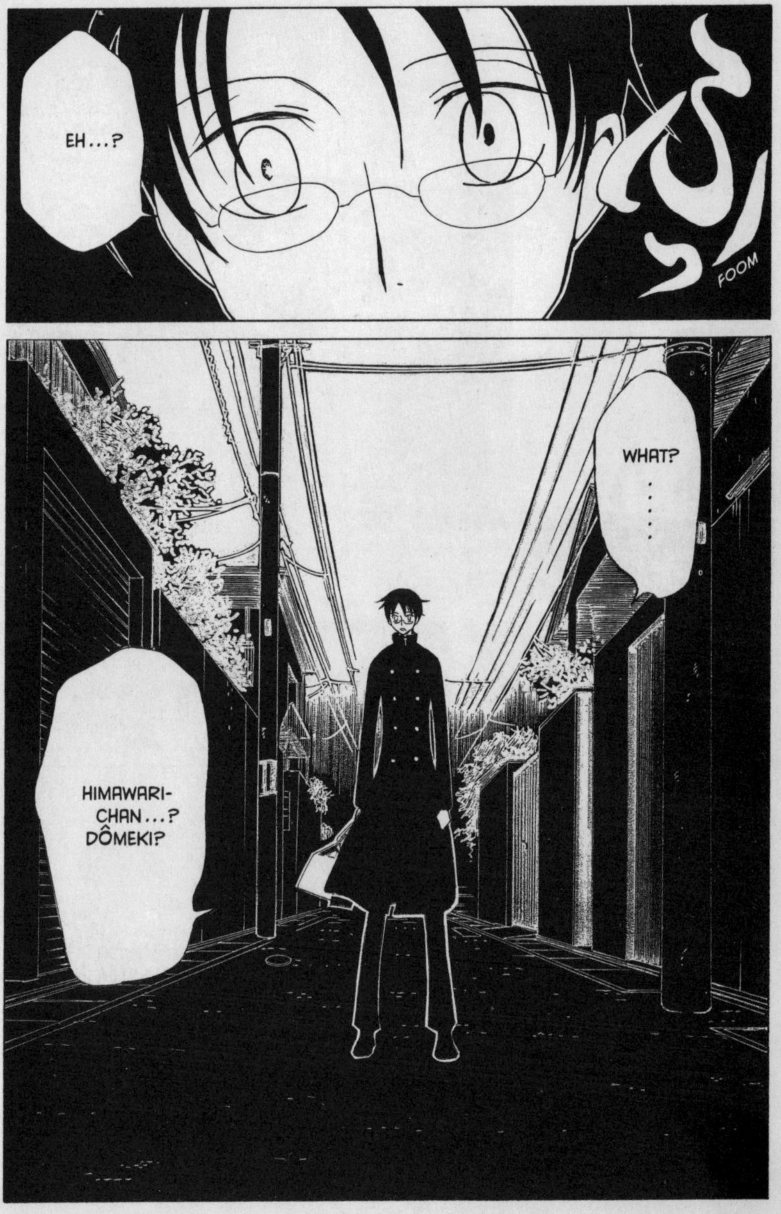
EH...?
FOOM
WHAT? ......
HIMAWARI-CHAN...? DÔMEKI?

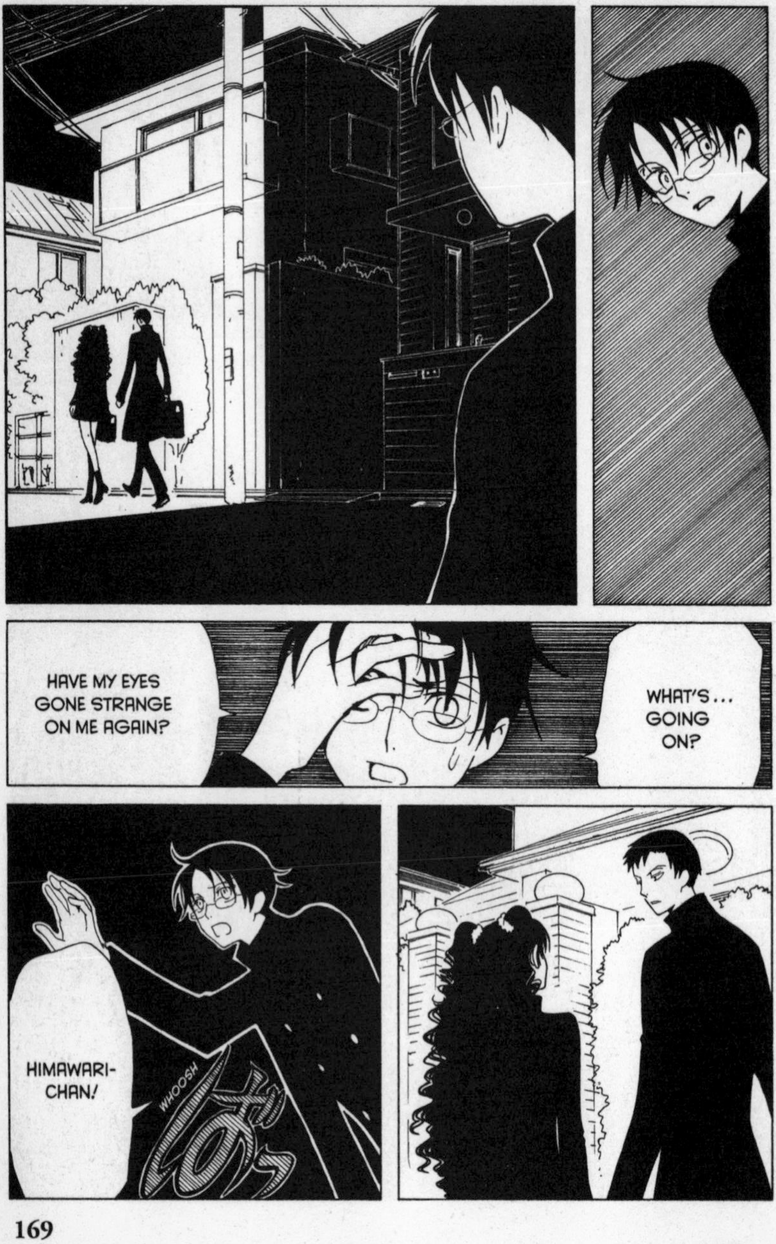
WHAT'S... GOING ON?
HAVE MY EYES GONE STRANGE ON ME AGAIN?
HIMAWARI-CHAN!
WHOOSH

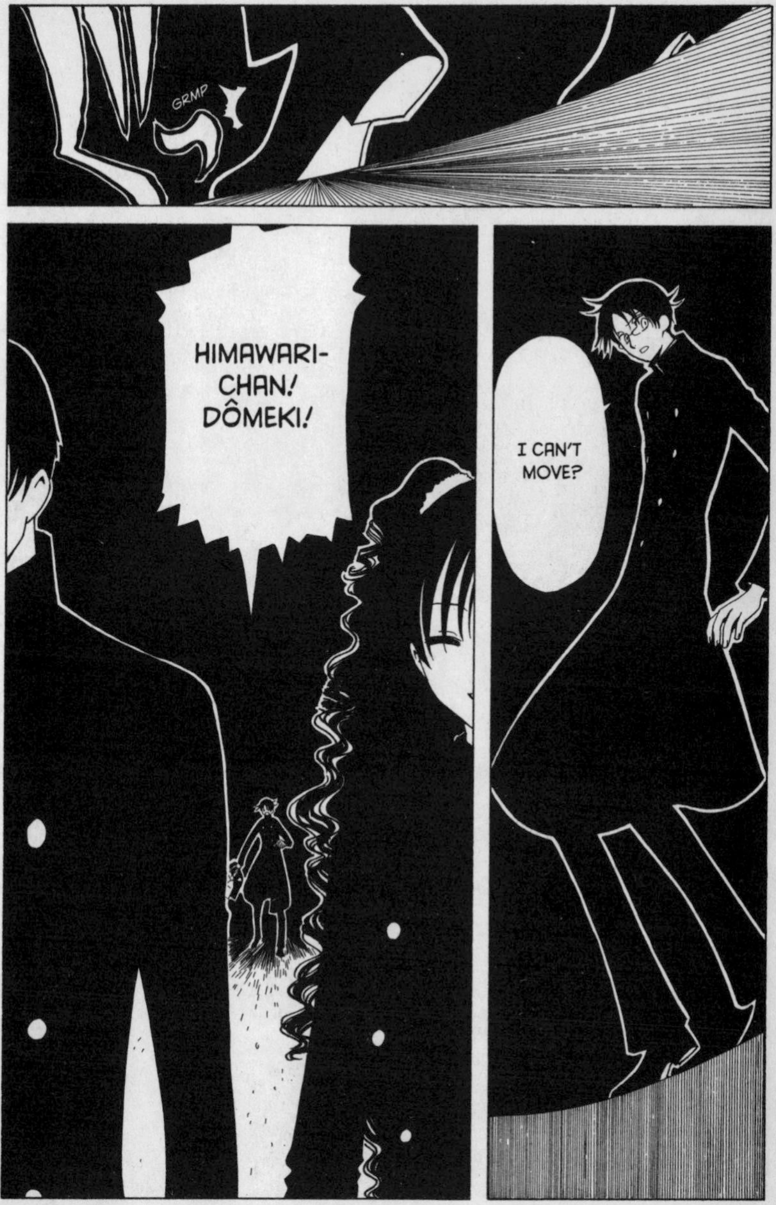
GRMP
I CAN'T MOVE?
HIMAWARI-CHAN! DÔMEKI!

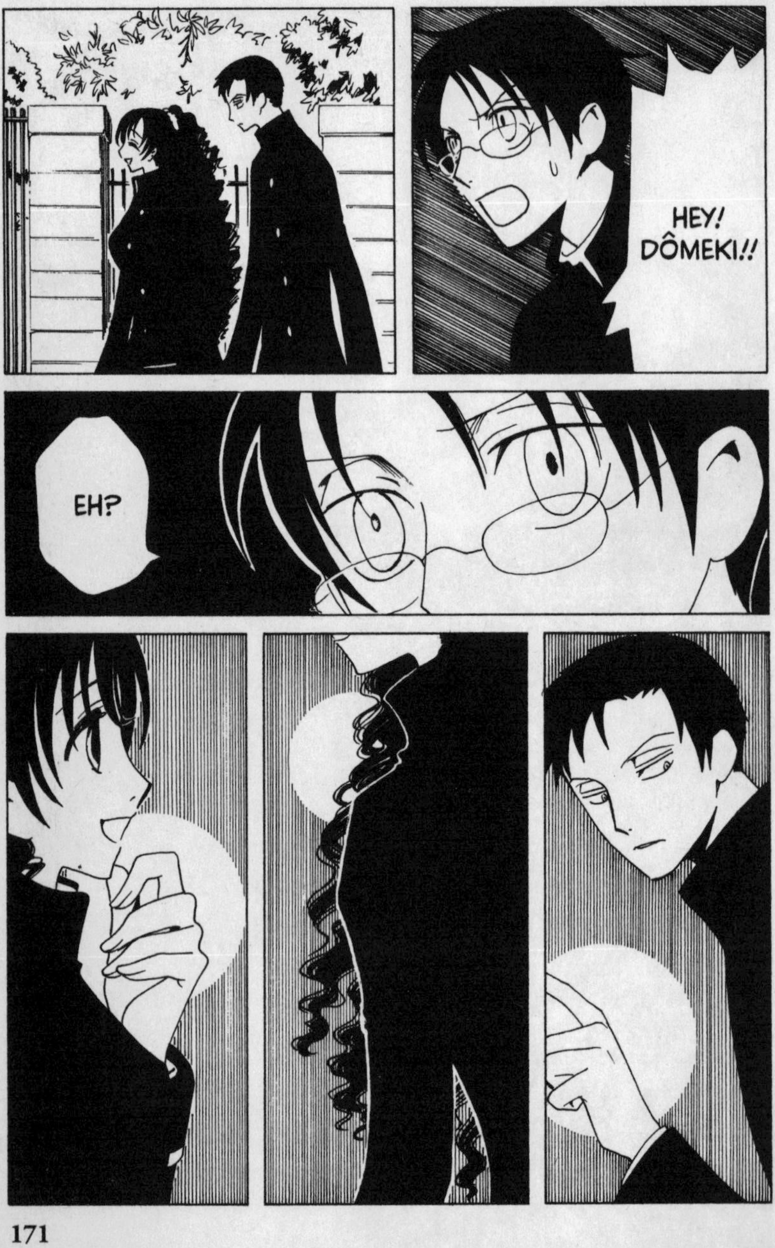
HEY! DÔMEKI!!
EH?

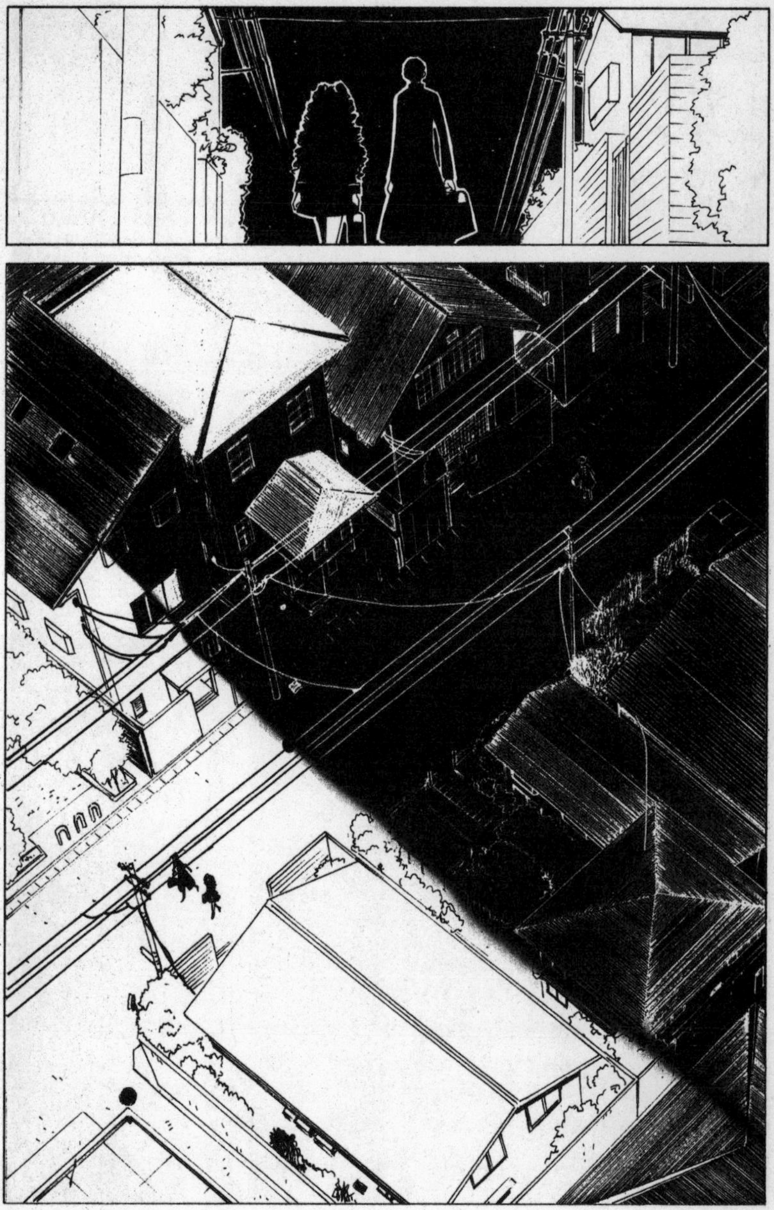

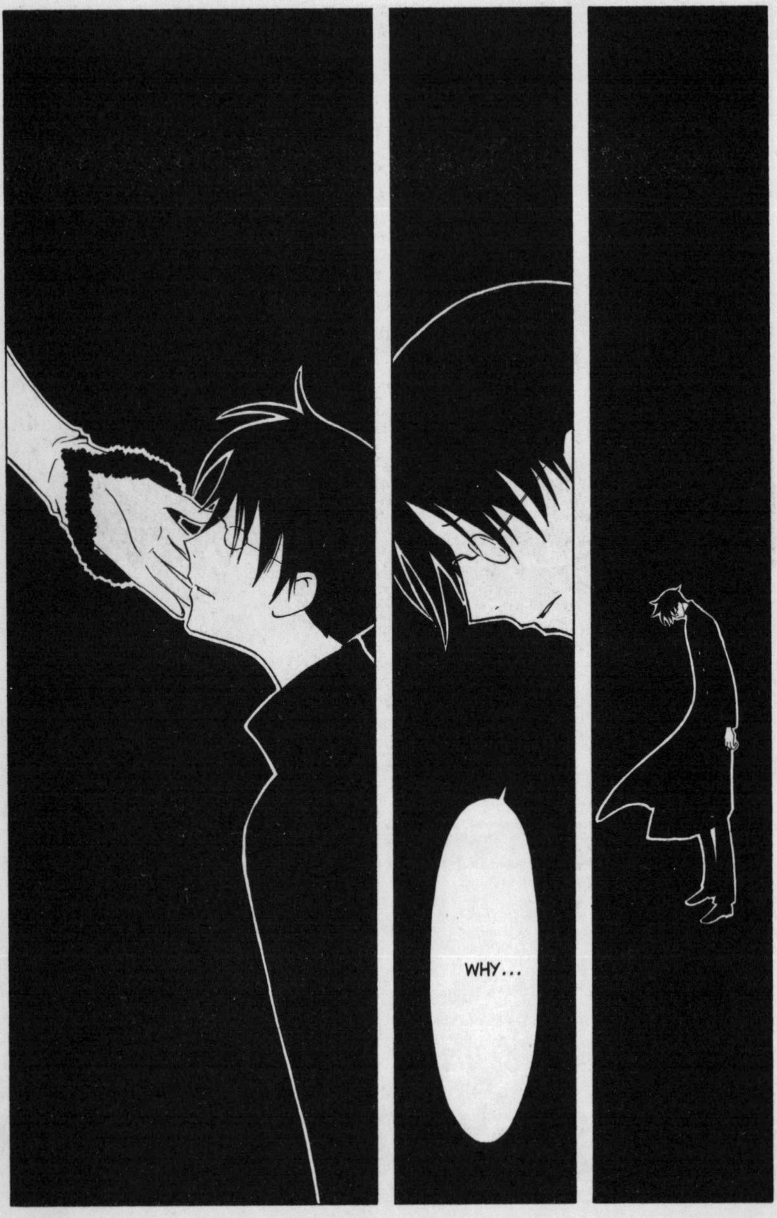
WHY...

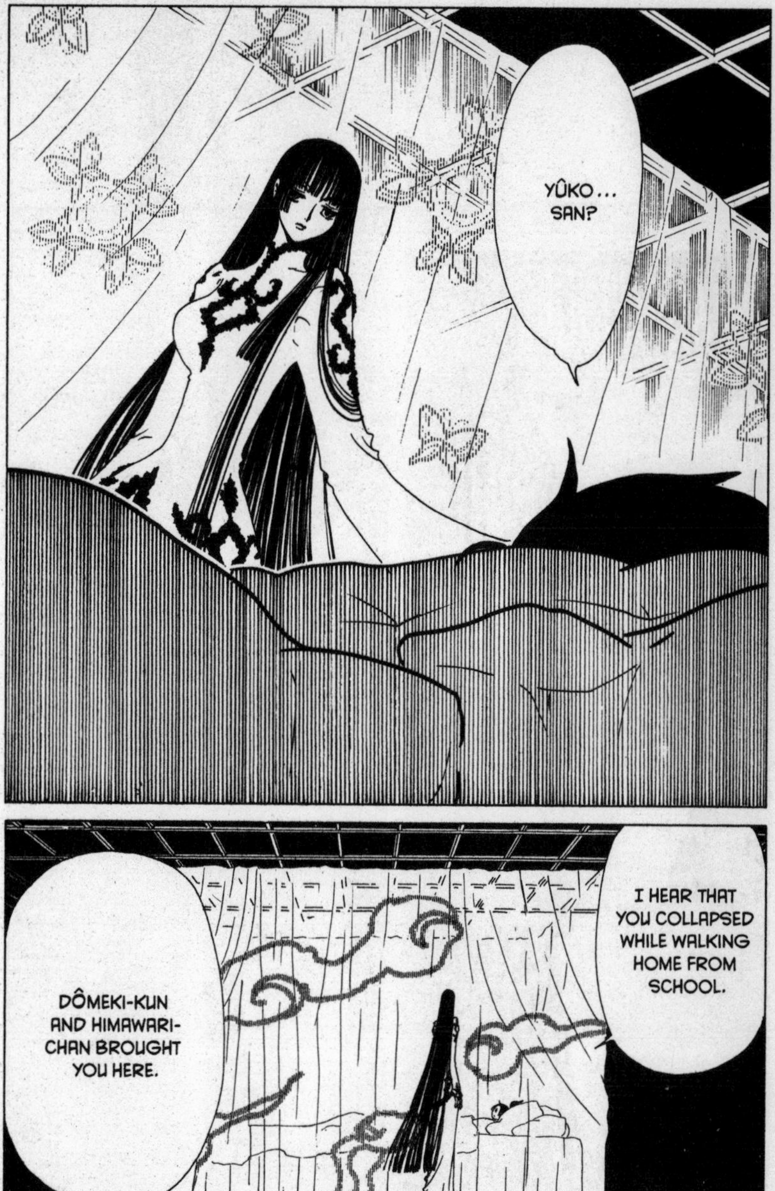
YÛKO... SAN?
I HEAR THAT YOU COLLAPSED WHILE WALKING HOME FROM SCHOOL.
DÔMEKI-KUN AND HIMAWARI-CHAN BROUGHT YOU HERE.

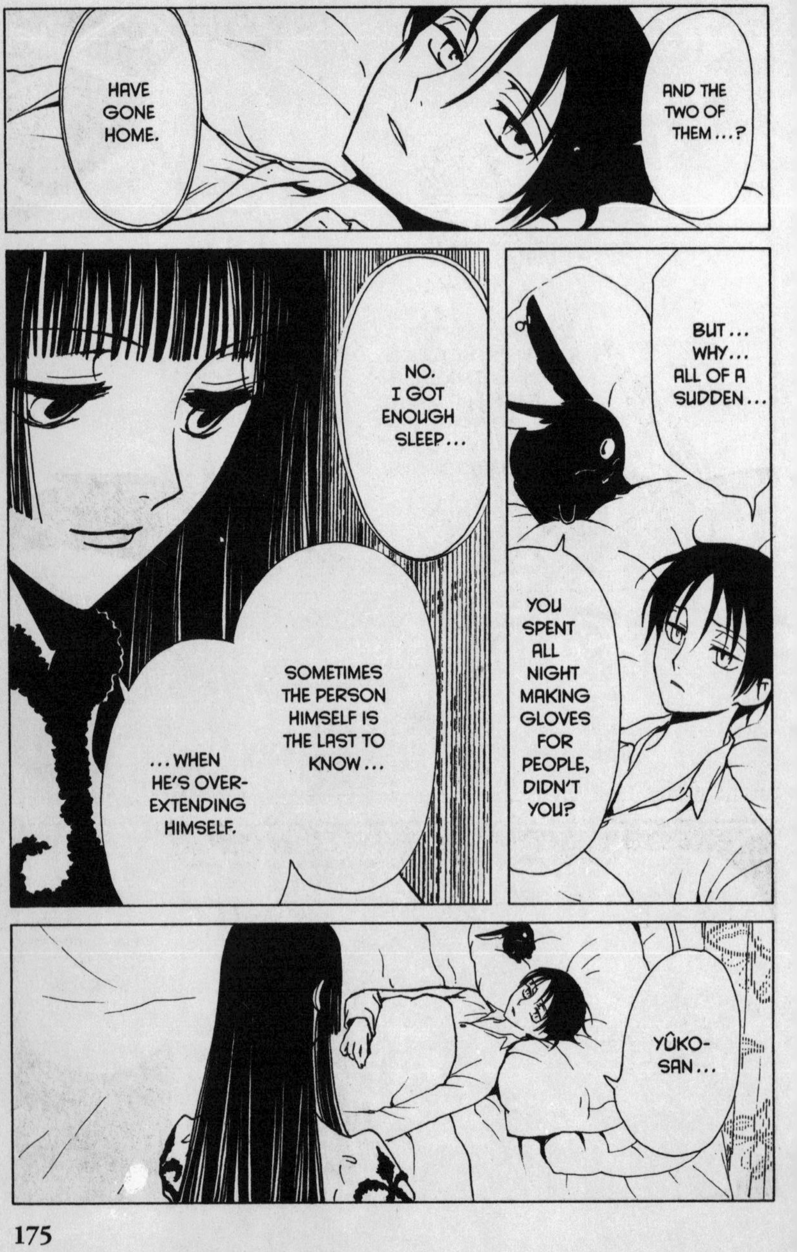
AND THE TWO OF THEM...?
HAVE GONE HOME.
BUT... WHY... ALL OF A SUDDEN...
YOU SPENT ALL NIGHT MAKING GLOVES FOR PEOPLE, DIDN'T YOU?
NO. I GOT ENOUGH SLEEP...
SOMETIMES THE PERSON HIMSELF IS THE LAST TO KNOW...
...WHEN HE'S OVER-EXTENDING HIMSELF.
YÛKO-SAN...

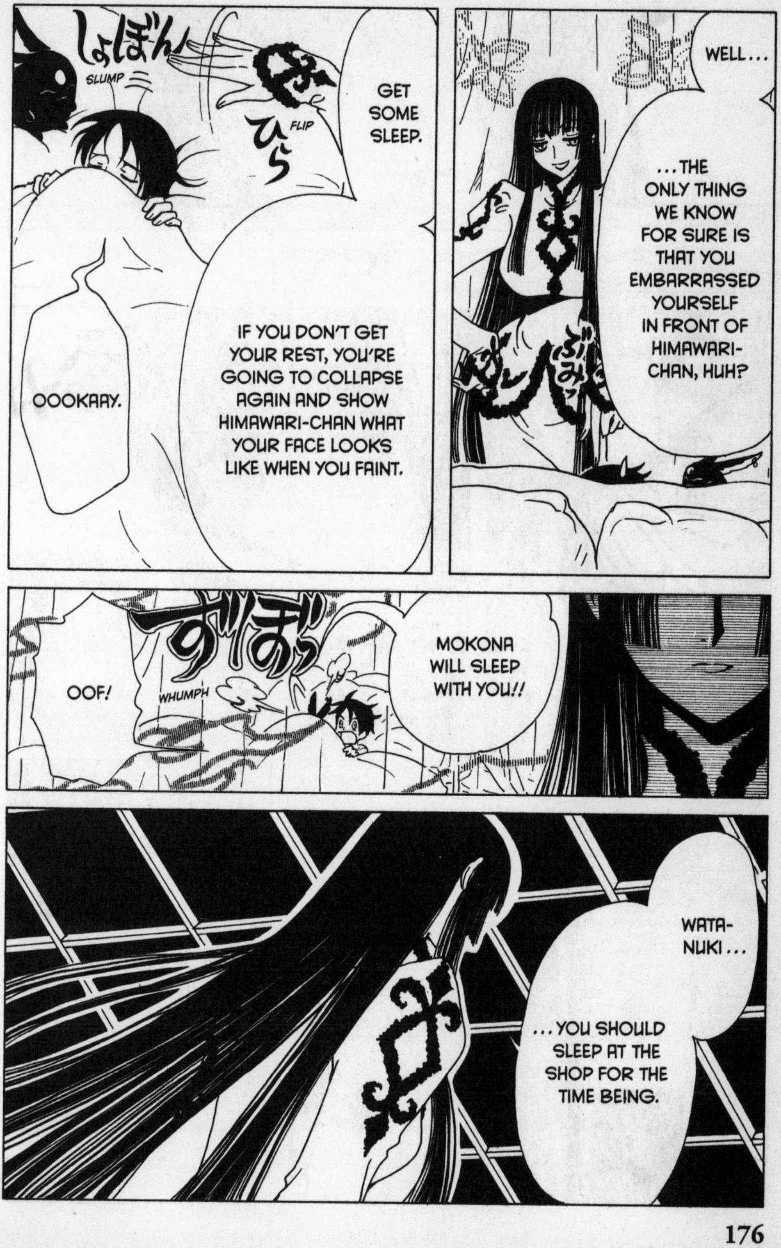
WELL...
...THE ONLY THING WE KNOW FOR SURE IS THAT YOU EMBARRASSED YOURSELF IN FRONT OF HIMAWARI-CHAN, HUH?
GET SOME SLEEP.
FLIP
SLUMP
IF YOU DON'T GET YOUR REST, YOU'RE GOING TO COLLAPSE AGAIN AND SHOW HIMAWARI-CHAN WHAT YOUR FACE LOOKS LIKE WHEN YOU FAINT.
OOOKAAY.
MOKONA WILL SLEEP WITH YOU!!
WHUMPH
OOF!
WATA-NUKI...
...YOU SHOULD SLEEP AT THE SHOP FOR THE TIME BEING.

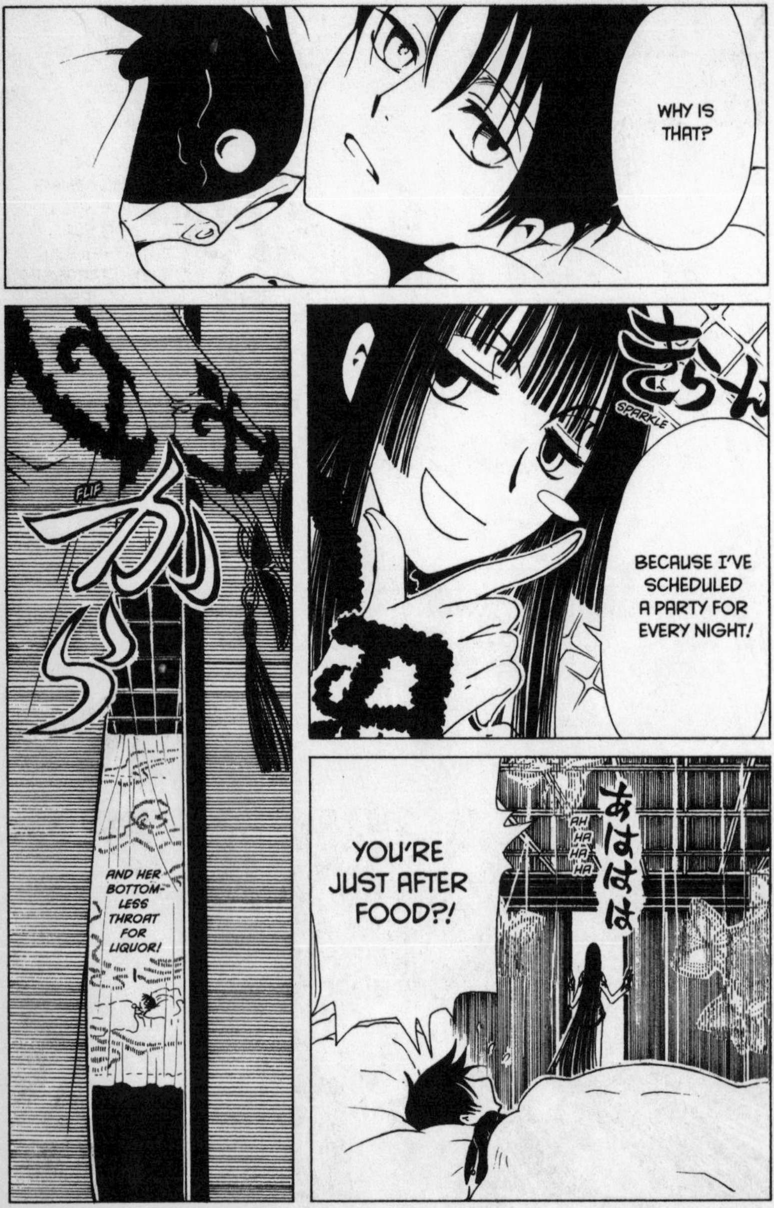

WHY IS THAT?
きらん
SPARKLE
BECAUSE I'VE SCHEDULED A PARTY FOR EVERY NIGHT!
あははは
AH HA HA HA
YOU'RE JUST AFTER FOOD?!
FLIP
AND HER BOTTOM-LESS THROAT FOR LIQUOR!

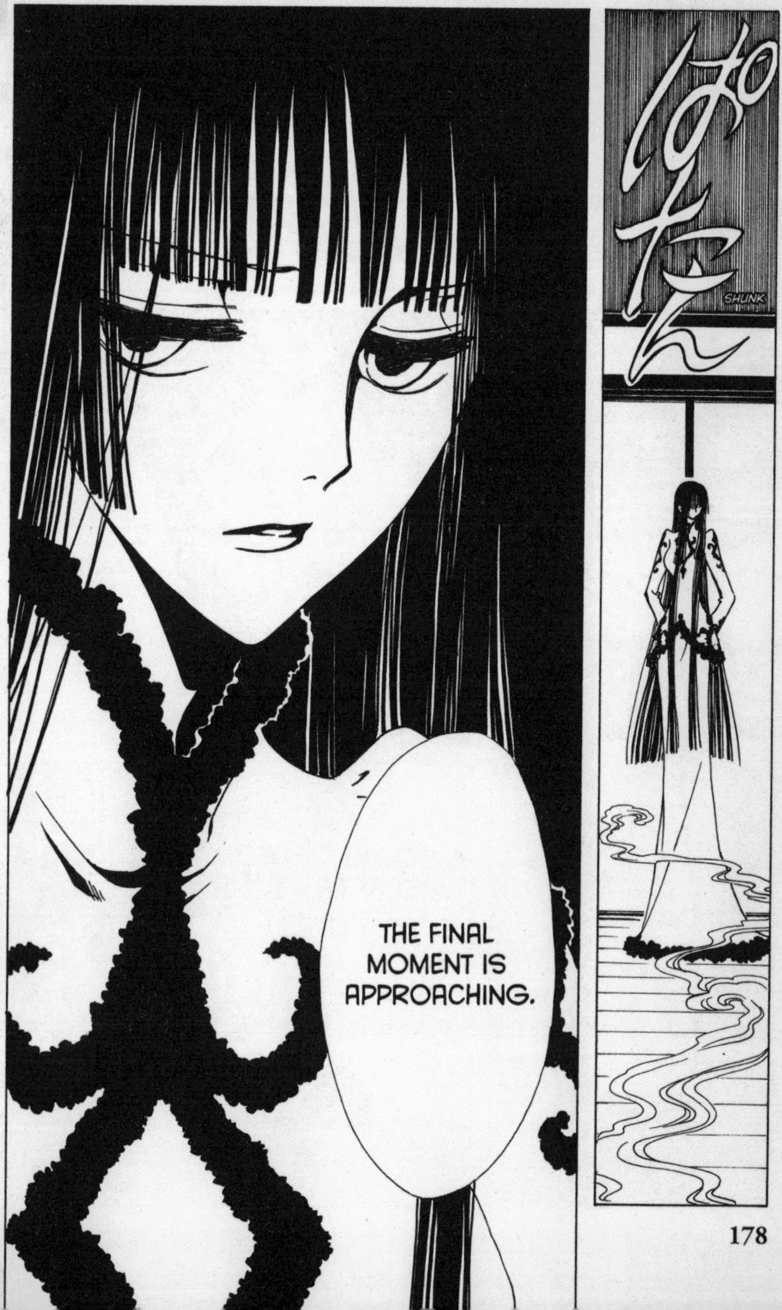
ぱたん
SHUNK
THE FINAL MOMENT IS APPROACHING.

⊰ Continued ⊱

in *xxxHOLiC*, volume 12

About the Creators

CLAMP is a group of four women who have become the most popular manga artists in America—Satsuki Igarashi, Tsubaki Nekoi, Mokona, and Ageha Ohkawa. They started out as *doujinshi* (fan comics) creators, but their skill and craft brought them to the attention of publishers very quickly. Their first work from a major publisher was RG Veda, but their first mass success was with *Magic Knight Rayearth*. From there, they went on to write many series, including Cardcaptor Sakura and Chobits, two of the most popular manga in the United States. Like many Japanese manga artists, they prefer to avoid the spotlight, and little is known about them personally.

CLAMP is currently publishing three series in Japan: Tsubasa and xxxHOLiC with Kodansha and Gohou Drug with Kadokawa.

Translation Notes

Japanese is a tricky language for most Westerners, and translation is often more art than science. For your edification and reading pleasure, here are notes on some of the places where we could have gone in a different direction or where a Japanese cultural reference is used.

Page 4, Sick Bed Visit (*Omimai*)

The Japanese traditionally make bedside visits to someone very sick or hospitalized. Normally one brings a gift of fruit, nuts, sweets, or flowers, then after presenting it sits down and converses with the patient for a while.

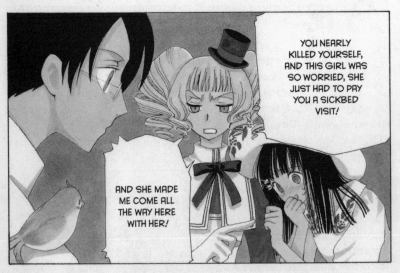

YOU NEARLY KILLED YOURSELF, AND THIS GIRL WAS SO WORRIED, SHE JUST HAD TO PAY YOU A SICKBED VISIT!

AND SHE MADE ME COME ALL THE WAY HERE WITH HER!

Page 15, Gonta-kun

There was an NHK public-television children's show in the '70s and '80s named "Dekirukana" (I Wonder if I Can Make This). In it a

showman named Noppo-san, whose talents included pantomime and tap dancing, was helped in various kids-style build-it projects by a big, silent, brown cross between H. R. Puf'n'stuf and a gopher, a character named Gonta-kun. Gonta-kun wanted to be like Noppo-san, so he'd try all the projects and constantly fail. The series ended about the time Watanuki would have been born, so he would have had to hear about the show from some adult (Yûko) rather than watch it himself.

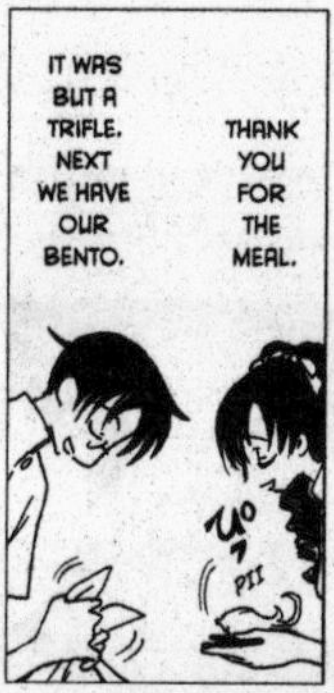
THANK YOU FOR THE MEAL.
IT WAS BUT A TRIFLE. NEXT WE HAVE OUR BENTO.
PII

Page 24, Thank You for the Meal

This is the best I could come up with as an English rendering of the standard Japanese phrase *Gochisô-sama deshita*. "It was but a trifle" is an English translation of a formal (but not so often used) response to *Gochisô-sama*: *Osomatsu-sama deshita*, or "it was, in fact, a poor performance."

Page 24: *Bento*

As described in the notes of earlier volumes, *bento* is the word not only for the traditional-style Japanese lunch box but also for the lunch inside. One can buy *bento* in convenience stores, although the box they come in is simply a standard Styrofoam tray. In Watanuki's case, his hand-made lunch is packed in a traditional *bento* box.

Page 44, Mugetsu Shôchû

Shôchû is a clear liquor most commonly made from rice or potatoes (see notes in volume 10 for Soba Jôchû). Mugetsu is a *shôchû* that is made in Miyazaki prefecture near the southeasternmost tip of the southern island of Kyushu.

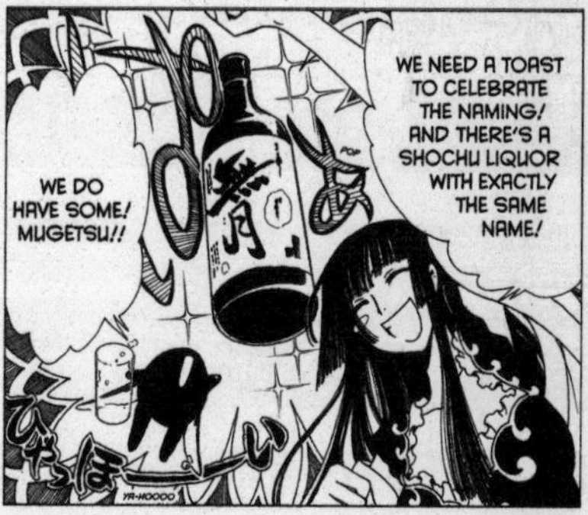
WE NEED A TOAST TO CELEBRATE THE NAMING! AND THERE'S A SHOCHU LIQUOR WITH EXACTLY THE SAME NAME!
WE DO HAVE SOME! MUGETSU!!

Page 69, Broiled *Harasu* with Salt

Harasu is the belly portion of salmon, and *shioyaki* is to broil fish with salt. Most Japanese gas ranges include a gas broiler designed especially for fish. That is probably what Watanuki would use for his *shioyaki* broiling of the portion of salmon.

Page 69, *Gokoku* Rice

Gokoku is a mixed rice dish containing rice, wheat or barley, beans, and two different kinds of millet.

Page 81, *Kanmiya*

A *kanmiya* is a Japanese-style sweets shop. Many of the sweets in a *kanmiya* are based on *an*, a sweet-bean paste that is found in a lot of Japanese confectionary, but many other kinds of desserts can be found in such shops.

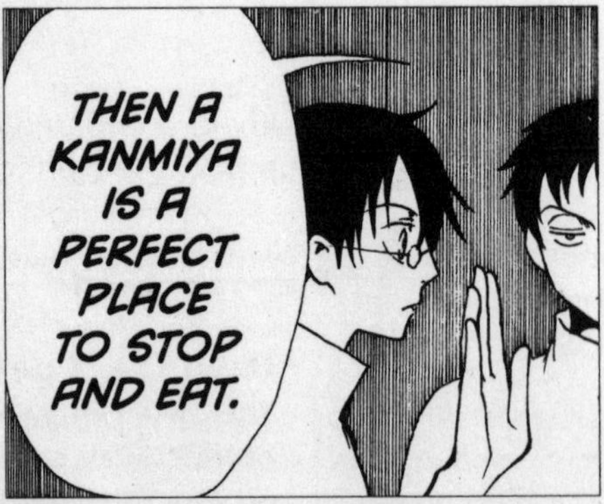
THEN A KANMIYA IS A PERFECT PLACE TO STOP AND EAT.

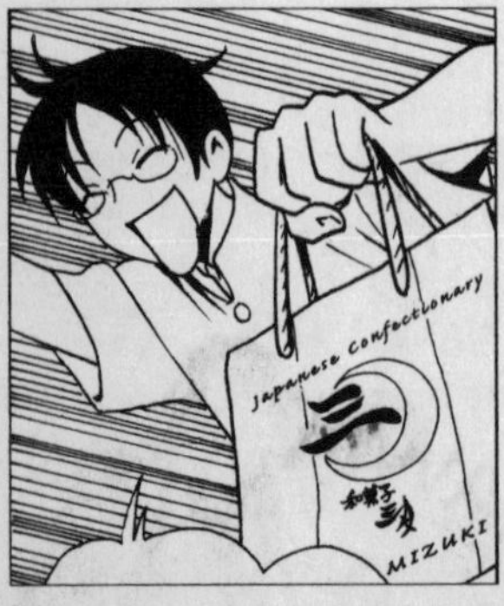
Japanese confectionary
MIZUKI

Page 84, *Kuromitsu Kanten*

Kuromitsu is a syrup made from brown sugar and water, and *kanten* is a type of Japanese gelatin. So the sweets that Watanuki brought back are gelatin squares flavored with a sweet, dark-brown syrup.

Page 92, Entering a House with Shoes on

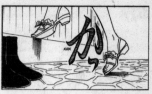

The second panel on page 92 may not have been noted by some Western readers, but Japanese readers would recognize the significance of it. It is an ingrained habit of the Japanese to take off their shoes before entering a home or traditional-style place of business such as Yûko's shop. To step into such a shop with one's shoes on is a measured insult. The girl didn't just forget to take off her shoes, she used the gesture to indicate how displeased she was.

Page 122, *Nabe*

Nabe is the word for a boiling pot used to make stews and similar dishes, but it is also used for the food that is cooked within the pot. One tends to crave *nabe* on cold days, since it is associated with a hot stewy soup filled with meat and vegetables.

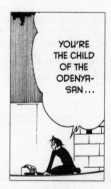

YOU'RE THE CHILD OF THE ODENYA-SAN...

Page 124, *Odenya-san*

The owner of a shop specializing in a single product may be called by the title of product-*ya-san*. For example, the owner of a ramen shop may be called a *ramenya-san*. An owner of an electronics shop may be called a *denkiya-san*. In this case, the parent fox spirit who makes *oden* is an *odenya-san*. You can find out more about *oden* in the notes for volume 3.

Page 124, *Hyakki Yakô* and Being Saved

Watanuki and Dômeki were discovered as the only humans in a parade of spirits and magical creatures in the first story in volume 6, after which they were saved by the young fox spirit Watanuki met in volume 3. There is more information on the parade (the *Hyakki Yakô*) in the notes for volume 6.

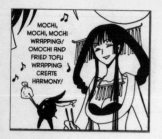

MOCHI, MOCHI, MOCHI WRAPPING! OMOCHI AND FRIED TOFU WRAPPING CREATE HARMONY!

Page 127, Mokona's Songs

Not for lack of trying, but I couldn't find out whether Mokona's songs were made up by Mokona or if they're actual songs about *oden*. In any case, Mokona sings about the traditional triangular fishcakes that one finds floating in the *oden* broth. The second one is about rice paste (*mochi*) that is stuffed inside a "skin" of thin, fried tofu. The *oden* treat is the same as *inari* sushi but with rice paste inside rather than sweetened rice.

Page 161, *Tamago-yaki*

The *tamago-yaki* that Watanuki is talking about is *dashimaki tamago*, an egg dish similar to an omelet that is spiced with soup stock and rolled into a thick cake. See the notes in volume 10 for more details.

Page 163, *Hanazushi*

Hanazushi is rolled sushi that in one way or another resembles a flower. One way to make it is to arrange colored rice and vegetables within the roll so that when it is cut, the rice and other foods form the picture of a flower on the face of the roll. Another is to have the vegetables and other ingredients extend out from the rolled sushi as if it were a flower arrangement.

TOMARE!

[STOP!]

You're going the wrong way!

Manga is a completely different type of reading experience.

To start at the *beginning*, go to the *end*!

That's right! Authentic manga is read the traditional Japanese way—from right to left. Exactly the *opposite* of how American books are read. It's easy to follow: Just go to the other end of the book, and read each page—and each panel—from right side to left side, starting at the top right. Now you're experiencing manga as it was meant to be!

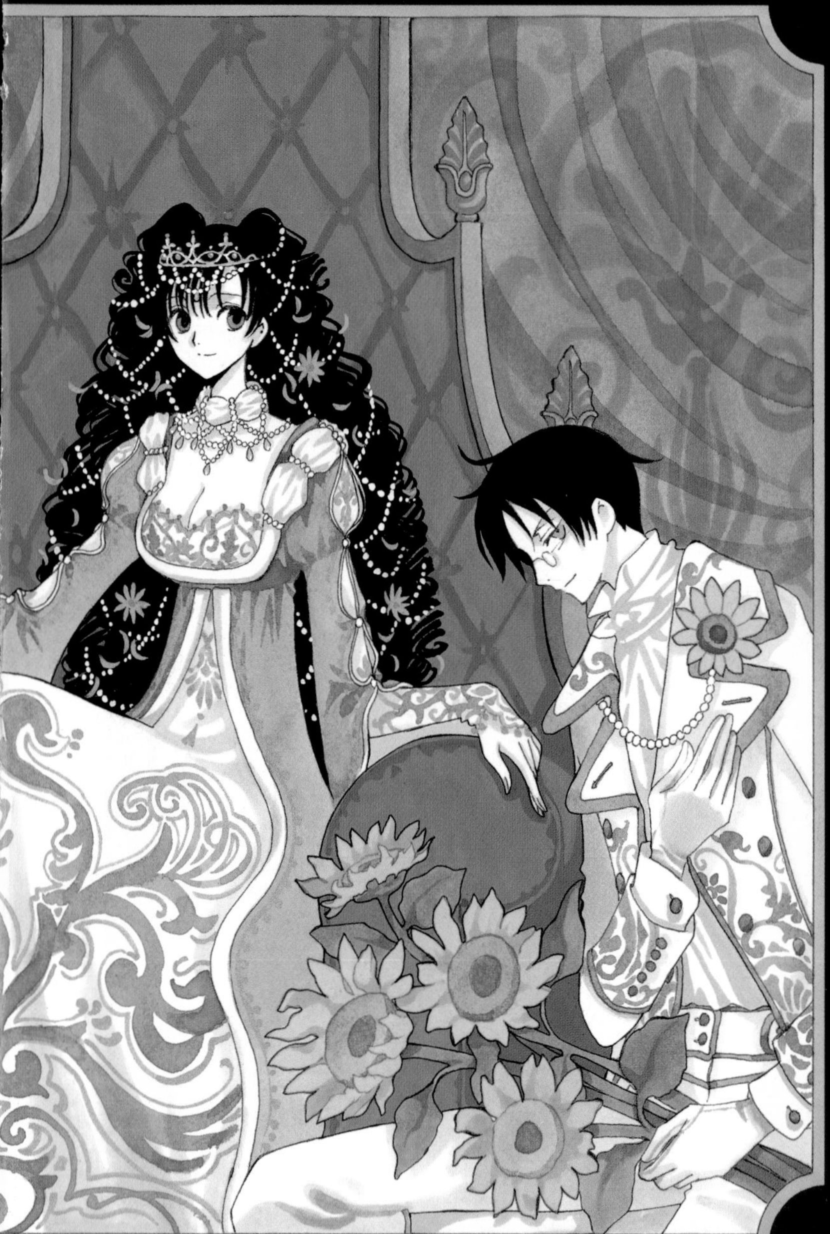

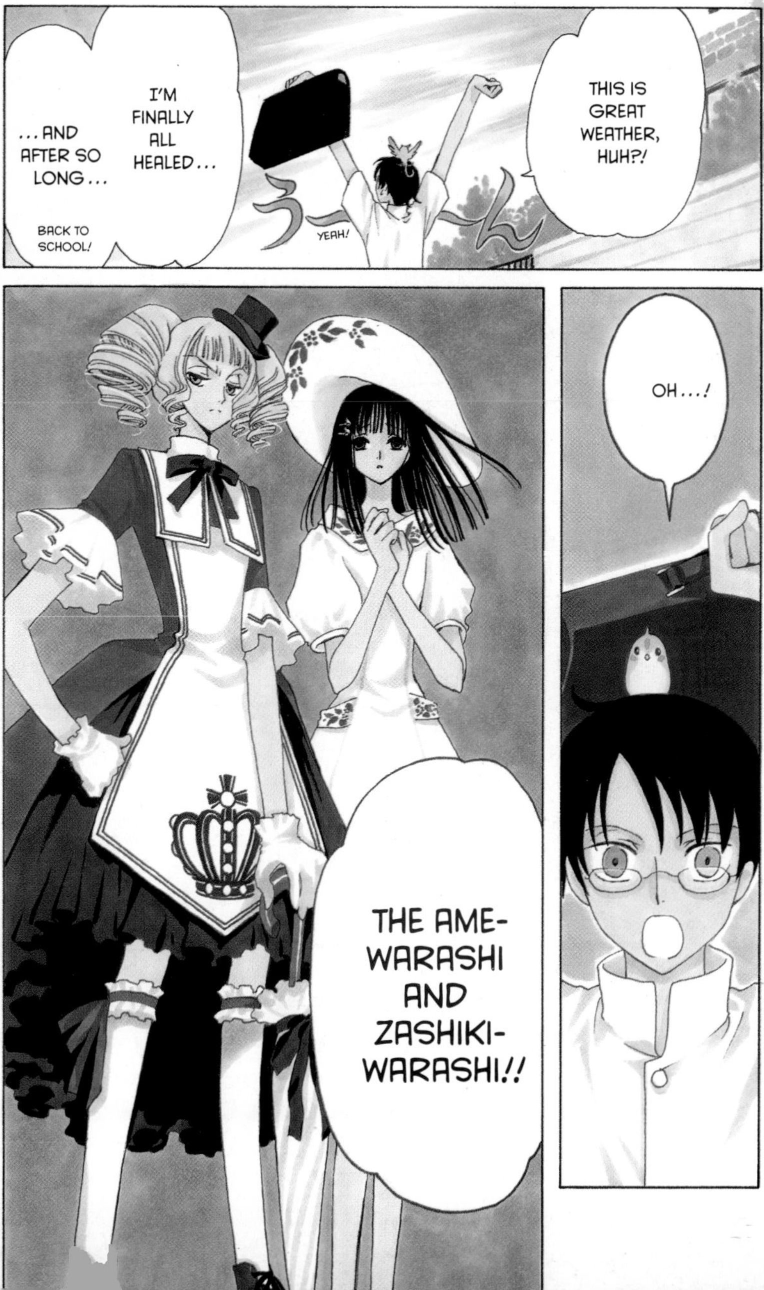
THIS IS GREAT WEATHER, HUH?!
うーん
YEAH!
I'M FINALLY ALL HEALED...
...AND AFTER SO LONG...
BACK TO SCHOOL!
OH...!
THE AME-WARASHI AND ZASHIKI-WARASHI!!